TO AMERICA WITH THE DOUKHOBORS

This book has been published with the help of a grant from the Minister of State for Multiculturalism.

TO AMERICA WITH THE DOUKHOBORS

L.A. SULERZHITSKY

translated by MICHAEL KALMAKOFF
introduction by MARK MEALING

CANADIAN PLAINS STUDIES ■ 12
JOHN ARCHER, GENERAL EDITOR

CANADIAN PLAINS RESEARCH CENTER
UNIVERSITY OF REGINA

Canadian Cataloguing in Publication Data

Sulerzhitŝkiĭ, L.A. (Leopol'd Antonovich),
    1872-1916
        To America with the Doukhobors

(Canadian plains studies, ISSN 0317-6290 ; 12)
Translation of: V Ameriku s dukhoborami.
ISBN 0-88977-025-5

    1. Doukhobors.* 2. Russians—Canada.
I. University of Regina. Canadian Plains
Research Center. II. Title. III. Series.
BX7433.S8213 1982   289.9   C82-091178-X

48, 212

Cover Photograph: THE FIRST SHIPLOAD OF DOUKHOBORS
ARRIVING AT HALIFAX
Courtesy of Blaine Lake Doukhobor Society

TABLE OF CONTENTS

EDITOR'S NOTE

This is one of the most important diaries bearing on the settlement era of Western Canadian history. Because of its importance, and since translation necessarily does some violence to the grammatical structure, every effort has been made to express philosophy and meaning. This is not a slavish rendering of words of one language to another.

The original diary was written by L.A. Sulerzhitsky, himself a Russian and not a Doukhobor. He was much in sympathy with the Doukhobor way of life hence his devotion to the welfare of those Doukhobors who emigrated to Western Canada. Sulerzhitsky wrote in his diary as he found time and opportunity. Events were recorded as he saw them take place or as he remembered them a day or more later. The author pauses to reflect on the Doukhobor way of life and his own attempts to make easier the physical movement of the people from one country to another, a movement which involved changes in law, custom, language and environment. The original text, therefore, shows sudden changes of tense, mood, even person. The editing involved some changes felt necessary to better reveal the spirit of the diary to the reader of English.

This is a very human document. While the author makes no attempt to hide the human frailties of the Doukhobors or the racial prejudices of the times, he manages to portray, with sympathy and understanding, the great reserves of spirit and will which carried the Doukhobors through trials and tribulations from one continent to another, in search of a home where they might live according to their interpretation of God's will. It gives a clear insight into one of the unique threads that make up the mosaic of an emerging society on our western plains.

John Archer,
Regina

TRANSLATOR'S NOTE

I first learned of this material when I acquired the 1960 issues of (ISKRA) magazine in which this book was published, serially, in Russian. As I read it, I came to feel it should be made more widely available, not only to young Doukhobors unable to read Russian but also to others interested in the Doukhobors or in the history of early settlement of the Prairies.

While looking in book stores for reading material in Russian, I came across Maxim Gorky's *Literary Portraits*. My interest was drawn mainly by a lengthy article about Tolstoy, but in perusing the book I found it also contained an article about Sulerzhitsky, who had died in 1916. It seemed significant that Gorky should have written about Sulerzhitsky as he had written about famous writers, artists, etc. Later I discovered there is much more material about Sulerzhitsky written as memoirs by his friends and fellow workers in the Moscow Art Theatre and others.

Among these was Tolstoy's eldest daughter Tatiana Sookhotina-Tolstaya who attended the Moscow School of Art and Sculpture with Sulerzhitsky and brought him into the Tolstoy home. She states his philosophy as:

Life must be beautiful.
People must be happy.
To bring about these aims one must not neglect the simplest actions.
If one can produce merriment by an amusing story or funny anecdote, it must be given.
If life can be beautified by a picture, performance or song and for this labour is needed, it must be given willingly and happily.
If suffering is needed to bring about the happiness of people, one must accept the suffering boldly, confidently and joyfully.

Upon his return from Canada, Sulerzhitsky joined Stanislavsky's Moscow Art Theatre where he did outstanding work as director of plays in the first studio.

He published this book in Moscow in 1905 based on a diary he had kept.

In translating, my aim has been to preserve the author's ideas and expressions as fully as possible so as to preserve the historical value of the work. For example, it may seem more accurate to call the book "To

9

Canada with the Doukhobors." But the important thing about going to Canada at that time was the fact that it meant going to the New World and America was almost synonymous with New World. Therefore going to Canada was looked upon as going to America.

In addition to my gratitude to the Multiculturalism Directorate of the Department of the Secretary of State of Canada for a grant to cover expenses and to compensate in part for my time on this work, I wish to express my appreciation to Dr. Mark Mealing, Head of the Institute for Doukhobor Studies of Selkirk College, Castlegar, B.C., for writing the Introduction and for working on the English translation in order to improve its readability. Dr. John Archer was responsible for the final editorial changes. Both of these scholars have spent many hours on these tasks and contributed immeasurably to the final product. I also thank my daughter Dorothy Jane Kalmakoff for typewriting a large part of the original hand-written manuscript and suggesting many improvements, and Mrs. Carole Patterson for an excellent job of the final typing of the complete, edited manuscript.

Michael Kalmakoff,
Nelson, B.C.

INTRODUCTION

F.M. Mealing
Institute for Doukhobor Studies, Castlegar, B.C.

Dukhoborets tot . . .

A Doukhobor is one
> whom Christ has chosen
>> for His incarnation

godliness dwells on earth
> in flesh

>> from which eternal wisdom is revealed

Jesus Christ must have a body
> must be a person

for through a human mouth
> the Lord speaks out!

the Church Apostolic and
> Mountain of Zion
>> this is the Community of Doukhobors

amid the mountains lives the Spirit of godly wisdom
> the power of God
>> among men

dwelling with them   the spring of living waters
>> joyously bringing forth eternal life

their good deeds
> good way of life
>> will triumph over the earth
>> and over worldly kingdoms
>>> whose end comes soon

then the Doukhobors will be made known to all peoples
> and the One Christ shall be the worthy King
>> about Him   shall all folk gather

but a time of grief and trials shall come before their glory
there shall be a horrible struggle
but
> indeed
>> they shall win victory
>> and shall establish the Kingdom of God in the earth.

This venerable psalm—Legebokoff (1978, p. 88) notes that von Haxthausen reports it no later than 1847—epitomizes the Doukhobor belief by which faith and history are concorded: beyond Doukhobor witness and suffering is the approach of total human reform. The events Sulerzhitsky sets down are in accord with the Doukhobor view, then and now. The origins and development of this view may in part be recounted. I say "in part" because not only are the records and evidence of Doukhobor origins distant in time and place, but the essential qualities of Doukhobor philosophy disdain much of the literate West's preoccupation with objective fact, focusing instead upon a transcendent and timeless process. As in our own world, this process may be much obscured by carnal political wrangling; but its apparent failures should not blind us to its achievements.

In the Middle Ages, Great Russia was on the far rim of Europe. It is arguable whether the Christianity brought to it from Byzantium was ever established with spiritual and administrative clarity, though beyond question great wisdom and enlightenment appeared at certain times and places. Inequities, corruption, and rigidity made room for the intermittent growth of sectarian groups and doctrines; these were sometimes fueled from Byzantium itself, as in the case of the *Ikono-bortsi* or Iconoclasts, puritans who rejected the most visible apparatus of worship. In 1652 the reformist Patriarch Nikon's centrist policies inspired a major movement of reaction, the *Raskol* or Schism, spawning a host of sects to left and right—favouring either no such change, or yet greater change. Among such events, the ministry of Daniel Philipov survives in Doukhobor memory: finding bible translations, liturgy, and clergy all imperfect guides to spirituality, Philipov preached that the only reliable guide was the voice of God within the believer.

Doukhobor doctrine has evolved from this essential concept, taken one step further. If God speaks within any of us, then God is indeed with us; and, if so, then to kill a person—even at the state's behest—is to commit the profound sin of attempting to destroy a part of God. Doukhobor believers, then, from the first time they appear as a distinct sect, were doctrinaire pacifists. Repudiating the authority of the church (as corrupt) and of the state (as the power of AntiChrist), they came under the most bitter persecution. They were the more put down in the 18th century because of their exemplary society: thus the Governor of Ekaterinoslav, said in 1792 (Mealing 1975, p. 12):

> . . . those infected with the movement merited no mercy . . .
> (because) of their exemplary conduct . . . they avoided drunkenness and idleness, gave themselves up to the welfare of their homes and led a moral life. . . . (They) paid their taxes regularly and fulfilled their social duties, often even to excess as compared with other peasants. . . . (They were) monsters and breakers of the general peace. . . .

to a state unable to tolerate a community that gave its own standards the lie.

We know little of the life of the Doukhobors before the mid-18th century, when the People of God (as they knew themselves) first acquired leaders. The models for Doukhobor leadership are alien to us; they are a blend of the lore of the biblical patriarchs and the superimposition of Doukhobor ideals upon the example in the world, the feudal lord. God is in every person but is not, Doukhobors note, equally welcomed. The person who most intently nourishes the divine spirit within must in the most natural way become the Doukhobor leader—and necessarily is followed, for in such a person the voice of God must speak most clearly and fully.

A persistent legend records that a stranger taught the Doukhobors in the village of Okhochem, Kharkov district, about 1715, with a message "much in the style of Quaker teaching" (see Mealing 1975, p. 11). The first leaders we know by name are Sylvan Kolesnikov, who formed a community in the village of Nikolai, Ekaterinoslav district, and Ilarion Pobirokhin, active in Goreloe, Tambov province, and who replaced Kolesnikov at his death in 1765. These men were intelligent, literate, and consistent in their philosophy and authority. Apparently it was under Pobirokhin that the role and status of the leader in the community was compared with that of Christ and the disciples— language which led pious Doukhobors from that time to the present to see a leader as an incarnate Christ in their own time and place. In 1790 Pobirokhin died, to be replaced by the already influential Savely Kapustin.

In that decade the continuing brutalities to which the Doukhobors were subject as sectarians and draft resisters were brought before the sympathetic Czar Alexander I, who resolved the enigma facing both Doukhobors and state by making a land grant in the Crimea. From all parts of southern and central Russia west of the Urals came families of Doukhobors; some appeared from dungeons and prisons, released unexpectedly from bitter servitude. They went to the *Molochnie Vodie* (Milky Waters) region in Tavriz province, and there, with commendable speed, set up farming communities that prospered until 1818, when changes in government brought about renewed persecution.

At that time a confusing event took place, for which no clear explanation exists. Kapustin died in 1820, and was replaced by his son Vasili Kalmikov. The ideal of spiritual excellence had been modified by the feudal value of primogeniture and aristocracy—who more likely to be excellent than the son of the excellent? But Vasili proved to be a dull-witted, self-indulgent drunkard who upon his death left a worse son, Ilarion Kalmikov, a confused and impotent alcoholic upheld as leader by more powerful associates at the age of sixteen, to die only eighteen years later. Under this debatable leadership, a tragic event took place in the Milky Waters region. As reported at the time by unsympathetic sources, between two and four hundred Doukhobors were murdered and buried in mass graves for rebellion against community policy. Another source suggests that twenty Doukhobors were killed by an army patrol as punishment for harbouring deserters. At all events, persecution by the state resumed, and a new exile to the Wet Hills district of Tiflis province in the Transcaucasus began. Whatever the facts—and paramount was the hostility of the state and its power of propoganda—the Doukhobor community submitted with unfamiliar complacency, and preserved a legend accepting the circumstance of the murders but assigning a double cause. The legend argued (Mealing 1972, p. 371) that not only Doukhobors emigrated to the Milky Waters in 1801, but also bandits claiming Doukhobor identity to escape imprisonment. The bandits were given land, but the 'true Doukhobors' did not accept them socially, "God had forgiven them but Man had not," and the bandits murdered to make room for themselves in the community. It is noteworthy that the legend ascribed two forms of blame: that of the unreformed bandits who acted directly, and that of the devout Doukhobors who provoked that action by their inability to accept fellow humans (Woodcock and Avakumovic 1968, p. 55-60).

Ilarion Kalmikov was succeeded in 1850 by his son Peter, a competent and effective leader carried off in 1864 by illness, and succeeded in turn, unconventionally, by his wife, the remarkable Lukeria Kalmikova. Lukeria blossomed as a talented administrator in business affairs, a motherly counsellor when dealing with personal and village matters, a friend of children, and a shrewd diplomat when dealing with agents of the state. Under her hand the community prospered in the relatively inhospitable Transcaucasus. When the Crimean War intruded upon community life, Lukeria's elegant compromise between the demands of Doukhobor ideology and the militant state was to send food, wagons, and wagoners to supply the Russian army and provide ambulance service, thus avoiding a direct draft of Doukhobors as soldiers. For the second time in the century, Doukhobors prospered and were at peace with the state.

Lukeria selected Peter Vasilievich Verigin as her successor. Verigin was a man of striking appearance and intellect, charismatic, energetic; he was also her nephew and thus suitable for the leadership succession, for Lukeria had no children that survived childbirth. (It is a measure of the influence of both Lukeria and Verigin that pious legends aver he was indeed her son.) Lukeria exercised strong control over Verigin's training: he became a part of her household, and his former marriage was dissolved—to create, ultimately, a rift between Verigins and the Kotelnikovs, the family of his wife and son, a rift that no doubt affected the policy of the latter when he succeeded to the leadership in the 1920s. In long private sessions, Lukeria imbued the receptive Peter with traditions and principles of his anticipated role as leader of the Doukhobors.

In 1886, five years after her adoption of Verigin, Lukeria died leaving no clear statement on the succession. Alesha Zubkov proposed Lukeria's brother, his pawn Michael Gubanov; Peter Verigin, on the other hand, moved about the community with words and actions appropriate to one who was already the viceroy of God. When Zubkov was convinced that the majority supported Verigin, his 'Small Party' chose to denounce Verigin to the government agents as a man preparing to foment religious insurrection. Tsarist officials, at best paranoid, responded by throwing Verigin into Siberian exile. It is a matter of record that his imprisonment was minimal and allowed him time not only for broad reading in Scripture and Tolstoy, but also for writing letters to the home communities. These letters, it appears, were designed to stimulate discussion of religious ideals and social policy; but the faithful received them as apostolic epistles to be accepted with no question beyond the planning for implementation of their contents or goals.

Doukhobors were passing through more changes than, perhaps, they knew. They had lost a powerful and pacific leader; they had suffered division over the question of succession, and, their present leader in exile, still lacked immediate direction. The policies and attitudes of the state, also, had changed, improved communication technology expediting information and control. While Verigin's letters enlarged theory and argument toward a renewed Doukhobor philosophy, the government renewed conscription of the Doukhobors. On Easter Monday, 1895 (o.s.), some 60 young Doukhobor inductees on the parade square laid down their guns, swearing never to take them up again; they were punished with barbaric harshness and were exiled to Siberian labour camps. When the news came to the southern villages, the Doukhobor community perceived that it was again on a knife-edge between the integrity of its ideals and the assaults of the godless state, and it fell back upon its proven means, that of survival gained through suffering and witness.

When the Doukhobors first came to the Transcaucasus, then controlled largely by pagan Tartars, they had been issued obsolete muskets for defense; never used, these were left to rust in cottage lofts. But now the old guns were seen as a sign of intolerable compromise; and so, on June 29, 1895 (o.s.), at Doukhobor centres in Tiflis, Elisabetpol, and Kars provinces, folk gathered about outdoor fires, praying and singing hymns while their guns burned and lost their shape, their usefulness.

More political than spiritual, the state authorities perceived these fires as the signs of general rebellion. Some local officials merely chided the Doukhobors till their superiors in turn roused them to action; in other areas, the fiercest punishments were at once applied. People of all ages were thrashed, their homes were ravaged; Cossack troops were sent and billeted on them, taking food, smashing furnishings, beating males and raping females without check or rebuke. Whole villages were relocated, without supplies, to meagre Tartar settlements, to scrape by as best they might, or survive upon whatever charity the Tartars dared give them under threat of execution.

But the same improved communications that expedited the state's overreaction also carried news of these atrocities to sympathetic ears. The Populist movement had observers in the area studying the systems whereby dissident groups organized their societies in lieu of state administration. These political philosophers and theorists apprehended an early collapse of the Russian state, and believed that the most suitable seeds of a new Russian order might be found among those indigenous communities that were Russian in spirit yet different in function. Among these observers were students of Tolstoy, by now elderly yet no less a figure of great moral influence. The reports they returned to Tolstoy and to other sympathetic Russian intelligentsia were not, perhaps could not be, wholly objective; they not only recounted accurately the horrors inflicted by the state, but also, as though by reflex, depicted the Doukhobors not as a community of generally sincere people struggling to define their place in creation, but as an unhoused church of martyred saints, flawless in spirituality and virtue. This image, as may be expected, produced problems when tested.

Tolstoy, aroused by the apocalyptic nature of these events, laboured through many channels for the relief of the Doukhobors. He exerted his influence at all levels of official government. He wrote his final novel, *Resurrection*, and devoted its profit to Doukhobor relief. He also communicated with his British publisher, the influential Quaker Aylmer Maude. Maude, working through the London Yearly Meeting of the Society of Friends, secured the aid of the Philadelphia Yearly Meeting, and British and American Quakers also worked— through donation of money and goods, and through diplomatic channels—for Doukhobor relief.

When the Doukhobor case was recounted in Philadelphia, a visiting Toronto Friend, Arthur St. John, commented upon his tour of the Canadian Prairies some years before with the Christian Anarchist Kropotkin, stating Kropotkin's view that the Prairie would be an ideal region for Russian settlement and steppe-style agriculture. The result of this comment was a quiet campaign by the London Friends to arrange Doukhobor exodus and settlement in Canada, whose external affairs were at that time administered by the British Foreign Office. The Russian state favoured the departure of the Doukhobors, whom it perceived as a troublesome and insoluble problem. The first group to depart were settled experimentally in Cyprus, but their diet, their agricultural technology, and their dawn-to-dusk work habits accorded not at all with the resources, diseases, and subtropical climate of that island. Many died, and emigration of the rest to Canada was expedited. Others were already on their way.

In the summer of 1898 Tolstoy chose a representative to assist the emigrants directly. This was the mercurial and energetic Leopold Sulerzhitsky. Sulerzhitsky, till that time a man apparently without a clear role in life, threw himself into this amorphous task with a characteristic goodwill and vigour, eventually functioning not only as a kind of on-the-spot Tolstoy, but also as business agent, pastor, interpreter, trouble-shooter, nurse, teacher, and finally chronicler. In winter 1898 he oversaw the loading of the Lake Huron at Batum, and conducted the first contingent of Doukhobors to the interior of Saskatchewan to undertake the initial phases of settlement. When he reached Winnipeg on the first leg of his return to Russia, news of the failure of the Cyprus experiment came through the Quaker network, along with promises of funds to aid Doukhobor transportation. The Quakers asked Sulerzhitsky to conduct the Cypriot Doukhobors to Canada. He not only saw them through the hardships of the Atlantic crossing, and accompanied them travelling once again across Canada to the Prairies, but spent some months observing the establishment of the first Community Villages and the inception of the Christian Community of Universal Brotherhood, the great Doukhobor communal enterprise. Perhaps aware at last of his own powers, Sulerzhitsky returned to Russia and moved into the heart of the life of Russian theatre. During this movement—no rapid matter—he wrote the remarkable record of *To America With the Doukhobors.*

In all, some 5,747 Doukhobor souls arrived in Canada. They were granted land in hamlet configuration, according to the precedent granted Mennonite settlers of the previous decade—by the Liberals' Secretary of the Interior, Clifford Sifton. The Doukhobors raised orderly villages, forty homes to a village, perhaps two families in a home, each site with oven, barn, and garden plot. With some money, with some goods, with little equipment and no draught beasts, women and elders broke the prairie that first spring, while more able men worked away from the villages for cash for animals and tools. Labour was hard and unceasing, but the Doukhobors persevered in a landscape harsher than that of Russia but less alien than Cyprus. Isolated and peaceable as they were, they were not to be untouched by the North America of the early twentieth century.

Firstly, the government changed, introducing a new and unsympathetic Secretary of the Interior, John Oliver, to the scene. The Doukhobors had been settled under the Homestead Act, and had conformed to its requirements for land clearing and home construction, but they had rebelled at the Oath of Allegiance—in Russia, the first action required of a conscript was an Oath of Allegiance to the Czar. They also avoided the registration of vital statistics, and directed their children away from schooling. The state school system they saw accurately as an instrument by which worldly, unGodly values might be imbued; but they failed to perceive that the system allowed some control by client communities, though less indeed than is presently the case. When, in 1905, pressure from Anglo-Saxon settlers increased, and the Doukhobors were no longer seen as a group useful for the development of the Prairies, Oliver not only insisted upon the Oath of Allegiance but, in an uncharacteristically harsh and peremptory manner, declared the original settlement arrangement retroactively void. The Doukhobors could not settle in their villages but must now conform to the prevailing—and, as later studies indicated, socially damaging (Smith 1922, pp. 72-73, 118-122)—pattern of isolated homesteads, newly registered under the name of each male.

The Doukhobors had abandoned all they possessed and knew, half a world away. They came to Canada expecting an undefined and ideal freedom. They had toiled without surcease to build not only homes and a productive land, but the restoration of their Doukhobor institutions and a new thing, a Communal instrumentality. In 1903, their Leader, released at last from exile, Peter the Lordly as all came to know him, was restored to them. They seemed to have come to the Kingdom of God on Earth. When the power of the state came down upon them again—for its own reasons, clear in its eyes, and doubtless expedient—they did not concede. 'Why should we bow down to George, who have left Nicholas on the other side of the world?' asks a proverb of the day, and the answer is given by a Psalm (*Questions Concerning Citizenship*, in Mealing 1972, p. 262-63):

> It is better to be peaceful servants of Jesus Christ
> than to be loyal bandits of the killer King!

While Verigin negotiated adroitly with Federal officials keeping them always off step, most of the Doukhobors refused the Oath of Allegiance. Some had discarded the concept of Spiritual Leadership; these had little difficulty in adapting to the Prairie reality as defined by the Canadian government. For those who saw matters in a different light, the choice was clear. They refused the Oath and they were forced off their land and improvements. With the income from their few years of farming and their Community institutions, they purchased land in the

West Kootenay of British Columbia, where most of the devout still dwell. Troubles and successes have come upon them, in ways and measure both unexpected, though that history goes beyond the scope of this book; yet much that Sulerzhitsky tells us casts a light upon not only the past but also the future.

*   *   *

Preconceived notions of Western Europe has led it to envision Russia, pre- as well as post-Revolutionary, as a dour and grey society, uniformly harsh and inhuman by contrast with the West's supposed enlightenment: wherever light begins to shine within some character or community, the forces of the state snuff and stifle it. But at least, during that age that was the threshhold of change, numerous social experiments were essayed and numerous characters—creative, luminous, intensely humane—appear and persevere. Leopold Sulerzhitsky is not the least of these.

Sulerzhitsky's permanent place was the theatre. As a child, he haunted theatres, and at the age of twelve produced a *Hamlet*; in his teens, he attended art school, first in his natal Zhitomir and later in Moscow; there he met Tolstoy's daughter Tatiana and learned through her of Tolstoy's doctrine, which he embraced enthusiastically. In 1894 his revolutionary speechmaking caused his dismissal from school, and he went to sea. When in 1896 he became a conscientious objector, he was sent first to an asylum and next to central Asia, where an army officer supervising his exile came to like him and expedited his rehabilitation. In 1898, Tolstoy persuaded Sulerzhitsky to represent him and expedite the migration of the Doukhobors to Canada (Magarshack 1950, p. 282-83; Stanislavsky 1948, p. 469).

Sulerzhitsky took up this task with a sensitive blend of energy, affection, competence, and caution. When officials and others neglected or could not fulfil essential duties, it was Sulerhitsky who more often than not undertook and completed the task. When Doukhobors came up against some problem they could not comprehend, it was Sulerzhitsky who led them through to the solution. Yet it is evident that he did not impose his views nor his aims upon those he helped: apparently he considered himself, in some novel sense, to be simply a skilled servant. When his aid was needed, it was there, wholly; but the will was that of those he helped. Gorky reports a comment of Tolstoy regarding Sulerzhitsky (Gorky 1963, p. 30):

> Lyovushka is the purest man I know. . . . if he does wrong, it's out of pity for someone.

Upon his return to Russia in 1900, Sulerzhitsky busied himself publishing banned works of Tolstoy and revolutionary pamphlets. He met Gorky while working as a stevedore, and began to attend the

Moscow Art Theatre, meeting Stanislavsky in 1901. Again he was arrested, confined, and exiled. In 1905, the year of publication of *To America With the Doukhobors*, he was called up to military service in Manchuria but was released on his arrival at base. He returned to Moscow, where Stanislavsky added him to the company of the Moscow Art Theatre. And it was with that institution that Sulerzhitsky remained associated—in spite of occasional quarrels, usually over theatrical policy—till the end of his days.

That end came too soon. Sulerzhitsky had contracted chronic nephritis during his sojourn in Canada, and his health collapsed in 1915. Stanislavsky attended him daily in hospital. Upon his death, he lay for two days in the theatre studio, and was borne to the cemetery by student actors (Magarshack 1950, p. 344).

*　　*　　*

Gorky writes twice of Sulerzhitsky: in the 'literary portrait' of Tolstoy cited above and in another essay, a memorial for Sulerzhitsky written in 1917, in which he comments upon *To America With the Doukhobors* (Gorky 1963, p. 46 ff.):

> The book is written in a somewhat disorganized way, and it leaves out many of Suler's interesting adventures. When I read the manuscript of the book, I urged him to add more detail to it, but he did not want to.
>
> "What have I to do with it?" he argued, "The Doukhobors are the subject; I am an outsider to this unnatural coupling of religion and politics. . . ." Leo Tolstoy once said of him, "What kind of Tolstoyan is he? He is simply 'the Three Musketeers', not one of them, but all three!"
>
> This was quite true, and Tolstoy could not have sketched Suler's vivid individuality more accurately, with his love of action and of work, his inclination towards quixotic adventure, and his romantic passion for everything beautiful.

Those close to Sulerzhitsky write of him with great warmth—'Suler.' In doing so, they mirror the loving nature of the man himself. As I write, I have before me a facsimile of an album of photographs apparently assembled by a young American Quaker, the Hannah Bellows who accompanied her father William from Cyprus to Saskatchewan. Sulerzhitsky appears in a number of shipboard scenes. He is a stocky, bearded young man in sunhat, shirt, and white trousers; his sleeves are rolled up, ready for heavy work; he is always talking to someone, always cheery, and evidently most willing to flirt with the attending nurses.

His books gives us portraits, stories, narratives, anecdotal detail—a wealth of information at many levels. Of special interest is his account of decision-making processes within the community, and of the slow, grass-roots evolution of the Christian Community of Universal Brotherhood, arguably the greatest economic experiment under-taken in Canada. All scholars must welcome this detailed resource encompassing a crucial period in the histories of the Doukhobors and of the Canadian Prairies.

But Sulerzhitsky, a profound humanist, does more than serve a thirst for factual knowledge: he is deeply sensitive to the breadth of human feelings. Story upon story counterpoints the bald details of the basic chronicle, in startling variety. Three stories particularly linger in my own mind: the account of the ancient couple Mischa and Markovna who almost lose their train and recount their trials in almost comic dialogue (p. 42); the reflective yet stark account of the shipboard death of Grigori's little son and his mournful sea-burial (pp. 57-60); and the story of the burly tangling between Doukhobors and self-righteous 'Englishmen' at the little settlement of Land Office (pp. 158-62). Sulerzhitsky portrays scenes of pathos, horror, determination, uproarious good humour, dedication and devout faith, yet never, despite the waiting pitfalls, descends to bathos or sensationalism. The English reader will be delighted to meet a new writer—one who must be added to the small roster of great travellers to Canada—whose work can be respected beyond the dry requirements of scholarship. Sulerzhitsky is accurate and informative; but he is also credible, passionate, and in the old sense, sentimental. Reason and feeling are tempered each by the other. His portrait of Doukhobor society of the time is complete, aesthetically as well as factually.

Sulerzhitsky does not seek to find his own ego in this chronicle, and only obliquely do we discover his character through his words. He is moody, competent in organization, unobtrusive. He does not thrust himself upon the Doukhobors, and above all he does not indulge himself by association with them. Though he reports their feelings and deeds, and his own, in depth, we do not come away with the sense of a do-gooder, a busybody, a bleeding-heart, or a professional angel. Sometimes a purely personal question is visible, a sense of melancholic isolation for which all this outgoing energy is the self-induced cure. Sulerzhitsky does not presume to interpret the Doukhobors to us, but instead presents them so that we may interpret them honestly for ourselves. It seems to me that he succeeds in this high aim; and further that he succeeds, not as if he were a conscientious enthnographer secure in his academic method, but because he has committed himself to a passionate experience in which nothing is more important than these people, these times. "The Doukhobors are the subject."

BIBLIOGRAPHY

I am deeply indebted to Jack McIntosh, Slavic Librarian attached to the Special Collections Department of the Library, the University of British Columbia, who has supplied not only detailed bibliographic data but also copies of scarce materials and translations of some Russian texts.

Mr. McIntosh notes that the Moscow Art Theatre Museum holds Sulerzhitsky's papers.

Gorky, M. "L.A. Sulerzhitsky," in his *Literaturnye portrety (Literary Portraits)*, Moscow, Gosudarstvennoe Izdatel' stro Khudozhestvennoi Literaturny, 1963.

Legebokoff, Peter, and Anna Markova, eds. *Sbornik: Dukhoborcheskikh Psalmi, Stikhi, i Pesni (A Collection: Doukhobor Psalms, Hymns, and Songs.)*. Grand Forks, B.C., Union of Spiritual Communities of Christ, 1978.

Magarshack, David. *Stanislavsky: a Life*. London, MacGibbon & Kee, 1950.

Markov, P.A. "Pervaia studiia. Sulerzhitskii-Vakhtonov—Chekhov. 1913-1922." (The First Studio: Sulerzhitsky, Vakhtonov, Chekhov, 1913-1922). In the book *Moskovskii Khudozhestvennyi teatr Vtoroi (The Second Moscow Art Theatre)*. Moscow, (?), 1925.

Mealing, F.M. "Our People's Way: A Study in Doukhobor Psalmody & Folklife." Unpublished doctoral dissertation, Department of Folklore & Folklife. Philadelphia, University of Pennsylvania, 1972. (University Microfilms # 72/25, 633)

————*Doukhobor Life*. Castlegar, B.C., Cotinneh Books & Kootenay Doukhobor Historical Society, 1975.

Smith, William G. *Building the Nation: a study of some problems concerning the Church's relation to the Immigrants*. Toronto, Canadian Council of Missionary Education Movement, 1922.

Stanislavski, Constantin. *My Life in Art*. tr. J.J. Robbins. New York, Theatre Arts Books, 1952.

Woodcock, George and Ivan Avakumovic. *The Doukhobors*. Toronto, Oxford University Press, 1968.

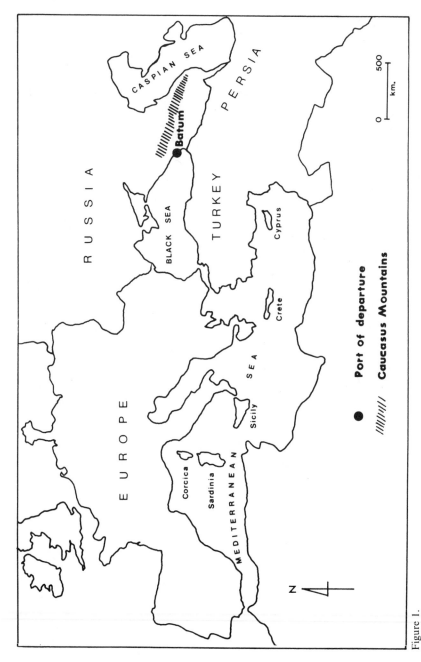

Figure 1.

The above map shows the Port of Batum on the Black Sea and the island of Cyprus. Four shiploads of exiled Doukhobors left Batum and Cyprus for Canada. Sulerzhitsky travelled on the ship the *Lake Huron*, which left Batum on December 10th, 1898, with 2,140 Doukhobors, and on the ship the *Lake Superior*, which left Cyprus on April 15th, 1899, with 1,010 persons.

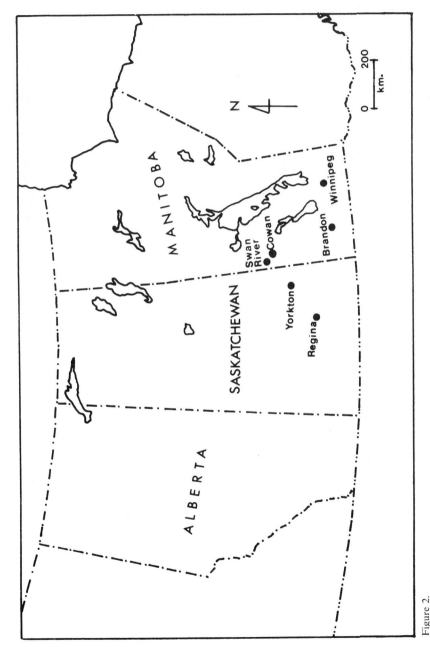

Figure 2.
The above map of the prairie provinces shows the communities of Cowan, Swan River and Yorkton, around which the first groups of Doukhobors in Canada settled.

25

TO AMERICA WITH THE DOUKHOBORS

FROM THE AUTHOR

In recent times many interesting articles about Doukhobors have appeared in Russian print giving adequate presentation of the external, material conditions of their existence as well as of the internal content of this impressive peculiar group of Russian people appearing, as fate had willed it, in the distant American prairie (See: Education: V. Bonch-Bruevich: Doukhobors in the Canadian Prairies; *Russian Gazette,* Tan: Russians in Canada; *and many others.)*

However, about the migration of the Doukhobors to America and about how they felt in Canada at the earliest time of their arrival in the new land, there is no information. This void gave me the idea of filling it with information I had. It was my lot to take an active part in this migration during which I sometimes kept a diary in the form of brief notes of all that happened around me. This diary, in a somewhat reworked form, I now offer to the reader, first apologizing for its brevity and incoherence which, in large measure, is explained by the fact that I recorded everything I saw without any preconceived plan.

L.A. Sulerzhitsky

I shall not speak here of the events of 1894, when some of the Doukhobors (about 4,300 persons) were taken from their homes in Kars Province (Wet Mountain Area) and settled (exiled) in the Georgian villages of Tiflis Province.

Nor is this the place to tell about the conditions they faced in the burning hot, fever-infested valleys of Tiflis Province, where they were split up and placed, two or three families per village, among people who were strange to them, who could speak neither Russian nor Tartar.* They were without land, without homes, and without chance of employment, forbidden to move from place to place and so on. All this has been written about elsewhere. Suffice it to say that, in three years of this existence, out of 4,300 persons, nearly 1,000 died.

It is important only to note here that the idea of emigrating from Russia came to the Doukhobors not so much as a result of their difficult living conditions as from the uncertainty of their situation and

---

*Tartar—In places where the Doukhobors lived earlier their neighbours were Tartars and many learned the language.

complete ignorance of what would become of them in future.

But, as has been said, the uncertainty of their situation did not permit them to get established.

Whatever the conditions of life in the places where the Doukhobors were ordered to settle at this time, they probably would have established themselves as well as they had in other places on previous occasions. In the "Wet Mountains" of the Caucasus, for example, to which the Doukhobors had been moved earlier from the Province of Tavria, they became the most prosperous inhabitants—not only of the Caucasus but probably of all Russia. Some of the exceptionally well-to-do individuals handled tens of thousands of roubles,* had large reserves of wheat, flocks of sheep and horned livestock while even the poorest proprietors had four or five horses and five or six head of cattle. Their prosperity may be judged by their communal capital which amounted to hundreds of thousands of roubles. Moreover, they achieved this prosperity in spite of great handicaps. In the "Wet Mountains" they had been settled at an altitude of 6,000 feet above sea level and, in the first years, even barley did not ripen due to early frosts. For firewood they had to go 25 to 30 versts** from the settlement.

Doukhobors are their own carpenters, weavers, smiths, tailors, joiners and masons. They buy nothing and, wherever they go, they take with them everything necessary for the creation of a full and prosperous life. Hard work and cooperation, which constitute the distinguishing features of the Doukhobors, would have helped them to attain the same well-being in the fertile valleys of Tiflis Province in spite of the unhealthy conditions they faced there.

"Had they told us," they said more than once, "that we were to remain here permanently, or had they set a time limit, we would know what to do. We wanted to buy land here, to build and to plough; but we cannot do any of this as no one knows what will happen to us. Perhaps tomorrow we shall have to prepare to go to another place—or possibly home. We know nothing!"

Having spent three and a half years tensely awaiting some kind of decision concerning their lot, they decided to emigrate.

The exiled Doukhobors (there were about 35,000 persons at that time) had set aside about 50,000 roubles for the possible emigration, which they had apparently been considering for a long time, even before being sent to Tiflis Province. This money was preserved intact despite their extreme need. Concerning migration, there had been a tradition among the Doukhobors that the time would come when they would have to leave Russia and go to some new country. According to their elders that time had now come; and in the summer of 1897

---

*roubles—one rouble was worth about 50 cents.
**versts—one verst = .64 mile.

Doukhobor representatives personally petitioned Empress Maria Fedorovna, who was in the Caucasus at the time. In the petition, the Doukhobors asked for permission to emigrate from Russia. At the beginning of 1898 the Doukhobors received official permission to leave—but with the condition that, having emigrated, they would lose the right to return to Russia.

Once the matter was resolved in this way, the Doukhobors sent two of their delegates to Leo Nicolaevich Tolstoy with a request for help in choosing a country, finding the means and organizing the process for migration.

L.N. Tolstoy disapproved of emigration and urged the delegates at length to reject all thought of leaving Russia, citing moral as well as purely practical reasons against it. In support of his view he quoted a letter from Peter Verigin, the chief leader of the Doukhobors, who at that time lived in Obdorsk. In this letter Verigin wrote that he did not know all the conditions of their present situation but, regardless of what these conditions might be, he was "in any case opposed to emigration."

Upon hearing out Tolstoy, the delegates returned to the Caucasus. At one of the largest meetings assembled, a letter from Tolstoy was read in which he strenuously urged the Doukhobors not to leave Russia.

In spite of Tolstoy's view, which was highly respected by the Doukhobors, and the letter of Verigin—and the will of the latter was their law—delegates from the Doukhobor society eventually came to Tolstoy again, to convey to him that emigration had been decided upon conclusively, and that they were again requesting his earliest assistance, as they must emigrate before winter.

After making a few more efforts to dissuade the Doukhobors and after writing a few letters in that tone, Tolstoy, seeing that emigration, one way or another, was unavoidable, turned to his friends in Russia and abroad for gathering advice in choosing a country and, at the same time, gathering resources for emigration.

Only at that moment did private persons begin to play a part in the migration of the Doukhobors, partly at the request of Tolstoy, and partly at the invitation of the Doukhobors themselves.

First of all it was necessary, of course, to decide where to emigrate.

This question was considered outside of Russia in the main, by Captain Vladimir Chertkov, D. Hilcoff, and the English Quakers who had previously organized a special committee in London for collecting funds for needy Doukhobors. Chertkov, as a member of this committee, informed the Quakers of the intention of the Doukhobors to emigrate, and the Quakers at once began to gather donations for a special Doukhobor Emigration Fund.

The most suitable country for the Doukhobors, in a material way and in other respects, was undoubtedly Canada, and Hilcoff, particularly, insisted on this choice. At the same time, emigration there seemed to be impossible because of the excessively high cost of transportation.

Looking for places nearer to the Caucasus, the Quakers suggested the island of Cyprus (which belonged to England).

In the first days of June 1898, in order to reach a final decision in this matter, two representatives of the Doukhobors went to London. They were Ivan Evin and Peter Makortoff. Canada seemed to them to be the most desirable place for settlement but, as has been said, to move there seemed, at the time, to be impossible as their resources were inadequate. They were unable to wait until the necessary sum was raised as they were hurrying to move before winter. For this reason they agreed to a temporary move to the island of Cyprus.

After a lengthy correspondence a telegram was sent to the Doukhobors in the Caucasus saying they should now secure passports, hire ships and prepare to move to Cyprus.

Immediately 1,126 Doukhobors, who were to form the first party, sold their remaining property, secured passports and moved to Batum to await the ship hired by them for moving to Cyprus. Then, unexpectedly, they received a telegram telling them to remain.

The reason for this was that the English government, never having dealt with this situation before, required of the Doukhobors a monetary guarantee of 250 roubles per person so that, if the Doukhobors should fall into need, the English government would not have to keep them at its expense.

Such a guarantee the Doukhobors, of course, could not provide and to return home from Batum to wait until sufficient funds were gathered for moving to Canada was no longer possible.

The situation was critical and the Doukhobors sent telegram after telegram from Batum to England: "Tickets (i.e. passports) are expiring," "We are not permitted to stay in Batum," "There is no time to consider new countries," "The ships are hired" and so on.

The Quakers saved the situation. They energetically undertook the elimination of difficulties, and began by persuading the English government to reduce the guarantee requirement from 250 roubles to 150 per person and ended by collecting 100,000 roubles among themselves in just a few days. This, together with the 50,000 roubles gathered earlier, constituted the necessary sum for the guarantee.

On August 6, 1898 the French ship *Durau* left Batum, carrying 1,126 Doukhobors bound for Cyprus. Emigration of the remaining 2,200 persons from Tiflis Province was put off indefinitely.

About this time I received, through L.N. Tolstoy, an invitation from the Doukhobors to help organize the move. But, because of some difficulties, I did not arrive in Batum until the 6th of August—that is, when the Doukhobors were already getting on the ship—so that in this case I was unable to help them with anything.

The Doukhobors were very poorly accommodated on this ship. They had to sleep on dirty, stinking decks, without facilities for cooking food. Looking over the kettles I could see that in one day only half the passengers could get boiling water. But there was nothing to be done; the money for the ship had already been paid.

Very fortunately for the Doukhobors the weather was calm during the voyage to Cyprus.

On their arrival, the Doukhobors quickly realized that it was impossible to live there. The high percentage of those who suffered from fever in the Caucasus was increased in Cyprus, where fever often ended in death. Soon nearly everyone fell ill, and more than sixty people died. Only with the coming of winter did the rate of sickness and death decrease.

The Quakers supported this party of Doukhobors during the whole period of their stay in Cyprus and promised to transport them at the Society's expense to the country to which the remaining Doukhobors would migrate from the Caucasus.

The sad fate which befell the Doukhobors in Cyprus forced the remainder to reject the thought of continued migration to this island. Instead, the Doukhobors and the persons organizing the migration decided that everything possible must be done to arrange emigration to Canada—not only by the Doukhobors remaining in the Caucasus but by the 1,126 in Cyprus as well.

In the last days of August the Doukhobor representatives, Evin and Makortoff, together with Hilcoff, left England for Canada, to investigate the land and the conditions of life there. The energetic, businesslike Englishman, G. Mood, who was close to the Quakers and was very sympathetic to the Doukhobors, went with them to negotiate officially with the Canadian government.

Soon the Doukhobors began to receive letters from these representatives in which they praised Canada, saying that "a better destination is not to be found." At the same time G. Mood reported that the Canadian government had agreed to the immigration. Also, thanks to his efforts, the Canadian Pacific Railway, on which the Doukhobors would have to travel from the port of disembarkation to the place of settlement (about 2,000 miles), agreed to give them a discount of 50% from their normal tariff.

Besides the 2,140 persons in Tiflis Province, 4,500 of the Kars and

Elizabetpol Doukhobors, who belonged, by their convictions, to the same party of vegetarian Doukhobors as the 2,140, wished to go to Canada.

The Kars and the Elizabetpol Doukhobors were living in their homes and only a small number of them had been exiled, some to Baku Province, and some to the Yakut region.

The impatience with which the 2,140 Doukhobors, living in Tiflis Province, awaited migration was getting beyond bounds; but the negotiations with the Canadian government were not yet concluded. More than once, when information from Canada was, for some reason, delayed, they asked that a cable be sent so as to hasten the final decision since winter was coming on and it was very difficult to wait; "or we will go to Turkey on foot!" they said.

Since Canada had not yet officially agreed to immigration, the Doukhobors sent two more representatives to London, N. Zeeboroff and I. Abrosimoff, to expedite the decision and to deal with the many details of this complex undertaking. With them went Sergei Tolstoy.*

At last in October 1898, we obtained the official agreement of the Canadian government to receive the Doukhobors, and the conditions under which they would be given land.

At once a desire to move more quickly to the new land seized the Doukhobors of Kars and Elizabetpol regions. They all wanted to move that winter. At the same time, the Canadian government warned that, during the winter, it could receive no more than 4,000 persons, as the immigration halls could not accommodate more settlers. The remaining 3,500 persons must move in the spring when those who had arrived during the winter had moved from these halls to their own lands.

Under these circumstances, the first to move had to be the 2,140 persons living in Tiflis Province, for it would have been very difficult for them to live there another winter. If they remained, they would have to begin spending the money which had been saved with such fearful privations towards the possibility of migration.

Next would go the 1,300 Elizabetpol Doukhobors, who, upon deciding to move, hastened to sell not only their homes, but also their chattels.

And last of all would come the 3,000 Kars Doukhobors, the most well-to-do and the least prepared for migration. They were in the least need of migration—much less early migration. But having been caught up in the passionate desire for the earliest possible migration, the Kars people received with disbelief the news of postponement of their move. Not wishing to wait for spring, they sent a telegram to Canada in which they said: "3,000 healthy Doukhobors wish early emigration for which

---

*Eldest son of Leo Tolstoy.

they will need no help from the government as they have sufficient means." In the telegram they call themselves "healthy," to distinguish themselves from the 2,140 living in Tiflis Province, among whom there were many sick and weak.

The Canadian government, taking a practical view of immigration, several times expressed the idea that sick and run-down immigrants were not desirable. It did state that it was indifferent as to who moved first; as long as not more than 4,000 persons came during the winter.

The Kars people, who had become over-impatient, were now embarrassed by their egoism, and at a big meeting called to establish the order of migration, the delegates of the Kars Doukhobors, Androsoff and Postnikoff, were reprimanded because they had sent such an important telegram without the agreement of the whole society, when they had been authorized only to hasten decision on the question.

At this meeting it was decided that the first to go would be the 2,140 persons from Tiflis Province. Then the Elizabetpol group with part of the Kars group—those subject to call up for military service in that year. And finally the remaining Kars Doukhobors.

Now, concerning the means and the routes by which the migration was to take place.

The first route proposed was as follows: from Tiflis Province by the Trans-Caucasian Railroad to Batum, from there by ship to Novo-Rossisk; from NovoRossisk by rail to Riga; from Riga by ship to Liverpool; and only then to Canada. By this route the fare to Canada per person would be about 100 roubles.

This plan seemed to me to be very expensive and unsatisfactory. In fact, where would it be possible to find the necessary help for the transfer of these thousands of people—among them women, children and the sick? How would they be fed along the way?

It seemed better to hire a big ship which would take a large party of Doukhobors directly from Batum to America without transfers of any kind. Enquiring at all the agencies, I found in Marseilles the lowest priced of all ships, *Les Andes*, which had all the facilities necessary for deck passengers and was asking 65,000 roubles for a voyage from Batum to Quebec. The fare on the Canadian Pacific Railroad would cost nearly 10 roubles per person. The total fare would be 75 roubles per person. This was so expensive that not everyone would be able to emigrate within the year because of the lack of funds.

Then I decided to hire a simple freighter without any facilities for passengers, and without service crew, except for the necessary minimum number of mechanical and steering staff. My aim was to adapt the ship myself for passenger travel and to organize a service crew from young Doukhobors.

When hiring the ship, we would have to stipulate the right to do the necessary construction, such as building bunks for passengers. The shipping company and the captain were relieved of all responsibility for the passengers. The whole ship was to be hired for the voyage with all its space, and the company would have no say in what I, the temporary user, would load it with in Batum.

With the help of the Matievich Office in Batum, after a long search in all the foreign ports, satisfactory ships—the *Lake Huron* and the *Lake Superior*—were found. Both of these ships sailed regularly between Liverpool and Quebec. Plans of both ships were sent, from which it was apparent that in construction and size the two ships were alike.

By my calculations, the *Lake Huron* could carry more than 2,000 persons. For the voyage from Liverpool to Batum, for which it would have to sail empty, and then from Batum to Quebec (or if the St. Lawrence was then frozen, to St. John) the shipowners asked 56,000 roubles.

Dividing this among the 2,140 people from Tiflis Province, whom I planned to take on this ship, the fare for each person would be only 27 roubles.

A contract was concluded quickly under which the *Lake Huron* came under my full authority.

Contract

Under the contract, the lessee may use all spaces on the ship except the cabins of the crew and spaces occupied by equipment connected with the sailing of the ship. The lessee may build new structures without interfering with the basic structure of the ship, and agrees, on arrival at the indicated port, to clear the decks of lumber.

The ship is to have a steam kitchen, an evaporator, and as many lamps as necessary to light up all dark places on the ship. The ship undertakes to stay in Batum not less than three days beginning 12 hours after the clearance of all port formalities, of which the captain must inform the lessee upon the issue of the official paper. For standing more than three days, the lessee pays 300 roubles per day for the first three days and then 600 roubles a day.

The shipowners are relieved of all responsibility to the Canadian Government for loading the ship. Half the money will be paid when the ship leaves Liverpool for Batum and the other half upon arrival in Batum. The ship must travel full speed from Liverpool to Batum and from Batum to St. John, not entering any ports. For unloading in St. John, one day is allowed. There must be a doctor and a pharmacy on board.

After several days, the *Lake Superior* was hired on the same terms, with the difference that it must stand in Batum seven days. This was necessary to lengthen the interval between the arrival of the two groups in Canada. The hirer of the second ship was Sergei Lvovich Tolstoy. Soon he arrived in the Caucasus to prepare his party for departure (1,600 Elizabetpol people and 700 Kars Doukhobors), to build the necessary structures on the ship, and take it to Canada.

As soon as the *Lake Huron* left Liverpool for Batum, Sergei Lvovich went to the office of the Trans-Caucasian Railroad to hire trains for the two parties, and to settle the arrangements by which they were to move. Migrants are usually taken on so-called "military trains"—that is, in freight cars where temporary bunks are built for 40 persons.

The Trans-Caucasian Railroad, having moved the 1,126 persons to Cyprus at the settlers fare, for some reason absolutely refused to move the remaining ones at the same fare and demanded the fourth class fare. The management of the railroad said the Doukhobors were not settlers. Hard as Sergei Lvovich worked for a change in this ruling everyone had to pay the fourth class fare which, for the whole group, considerably increased the cost.

Two delegates of the first party brought provisions for the sailing time of thirty days. Dried bread crusts had been collected in preparation beforehand, and now they had enough for the voyage. The remaining provisions consisted of reserves of rice, oats, wheat and other grains, potatoes, beans, flour, peas, butter, onions, salt, tea, sugar and cabbage. Since the Doukhobors are all vegetarians, this greatly simplified feeding en route as preservation of large stocks of meat would have presented an insuperable problem.

The assets of the first party were as follows: Of the 50,000 roubles which had been saved by the Doukhobors for the possibility of migration, 17,000 roubles had been used by those who went to Cyprus, so that 33,000 roubles remained. This is a list of expenses of the first party:

Rail fare to Batum	2,000 roubles
Lumber for construction on ship	1,200 "
Provisions from Batum to Canada	1,000 "
Ship (*Lake Huron*)	56,000 "
Fare on Canadian railroad	20,000 "
	Total 80,200 roubles

From the total it may be seen that they were short 48,000 roubles. English Quakers, notwithstanding their considerable expense in supporting the Cyprus Doukhobors, decided to help this party also. Assistance was also given by Englishmen living at that time in the agriculture colony of Purley, near London. They had helped the Doukhobors in the past, providing funds for the travel of delegates to Canada. Now they gave all they could. But the main help was given by

L.N. Tolstoy. Making an exception to his rule not to take royalties for his publications, he sold his novel *Resurrection* for the benefit of the Doukhobors. At the same time he turned to private persons for help and in this way the following funds became available:

English Quakers	2,800 roubles
Colonists from Purley	10,200 ″
From L.N. Tolstoy	34,200 ″
Doukhobor funds	33,000 ″
	Total 80,200 roubles

For wintering in Canada and acquiring stock and equipment, money was provided by the Canadian government in the form of the so-called "bonus." This is the money given by the Canadian government to the immigration agent or shipping company able to attract settlers to Canada. For each immigrant, regardless of sex or age, the agents or shipping companies, receive 5 dollars. But since Doukhobors were migrating by themselves without the help of agents, the whole bonus of 35,000 dollars (70,000 roubles) was paid to them through Mr. Maude as their official representative.

Certain precautions had to be taken to prevent the bonus from being claimed by the shipping companies on whose ships the Doukhobors would come to Canada. For this reason the contract said not a word about what we would be transporting from Batum. Sergei Lvovich and I gladly accepted the responsibility for overloading a ship, if it were to happen.* In this manner the bonus was completely protected from the shipowners.

The remaining Doukhobors included the 1,600 Elizabetpol and the 3,000 Kars Doukhobors, moved at their own expense; and the whole bonus, by general agreement was to be used only for the 3,300 exiled Doukhobors.

1) And so on December 10th, 1898, the *Lake Huron* left Batum with 2,140 exiled Doukhobors. Because of fierce storms en route, it took 32 days and arrived in St. John on January 11th, 1899. En route 10 persons died and one was born.

2) On December 17th, 1898, the *Lake Superior* left Batum with 1,600 Elizabetpol and 700 Kars Doukhobors, a total of 2,300 people. It was en route 27 days and arrived in St. John on January 15th, 1899, where it was detained in quarantine for 27 days because of the spread of smallpox on the ship. Six persons died en route.

3) On April 15th, 1899, the *Lake Superior* left Cyprus with 1,010

---

*In Canada, as in the United States, for ships arriving with immigrants there are established rules which limit the number of passengers a ship may carry according to its tonnage displacement. There are severe penalties for breaking these rules.

persons—Doukhobors. It was 26 days en route and arrived in Quebec May 10th, 1899. En route one person died and one was born.

4) At the end of January, 1899, the *Lake Huron* left Batum with 2,300 Kars Doukhobors. It was en route 27 days, and arriving in Quebec was held for 27 days in quarantine because of a smallpox epidemic on the ship. Four persons died en route.

In Batum
November 29, 1898 .

On November 21st, 1898, the *Lake Huron* left Liverpool for Batum. It was necessary that all passengers be in Batum by the time of its arrival.

The question arose: where to put the 2,140 persons for the several days that they would have to spend in Batum awaiting the ship. The local inkeepers refused to accept the Doukhobors, finding them unprofitable guests, since they ate their own food, and took no meat or liquor. They did not use tobacco.

The difficulty was resolved for us by a certain Mr. Richner, who offered the Doukhobors the use of all the buildings of his idle kerosene factory. The yard of this plant was filled with large warehouses; although these were open on one side, the protection of the roof and three stone walls kept out the rain and wind. There were also many sheds available for storing baggage and provisions.

Mr. Richner wanted no money for this stay, asking only that before leaving we would clean the yard and garbage holes at our expense.

Upon examining the buildings, we were convinced that they could accommodate more than 2,000 persons. Staying at this plant was convenient also because it was situated a half verst from the harbour beside a siding from the Trans-Caucasian Railroad, so that the Doukhobors did not need to hire transport for their baggage from the station to the plant.

Yesterday, the first train-load of 560 Doukhobors arrived in Batum. Sergei Lvovich and I, and the English Consul, Mr. Stevens, went to meet them.

From a distance, through the noise and whistles of the surrounding factories, the drawn out mournful sounds of the singing of the approaching Doukhobors was carried towards us. Around the corner the black locomotive appeared and rumbling past us came car after car in a long train. Tall Doukhobors in their blue work clothes stood at the open doors silently bowing to our welcome.

Moving undecidedly backward and forward several times, striking bumpers and chains, the train approached the factory and stopped.

The heavy doors of the cars screeched open. Men jumped out, setting up wooden steps on each car, and out came women, children and old men.

What a scene! A woman stands at the door of a car, hands a baby to the father standing below. The baby squirms and twists at the space opening up below him, preparing to roar with all his might, but he is held by familiar hands, and his howl is postponed to a more fitting time—especially since now hardly anyone will pay him attention. There are other matters. The old man and old woman have to be helped to get down, to bring out their goods—huge bundles of bedding, clothing, assorted barrels, troughs, pails, oven rakes, etc. People must find out where their fellow villagers will be, how they will cook dinner, where a comfortable corner may be found where they might bathe the baby?

Soon all the inhabitants of the cars are on the railway bank; from the wide doors now roll swollen bundles of bedding. Falling softly on the bank they roll to the bottom awkwardly, as if resisting, rolling over from side to side and flashing black letters indicating the owner. Next, the bundles, trunks, troughs and barrels are unloaded. Near the trunks, women bend over, busily tidying the rough canvas covers.

The grade comes alive. In the bright sunshine the colourful dresses of the Doukhobor women flash and the hurried speech of the busy crowd softly murmurs in the bright clear autumn air!

Several elders stepped forward from the throng and approached us. What tall, strong figures with wide backs and strong shoulders, as if cast of iron! Their movements were restrained, as is always the case with strong people. They came with a firm step; slowly, unhurriedly, heads raised with a feeling of dignity. The eyes looked straight ahead into one's face from under stern brows.

The faces of all were shaven, with large moustaches stretching down in the Little-Russian (Ukrainian) manner. Dressed in light blue work clothes that looked as if they might burst at the seams at the slightest careless movement, wearing sheepskin caps, they looked like Zaporozian Cossack leaders going to an official meeting.

As they came up to us, they stopped, took off their caps, and holding them in their hands over the head, bowed low, showing closely cropped heads.

"How do you do?"

We answered. They straightened up and continuing to hold their caps in their hands they bowed again.

"How is your family?"

Receiving an answer they put on their caps and stretched out their hands to us.

The Doukhobors have definite rules for greeting one another, and though we do not reply as fully as would be necessary according to their custom, they do this every time, omitting nothing.

In a meeting between Doukhobors the following conversation takes place:

"How are you?"

"God be praised. How are you?"

"Thanks. How are your people at home?"

"Thank you."

"Our people send greetings."

"Thank you."

At each phrase, the speaker bows with bare head. In the Doukhobor practice—which is something in the nature of a catechism—it is said that in greeting one's brother, the Christian must have a kind heart and gentle expression. All this is done sedately, without haste; and no matter what urgent matter might be before them, I have never seen them shorten or rush this ceremony.

After examining the places set aside for the provisions and baggage and the warehouses where the people were to stay, the elders returned to the buzzing crowd, and soon a line of people stretched across the yard from the sheds to the warehouses.

There was one man bent under a heavy bundle tied with crossed ropes; it seemed the earth sank under each step of his massive figure. Girls, conversing merrily in pairs, carried trunks hung from a carrying pole. On the road, two youngsters puffing, serious-faced, struggled with a barrel; they put it down on the ground for a rest and then could not lift it again. Barely moving their feet, old men came with sieves and troughs. Youths ran back and forth carrying bags of bread crusts.

Now there were two lines stretching across the yard. One was going to the train for goods and the other, loaded, was moving towards the warehouses. At the train, the portly figure of the elder Vasya Popoff stood out among the Doukhobors picking up their baggage and provisions as he directed the unloading of the cars. He spoke calmly, impressively. In a black sheepskin cap with red top and a new work suit, Vasya Popoff reminded me of Taras Bulba. I could not restrain myself and told him how striking he looked.

"Yes, the Georgians are saying, 'this is their senior,' " answered Vasya Popoff. "Even a policeman came up and asked 'They say you are the senior here.' 'Oh no, brother,' I said, 'we do not have seniors. This is not permitted with us,' I said. 'We are all equal.' It must be that the red top on the cap impresses them," he added laughing heartily.

Soon everyone was settled in the warehouses of the plant, their baggage and provisions piled in the shed. Throughout the yard campfires began to smoke under black kettles as women busily prepared dinner. Children fed the fire with the chips which were brought to us from the neighbouring plant. Here and there the fastidious Doukhobor women laundered linen. Young people gathered in a circle and in chorus sang their merry poems—"stikhi," as they call their songs.

Under the shed where the baggage was heaped, the owners crowded with bowls and bags in their hands. There Vasya Chernenkoff, a lively, excitable person, was handing out the common provisions—rice, potatoes, and other vegetables for dinner and supper. Impatient shouts were often heard from the crowd:

"Do not press."

"Oh, my God, brother! Let me breathe!"

"How many persons have you?"

"Now, where shall I pour this for you? Eh?"

There were 200 carpenters on the train, chosen by the people themselves to perform the construction work on the ship. To several more of the experienced I explained what would be needed for their future work, and they set off at once to the lumber yards to buy the lumber.

Today the second train came. On the journey two men and one little girl had hurt their fingers in the heavy door; I had to take them to the city hospital for bandaging.

On my return I saw in the yard a crowd gathered in a circle. I asked what had happened. It seems that two old people (husband and wife) travelling on yesterday's train, got off during the night at some small station and, absorbed in the strange sights, they failed to get back to their train on time. They arrived with today's party and were meeting their fellow-villagers.

In the middle of the circle, leaning on a stick, stood a thin, bent, very old man with a long, red nose and a sore eye. Beside him stood a stout, round woman. Both of them turning in all directions and smiling, replied to welcomes and described how they had spent last night. In telling this, both with happy faces like newlyweds, they glanced at one another.

"I see my old man has got off. 'Where are you going, Misha,' I said, and he, the old dear, did not hear and kept walking into the dark."

"I didn't hear, I didn't hear, that's true. I did not hear!" the old man confirms hurriedly, nodding in all directions.

"And I think: 'How lonely he will be without me,' and I decided to get off myself. At first they didn't let me. By the time I got to him the train started! I shouted and he shouted—but we got only hand-waving in return! We ran a little after the train, but there was no way! We stopped and began to weep."

There was laughter in the crowd.

"And what were you thinking, Markovna, that the old man had run away from you?"

"Oh, no," said the old lady. "The important thing is that he is sickly. That's the important thing. We went to the station and the station master, God save him—such a good fellow—said, 'Tomorrow another train will come with your people, they will take you. Meanwhile,' he said, 'sleep in this cabin.'"

"And he gave us bread and tea. And in the morning our people came. And so here we are!"

"It is so joyful, so good to be with our brethren, dear ones," said the woman smiling in all directions.

"But oh, how frightened we were, oh-h-h!"

The crowd laughed and took the old couple for a meal and to find them a place in the warehouse, with their fellow-villagers. And for a long time, they could be seen here and there, always together, telling about their adventures.

On the 25th and 27th of November, the remaining 1,020 exiles arrived. Now in Batum there were 2,140 people who were to travel on the *Lake Huron*. All the space at the plant was taken up. Under the huge shed lay mountains of trunks, bags and all kinds of domestic furnishings. Doukhobors were walking around everywhere—on buildings under construction, gardening, and in the harbour unloading ships—everywhere their large, neat forms appeared. It is hard to imagine how this large group will get onto one ship.

Batum
December 4, 1898.

The ship has been delayed and the weather has changed for the worse. Day and night, rain pours down, the yard fills with a thin mud, and the people, sitting still in the warehouse, are chilled—especially the children. It is difficult to cook food; the chips are wet, and the area with kettles is filled with smoke which, mixed with fog, floats up and reddens the eyes.

From the gloomy grey sky, almost lightless, come slanting streams of autumn rain. Feet slopping through the cold thin mud, sad figures wander in the choking yellow fog; one, covered with bags, bends over a campfire; others coax the smoking chips to burn.

At night a raw penetrating fog hangs over the huge warehouses. It is cold! A lantern burns, blinking dolefully, surrounded by a dirty yellow cloud of light. It squeaks mournfully on its rusty ring every time a cold draft puffs from outside. Rain drums loudly on the roof and bubbles and spatters monotonously in the pools that have gathered in the yard.

In the depth of the black night, someone seems to be bitterly weeping, sobbing, sighing loudly. The sound echoes through the warehouse and penetrates mercilessly with its icy chill. The people, who are scattered all over the floor with the children, press closer together. Then this living mass, lost in the terrifying darkness, stirs lightly. Dark figures move, trying to get warm under their cloaks; mothers murmur with concern, cover their children and press them to their breasts. Here and there people cough as if conversing—a dry sharp cough, like the bark of a dog. Sometimes in a distant corner as if by agreement there is a chorus of coughs. Somewhere a child weeps mournfully.

*　　*　　*

One night there was such a wind that the warehouse shuddered and the iron roofs rattled as if they were being torn off. It was impossible to sleep! We asked the owner for tarpaulins, and tried to hang them over the open side of the warehouses. The wind shook them relentlessly and the tarpaulins rattled and flapped like flags. The coughing did not subside that night.

Because of this weather people began to fall ill. Many complained of coughs, of dysentery, and especially of fever, which appeared more and more frequently. There was fear of an epidemic. I had to ask the city doctor to examine the Doukhobors; during the examination, it was found that many were sick. The doctor prescribed medicines, and in the evening Vasya Chernenkoff and I handed them out. Under such living conditions, the medicines could not help much. During the seven day stay in Batum, three children died: two from dysentery and one girl who had suffered earlier from cancer.

Once while examining the sick, the doctor discovered one girl with scarlet fever. For fear of the sickness spreading among the crowded people, it was necessary to isolate the girl and her family from the rest. A place had been set aside for quarantine for contagious diseases; but to do this was not easy. The sick girl and her relatives were deeply hurt by this separation from the people, and argued that they had similar sicknesses often at home, that it was not contagious, etc. Only with the help of the "elders," could we manage to move them and isolate them from the rest of the people, though it should be said that the elders were not keen to help in this matter.

Today one of the men came to me with an embarrassed look and spoke long and not too clearly—something about his wife, of the difficult conditions, that he is not guilty, and that I should not tell anyone. After a long conversation, it finally was clear that his wife was about to give birth and he was asking for a private place to be found.

I found nothing wrong with the fact that his wife was to give birth and it seemed strange that the man should speak in such a confused and apologetic tone. Later, the reason became clear. From the time they were exiled to Tiflis Province, three and a half years before, the Doukhobor men lived apart from their wives, finding that under these conditions it would be better not to have children. This had been decided by the whole society. For this reason, if a birth occurred, the society looked disapprovingly and with suspicion at such inexcusable weakness of spirit.

The wife herself and her husband, feeling their guilt exposed before the others, strove to make themselves as inconspicuous as possible and to have the birth away from the people.

Now I understood the reason for the lack of young children, which had previously amazed me.

The manager of the plant provided a delivery room. When I passed the door, I saw women running out with pails and tubs hurriedly whispering, and returning. While all the people knew what was happening in the little room near the office, none spoke about it aloud and each one, passing by, gave the appearance of not noticing anything unusual. The woman gave birth to a baby boy before the day was over.

Batum
December 7, 1898.

The lumber had been bought, and now it was necessary to move it from the lumber yards to the dock where the ship was to be berthed.

The cost of hiring teams for this purpose would have been considerable, so the Doukhobors decided to move it themselves.

Men, women and children—in total about 700 persons—formed a long line in pairs, carrying boards and rails on their shoulders. This line stretched through the whole city and sea-front, eliciting surprise and sympathy from passers-by. Picking up their skirts, the women merrily marched through the shining puddles in the light rain, and the next day all the lumber was piled at the plant.

But the ship had not arrived. Finally a telegram came from Constantinople saying that the *Lake Huron* would be in Batum on Saturday, December 5th.

All that day everyone searched the horizon, in case the smoke of a ship should appear. Not seeing anything by evening, they went to sleep. But the sleep was restless, as no one could sleep for the excitement. And then, not long before daybreak, through the damp fog from the sea came a steady hoot, then another, as if asking for something. Hearing it, many people came out into the dark, to the edge of the pier. Once again, hardly piercing the thick fog, came another hoot, this time short and uncertain. But through the fine rain, nothing could be seen. Yet the blustering wind howled, and with heavy sighs the icy waves broke against the dock, sending clouds of salt spray flying, mixed with drops of rain.

It was not until daybreak that we could see the black silhouette of a large three-masted ship gently rocking on the still water outside the harbour. It was the *Lake Huron*!

After several hours it entered the harbour and stopped near the factory, its side pressed against the pier. No one could board the ship since a customs examination was in progress.

At about three o'clock, we were finally admitted. In the ward room, we were met by a small heavy-set person with energetic, confident movements, who introduced himself as the captain of the ship. He had a good open face, clearly delineated lips, sharp grey eyes that looked intelligent and piercing; despite his short stature he was impressive. One felt this was a man of character, who knew how to handle himself and others.

We went around the ship with him, comparing it with the plan which had been sent to me earlier, and with which I had planned the bunks and other structures. In comparison with the plan, the ship turned out to be wider by one foot.

Now we could begin work! First the necessary lamps were set up on the ship. Carpenters came from the plant and I divided them into two shifts of one hundred each, so that the work would not stop for a minute, day or night.

At first the Doukhobors felt uncomfortable and timid on the ship, pressed together, and unable to imagine what they could do here with their axes and saws in this big iron box with iron ceilings and a network of tangled walk-ways.

After becoming familiar in general with the ship, work was begun on one of the stern decks. The places for the bunks were marked with chalk. Several experienced carpenters made the start, since it was necessary to find a pattern for the complex and unusual work. Those standing around watched. Little by little they joined the workers and soon all 100 were moving confidently to the deafening rattle of axes and the screech of saws.

Their dark figures were lit by the lanterns as they moved about the deck between rails, boards, and other lumber, the whiteness of which stood out from the surrounding gloom. The long shimmering shadows of the carpenters ran restlessly along the sides, now gathering into one dark spot, now quickly separating and going in different directions. They too, seemed occupied with some work of their own. From a distance, it looked as if this bustling, noisy crowd, lantern lights flashing among them, was doing some fearful, mysterious work.

The noise was unimaginable; it rang in the ears. The work proceeded very well. But by the end of the shift, towards two o'clock, the workers became noticeably tired. There was less shouting, axe blows were drawn farther apart. And the saws, heavier than before, screeched lazily, as if complaining. Perspiring faces, reddened eyes and furrowed brows were everywhere.

Time to rest!

At two o'clock, the second shift came. Ten persons who understood the work well remained from the first shift, to show the newcomers how to work. At first the work slowed down, but soon the axes hammered busily and the saws screeched once more.

At five o'clock I left this uproar and went to the top deck to see if enough lumber had been brought during the day, and was startled by what I saw there.

The sky was completely clear, the moon shone, the bay was quiet, very quiet. Somewhere far away, a sleepy bell tolled the time. And from below came the bangs of axes, shouts and noises, strange and out of place on such a beautiful, peaceful night.

Distant, the moon was not surprised, looking calmly and sadly at the earth as if not believing that it would ever see bustling, hostile people living wisely and loving one another.

Day was breaking and the sky was suffused with a pale light, while in the grey dawn a line of people carrying lumber stretched from the plant to the ship.

By noon today a significant part of the work was done. The captain announced that he needed workers to move coal from the hold to the coal bins today. He offered 80 kopeks per day and 1 rouble 20 kopeks at night; Doukhobors not occupied with carpentry undertook this work gladly.

Batum
Tuesday Morning, December 8, 1898.

All night the bunks were being built in the lower decks. The outside part of the top deck was finished. Tonight the noise on the ship was increased by the sound of winches moving the coal.

Batum
Wednesday, December 9, 1898.

All yesterday and last night the same work continued. On Tuesday evening the loading of baggage was begun, continuing till Wednesday evening. For this work, sixty more Doukhobors were called. They worked in the lower decks, stowing the baggage so that in the event of a storm it would not roll and break. Above, all spare space was taken up by bags of flour.

About noon today the bunks were finished. But the bunks and the decks had been covered with fine coal dust, when the coal was moved. It would not do to bring the people in without first washing the ship.

A fire hose was attached to the pump, as is always done for washing down the ship, and soon a strong current of hot water came splashing out. It reminded me of my previous work as a sailor, and I took hold of the hose. About thirty people arrived with long brushes and rags and vigorously scrubbed the deck and the bunks.

The work went noisily and merrily. The heavy stream of water carried away the dirt, and the Doukhobors, chattering clamorously, sometimes unnecessarily got in the way of the stream of water, as if wishing to show that such work was quite customary for them.

At five o'clock, after the ship was cleaned, a deputation, consisting of the captains of two ships standing in Batum and the English Consul visited us. They wished to see our makeshift arrangements for passengers. Walking through the whole ship, they approved of the construction, suggested re-inforcement in some places, and went away expressing surprise at the quick and sound work of the Doukhobors.

Tomorrow—Thursday—at twelve noon the period during which the ship can stay in Batum without charge ends. So we had to hurry with the loading of the passengers. But before beginning this work, we had to examine the baggage which people wanted to have with them so that the baggage not needed on the voyage could be sent to the hold, and would not take up space in the bunk area. During this examination, while taking the larger trunks to the hold, we often encountered resistance from the Doukhobor women.

You see a large number of bags, pails, barrels, boxes, as well as two trunks and you ask:

"For how many people is this baggage?"

"For four. And why?" asks the woman sometimes smiling and sometimes preparing to weep.

"I asked you to take with you as little as possible—tea dishes and change of linen. Trunks will be brought from the hold every week."

"But is this much? It seems there is nothing here for four! I cannot do anything without the trunk. It's true!"

"Well, what do you have there?"

"Well, what? Tea dishes!"

"This is for four persons?"

"Of course. Well there is thread, needles, patches, soap, three changes of linen. Burial clothes."

"Well, whatever you say, this trunk goes to the hold! Take out the tea dishes and change of linen, but the rest you can get from the hold."

At once the woman's face falls and, through tears she says:

"Yes. But for the Resantsevs you have left more than for me!"

"But they have 21 persons."

"Well then, take it," she says decidedly after sad contemplation. "Only be so good as to see that it does not get damaged. They say the trunks are thrown very carelessly, like nuts; the trunks, they say, just smash!"

At nine o'clock in the evening the elders were told of the plan for embarkation. The elders approved the plan, but nevertheless asked permission to go aboard by villages. They went around the whole ship and marked with chalk the place for each village.

The plan they proposed seemed undesirable for many reasons, but not having observed their organization at any time I decided to accede to their wishes. For the last time I examined the decks; there was a fresh feeling. There was no trace of the noise and disorder; the bunks seemed well built and ready for their passengers.

The first Doukhobors appeared at the entrance. Looking at one another we said, "Good day." The family came in timidly.

From the top deck one could see, as well as the night permitted, an endless line of people coming from somewhere in the dusk, with bundles of bedding on their backs and children in their arms.

Until about midnight, the movement went smoothly enough, but then little by little, people crowded at the spar deck, and at the entrance to the deck; and on the street near the entrance a noise was heard. The people at the back pressed those ahead, and those at the front called to those behind that there was no room although not half the ship was occupied yet.

I proceeded to the deck entrance and saw that there was no way to go ahead. The crowd blocked the steps all the way down.

I therefore, went down by another route and came upon an unimaginable mix-up. In the dusk dark figures of people struggled, shouted, pushed one another, in an incredibly tight space, arguing about which bunks were for the Orlov village people, and which for the Tambov village. But since it was not possible to find the answer in the complex plan of the ship, they crowded together with their bundles, blocking all entrances and exits.

No one was in the bunks, and it was impossible to consider how much space they would take. Only the children sat beside the untied bedding, and with wide open eyes looked at all that was happening around them.

The air was filled with dust and a kind of fog from close-packed humanity. Adults with perspiring faces and swollen veins on foreheads looked around confused and asked each other questions for which none knew the answers. When they saw me they rushed to ask:

"Where are we to sit? We are from Orlovka village. The elders said to the left as you enter but here are people from Tombovka and Efremovka. What trouble!"

"Their place is not here at all," answered the Tombovka people, "they are mixed up. They should go to deck number 2."

And so on.

Obviously if things went on this way they would never settle down. Hence I told them to sit wherever there was free space.

But this did not help immediately. Many standing near free bunks continued a persistent search for "their" places which had been occupied by others, and those who had taken places did not put their bedding on the bunks, but milled around in the passageway, so that it was impossible to get onto the deck or off it. I had to announce that the loading would stop until those already on the ship had settled down in their places. Soon everything came to order and the movement resumed. The river of people moved slowly, filling the ship, taking up the bunks one after another.

The last deck was already filled with noisy people, but on the dock, under the lamp flame flickering in the wind, there were still about 150 people standing or sitting in tired poses near their baggage. Apparently there was no room for them. Together with the elders, who were asking where these people were to go, I went around the decks where the loading had begun. We had not been there for five hours.

It was quiet. All were sleeping.

But one had only to look at the bunks to see that people were taking up twice as much space as they needed. Some lay across the bunks taking up space for two. Others preferred to lie diagonally, fencing themselves in with pails, troughs, bundles, and even with kegs. Here and there unoccupied places appeared. Though it was a pity to waken the people, tired from all kinds of excitement, it had to be done. But despite our shouting, not everyone awoke. We explained the problem, and asked all the people to move closer together in one direction. Those who awoke began to waken their neighbours and move children together with their bedding. Surplus bags, dishes, etc., were taken off the bunks and put on the deck. The people moved willingly, saying they must find space for the brethren. The women were especially cooperative saying:

"Dear people, still outside with little children! Oh, how much more of this suffering must we have!"

"That's all right," said others. "This is the last God will provide. Be patient a bit more."

People on one side of the deck moving closer together, freed space for about thirty people more.

In moving the people on the other side of the deck, we wakened one old man. He sat down not understanding anything in his sleep. Flapping his eyelids, he looked all around. His lips and chin pushed forward and his tousled beard and moustache made him look very funny. When he was asked to move in the direction in which others were moving, he silently moved in the opposite direction. The elders explain to him where he must move. With an angry and injured tone he shouted:

"Yes. Of course. I will not move far in that direction!"

"But why? Is it not all the same?"

"If it's all the same, there is nothing to talk about. I'll move wherever I wish."

"Understand, Shamshirin, that all are moving in the same direction so as to clear space at one end. There are still people outside, brother."

"Did I not move? Take a look. See how much space is opened up. Why are you after me with this nonsense. I will not go in that direction: I do not wish it! Understand?"

Little by little, the whole deck began to persuade him and only after prolonged arguments, the disagreeable old man moved, grumbling about persecution, which was pursuing him even along the way to Canada.

"And they said this would be the end. That end seems a long way off!" he grumbled moving his bed.

Batum
December 10, 1898.

It was eight o'clock in the morning when the last Doukhobor boarded the ship.

The cranes rumbled endlessly, loading the last provisions and the flour. Smoke came from the huge chimney. Steam was being built up in the boilers and from time to time the ship droned and shuddered as if impatient to be on the way. Soon the chief of police came with police officers and men.

A table was set up near the gang plank where the chief of police installed himself. When everything was ready, all the Doukhobors were sent off the ship to the dock. The police and customs officers examined the whole ship and announced to the chief that there were no Russian citizens on board.

The final loading began.

Each family came to the table and presented its documents. The chief of police found the corresponding passport, naming each member of the family, counted all and let them through on to the ship.

Foreign passports were not given to the Doukhobors, since they were leaving on the condition that they would never return to their native land. For this reason the passports went from the chief of police to the customs officers, who probably have them to this day.

At the entrance to the ship stood two ship's doctors, who examined each Doukhobor embarking. This was done to prevent the introduction of some contagious disease which could spread throughout the ship. If this happened, we would be subject to prolonged quarantine on arrival in Canada.

It was decided by general agreement, that Resantsev's family, which had had scarlet fever not long before, would be left on land. This had a terrible effect on Resantsev. He wept and begged, giving many reasons why it was essential for him to come now, but he had to give in. I was standing on the top deck, the spar deck, observing the last preparations, when the Resantsevs came past me, carrying their baggage off the ship. Coming near me Resantsev raised his pale face with hostile flashing eyes and through the roar of the ship, ready to depart, called:

"Well, thank you. This is all your work."

I knew that in seven days the next ship would leave Batum, taking Resantsev. Nevertheless, I was awe-stricken by these words, spoken in a voice shaking with restrained emotion. For a long time I remembered that face and those words of hurt and blame.

With a final hoot, we said good-bye to those remaining in Russia, and as soon as they got off the ship the last lines holding us to the land were taken away. The shore slowly moved away from us and with it the people standing on the dock. Over the stern, the propellers began to stir the water. The ship shuddered, turned smoothly, and slowly moved forward, surrounded by a flock of skiffs full of friends seeing us off.

The Doukhobors sang a psalm; the mournful drawn out sounds, full of hopeless sorrow, flowed out to the receding shore.

Thousands of voices now joined in a single cry of despair, sorrow, injury. Not only people, but it seemed all nature was stilled, shaken by the soul-searing sobbing of a crowd of thousands mourning their parting from their motherland.

With bared heads, sad and solemn, their eyes full of tears and sorrow, the Doukhobors stood with their faces to the land where they grew up, where their grand-parents and great grand-parents lived and died, where their leaders are buried, where they had to bear so much suffering, accept so many heavy losses.

The psalm flowed farther and farther out on an irresistible current, a psalm asking for forgiveness of the land for its sons leaving it. The shores moved farther and farther away, as life moves away, life itself never to return. It was felt that something incredibly inhumane was taking place, something that could not be corrected. Sometimes the wild, sharp screech of the ship's siren came through the dense tones of the psalm, as if horrified at what was happening here.

High in the air a rocket fired from the ship exploded, and in the distant sky the small white cloud left by it faded. The skiffs suddenly fell back: the ship was moving ahead at full speed. The singing stopped. The petrified crowd, faces wet with tears, silent, holding their breath, looked at the mist-covered, mountainous shore. In the stillness a woman could be heard crying somewhere by the mast.

Regaining awareness, we saw that the shore was far away and the ship was surrounded with a greater and greater expanse of dark blue water. The sounds of the city and of the land disappeared.

In the warm rays of the sun, the gulls circled above, breaking the silence with sharp cries. A fresh wind splashed small, brisk waves against the ship, reminding us of the fact that it was time to forget about the land and its life, that around us was another life, another power that we would have to consider in this unfamiliar, little-understood life, and we must depend on its laws alone.

The eyes of all turned uncontrollably to the bright calm line of the horizon beyond which the mysterious unknown awaited us, toward which our ship moved so confidently. And looking to that future, everyone on the ship, with a more or less heavy sigh thought:

"What could be waiting for us there?"

At Sea
Black Sea, December 12, 1898.

Out of the 2,140 Doukhobors on the ship, 94 young men were chosen as crew members. Responsibilities were assigned to them in the following manner:

Twenty persons were to be the water carriers. They must carry fresh water in pails from the cisterns to the kitchen. In the morning and evening they carry tea about the decks and at dinner, hot food.

Six persons were appointed as watchmen at two fresh water taps. Day and night in shifts, they must see that nobody besides the water carriers takes water, and that in filling pails the water is not spilt, as it is a thing of great value on board ship.

Two persons were lantern men. They look after all the lanterns on the ship, and see that they are clean. They trim them and light them.

Three persons, in shifts, watch the sea water taps, and see that people do not wash directly from the tap, do not wash dishes here, and do not let the water run on the deck floor.

Nine people were bread bakers, three shifts of three persons each. Two of them knead dough while the third bakes bread in a separate iron range. Each shift works twelve hours every other day.

Twelve persons were cooks—four per shift. Cleaning potatoes and other preparatory work is done by women.

Two persons issue provisions from the hold and keep account of them.

Twelve persons, in shifts, day and night, look after cleaning the latrines.

Thirty of the handier, more efficient persons were specially selected for the work of deck hands. They tie down all kinds of things in time of storm or rough seas, wash decks, look after the proper ventilation of all decks, close and open the hatchways as is necessary and so on. Among them are two carpenters. One of them looks after the readiness of the fire-hose with which the ship is washed, and also looks after the brushes and swabs, ropes, canvas ventilators, and so on.

At first there were many difficulties with inexperienced people. Every detail had to be explained, demonstrated. Some of the crew turned out to be slow. Many were sea sick. These had to be replaced by others.

The main shortcoming was slowness. They lacked the speed necessary for this type of work. At first, for example, in seven hours, they hardly managed to wash the two top decks. This was done at night so as not to interfere with Doukhobors going for a walk on these decks. Later, things worked in this order: during the day the lower decks were washed and every other day, or two, at night time, the two top decks. Soon, at any rate, the crew became accustomed to the task and the work proceeded more calmly and effectively.

On the second day of the voyage a fresh breeze began to blow. On the horizon heavy dark clouds appeared, there was some excitement as the ship began to rock lightly. We had to tie down the troughs lying on the deck, as well as the tables, the trunks and other small items. By the light of lanterns now that it was dark the crew were busy with ropes, attaching everything to iron benches. It was difficult for them to walk, for the deck was now leaping out from under their feet; or just when one decided to run down its slope, it suddenly rose before him as a steep hill. Tangled in ropes they suddenly all either ran or almost sat down, grabbing hold of one another, then flew in one direction as a group, taking hold of whatever was handy.

From a pile of items near which the crew was working, a heavy tub tore free and slid swiftly down the deck, knocking down one of the young men on its way. He was hardly able to straighten up when the tub, striking the side, turned and flew after him. The awkward young man spread his arms and almost caught it, but it suddenly changed direction and he grabbed the feet of his fellow crew member, instead of the tub, and slithered with him, after the tub, as if on a glacier.

At last the lively tub was caught by the combined effort of all, and tied down beside another wide tub, in spite of its angry efforts to break free.

The majority of the Doukhobors, of course, were sea sick although the pitching was only light. The elders, hearing the creaking of the ship sadly shook their heads. "Yes, we have got a cheap ship. If only we could avoid trouble. See how it creaks!" But learning that the whole ship including the under part was iron clad, all calmed down.

Morning brought no change of any kind. The grey sea bustled around the ship in the same way. There was not a soul on the decks; all lay in their bunks, except for several members of the crew standing at their places, and the water carriers, taking boiling water to the bunks. All day the people took nothing but black bread crusts, and tea. Only the children, obviously suffering less from the tossing, gladly ate some rice soup with potatoes.

Constantinople, December 13, 1898.

This morning land was seen on the horizon. A little later two white dots appeared. These were the beacons showing the entrance to the strait of Constantinople. As we came nearer we saw the angry waves dashing at the rocky shore, striving to reach its top and, breaking up into small spray boiling and foaming, falling back in powerless anger, licking the foot of the cliffs.

When word came that land was visible, whoever could handle their disobedient legs clambered to the top deck. Everyone asked whether we would get out on land, and being told that only a few would go on land for purchases, sadly shook their heads.

"We won't make it. No, we won't get there alive if we don't go out on land."

"Where?"

"Is it not visible?"

I took a long time to convince the passengers that they would get used to the tossing. As for going on land, even if it was possible, the Turks would not let us. The elders looked gloomy and repeated:

"It will not take much of this to ruin the people!"

But we are already in the strait, and the ship sails smoothly between beautiful shores thickly covered with tile-roofed houses. From among the buildings packed one beside another, sharp, well-shaped minarets rise towards the sky sparkling with whiteness.

All the inhabitants of the ship came to the top so as to get a view of the land even at a distance. Questions could be heard.

"Where does Arman-Pasha live?"

The majority asked if there will be more tossing, and does it come more violently than that through which we have come?

"How many versts is it to the bottom?"

"Why do we now have a cold wind instead of a warm one?" and so on.

As soon as the anchor was dropped, Vasya Popoff, Chernenkoff' and I set off for the shore to buy bread for the passengers. However, we were not admitted to the city and we had to return. To be admitted to the city one must have the passport and visa of the Turkish Consul. I did not have the visa while Popoff and Chernenkoff did not even have passports. So we delegated the purchase of bread to the captain.

In the evening the boat carrying the bread approached, accompanied by a little sloop. Therein to my joy, I saw A. Bakunin, a young Russian doctor, and his nurse M. Satz who, wishing to see Constantinople en route, had gone there by rail from Russia.

"This is the doctor himself?" asked the Doukhobors.

"How young he is!"

"And this will be our sister?" asked the women about M. Satz.

"You should see our little girl," someone said from the crowd.

After them came another sloop with Nicolai Zeebarev. This was a young doctor who had gained the highest respect of the whole society. He had been sent to England to clarify certain questions. As he had no right to return to Russia, yet wished to travel with his family, he had to board ship at Constantinople.

With him came a person with a well-worn coat, a worn-out fur cap, and long straight hair. His face, framed by a big beard, seemed to jerk before he began to speak, and the long hands, which he held in his pockets, restlessly handled something there. He was a sectarian, a stundist, and was being investigated in Russia for spreading heresy; he asked permission to go abroad. But reaching Constantinople, he became stranded, and having met Zeebarev by chance, he came to ask to be taken to America.

"I'm dying of hunger here, believe me," he said, stuttering with emotion, in his concern that he might be refused, looking mournfully from sunken eyes.

I saw no reason to refuse him.

He blinked his eyes with joy and was about to weep; embarrassed, he moved his cap to his forehead, then to the back saying:

"Now God be praised! Thank you!"

The whole shipload of people was now crowding around Zeebarev and a thin, dry woman, Zeebarev's mother, hugged him with weak old arms. Both wept. All those around had turned joyful faces. Everyone liked Zeebarev, so everyone wanted to greet him and to kiss him. Another crowd gathered around the stranger, who told them about his travels; and the Doukhobors asked him questions, trying to clarify how near this man was to them in his views on life and religion.

Mediterranean Sea,
Passing Cape Matapan.

On December 14th, the *Lake Huron* raised anchor and left Constantinople. The weather was excellent; it was especially good in the green archipelago. The islands there are scattered miraculously about the bright blue sea, covered with thick vegetation, appearing from a distance like furry caps coming out of the water.

High in the clear sky, busily circling, their white wings sparkling in the sun, the gulls were noisily whooping. At times a heavy cormorant, stretching out his neck, came down very close to the ship flapping his wings on the water, clumsily running in the direction of an island. Here and there was the angular sail of a fisherman's boat.

The Doukhobors gazed at the islands with enjoyment. Many did not come down from the deck till late evening. Others even spent the night above. On the ship in harmony with its surroundings, all was calm and quiet. The life of this floating city had become regular and orderly; so time went by unnoticed.

One morning after making his rounds of the sick, A. Bakunin requested that the hospital, as yet unused, be prepared. A five year old boy was ill with leukemia. His father and mother were put in the hospital with him, since the sickness was not infectious and there was no one else in the hospital. That night, after the washing of the deck, I entered the hospital and saw both doctors there. Bakunin and Mercer were busy beside the patient who was held in his father's arms.

In answer to a question about the condition of the patient, the doctor silently opened the boy's mouth and touched the teeth with a metal spoon. They were loose in the darkened, decomposed gums. From the boy came a heavy odour of decomposing flesh. His face was swollen. Looking significantly at me, the doctor said, "All I can do is to inject ether under the skin."

The boy tossed and wheezed, bending now to the window, now to his mother, seeking relief from the agonizing pain. With his helpless little hands, he took hold of the shoulders, then the neck of his grieving father, saying his name with difficulty.

"Grisha, dear father," he said hoarsely, "it hurts."

When they made the subcutaneous injection, he tossed even more.

"No—no, don't do that Grisha," he begged looking into his father's eyes. Carefully, with his large clumsy hand, Grigory quieted the boy lovingly saying with a low voice:

"There, there, now. It won't hurt, this will make it better. Now just wait a minute," and he threw a quick stern glance at his wife, who, weeping, kept taking the doctor's hands.

"Do not torture him unnecessarily," she pleaded. "He will die anyway: let him depart peacefully."

From the hospital which was lit by a small lamp, we walked out on the deck. Through the round window of the hospital we could see two figures bent sadly over the patient.

It was quiet on deck. The ship slept in a deep sleep. With the machinery regularly moaning, as if sighing, and the smooth sea running past the lightly shuddering ship with a hardly audible splash, the sea shone and played, silvery scaled, in the rays of a calm sad moon. And looking at this marvellous, well-proportioned picture, it was hard to believe that at that moment, a little being, in terrible suffering, was uselessly struggling with death, that shows no mercy for age nor condition.

In the morning the boy died. It was decided to bury him the same day.

On the bed in the hospital lay the little corpse, freshly dressed. Near him stood the father with head bowed and arms folded. Grief had diminished him. Deep wrinkles appeared on his face. But his sorrow was calm and full of dignity. There was no gesture of despair. But his whole giant body seemed to have become smaller. His shoulders sagged and his lips closed sternly.

And the mother looking with tender emotion at the peaceful face ravaged by sickness, whispered last words of love to him; covering her face with a handkerchief. Several times she started to weep uncontrollably, her whole body shaking with silent sobs.

It was crowded in the hospital and a choir of twenty persons stood on the deck near the open door. The choir sang psalms fitting the occasion. Relatives stood around the deceased. All were dressed cleanly in their best. Women with hands folded on their stomachs were holding clean, white, neatly folded handkerchiefs. All stood calmly with dignity as if fearing to waken the dead. The sad mournful psalm continued slowly with harmonious, drawn out sounds. One by one these were carried far out to the height of cloudless unknown distance and sunk there in the tranquil depth. When the singing was ended and the last strains had faded away a woman with a musical voice repeated a prayer with loving, pacifying intonations.

Grigory came to me on the deck and looking with tired eyes said: "I have been told that he should be sewn in a heavy canvas with an iron weight put at the feet. Then will you give me the iron? I will do it myself." But his face changed. "Would it be possible somehow to bury him on land? The shore, of course, is right here." With large fingers which one did not normally see shaking, he pointed to one side where Cape Matapan* could be seen.

----
*The southern tip of Greece.

58

Difficult though it was to refuse Grigory this request, it was impossible to grant his wish. That the little body would be dropped into the sea where there would be no grave by which one could, even mentally, go and sit—this thought particularly burdened the mother. It was hard for all the Doukhobors.

Moreover, nothing is said on this question either in the psalms or in the prayers; in their traditions nothing is said about burial at sea. This troubles many, since, while Doukhobors get along without ceremony and do not have priests to meet their everyday needs, nevertheless, in the important events of life, be it birth, marriage or death, they have developed established procedures. It is understandable that the majority assign to these formalities, established by custom, the same significance as to the essence of Doukhobor teaching. "The Christian form", "Real Christian Custom," could be heard more than once. But after all, where do people not confuse form with content, or even attach greater significance to form than to content?!

Grigory himself sewed his son's body into a thin canvas and then into a tarpaulin. He himself put into the foot, an old burnt out furnace bar brought to him for this purpose from the engine room. And only when it became necessary to sew the face, did he delay with the edges of the tarpaulin. It was a little too difficult for him to cover this dear face, knowing that he would never see it again.

The mother, standing beside him, wept so bitterly that it was impossible to see her without doing the same. Many other women were also near to tears. The whole crowd was saddened. Sighs and sympathies were heard.

"How is it, my dears, in the water? Right into the water?"

"What sorrow!"

"Is it altogether impossible on the shore?"

"They say, 'not possible.' "

A lad pulled the sleeve of his grandfather and asked loudly:

"Grandad, Grandad, will the fish eat him there?"

"Enough chatter," the old man answered angrily.

The little boy blinked his eyelids in question and looked at the dolphins jumping in the sea, trying to resolve this question on his own.

The corpse was sewn up.

Again the mournful choir sang, and slowly the crowd moved to the edge of the deck. At the front, with a stern face, went Grigory, holding in his hands a piece of old, folded canvas, the furnace bar awkwardly showing from one side. At the side where a part of the rail had been taken down, the sad procession stopped. The engines were not working and the ship rocked gently from side to side. The moving voice of a woman sang the last prayer, accompanied by the restrained sobs of the mother. The prayer ended. The mother kissed the package for the last time and embracing it, could not part from it.

"My loving one, why were you born, to be thrown into the sea?" she cried. She was quietly led away to one side. Grigory kissed the boy on the head and handed him to me with trembling hands. He suddenly turned pale as a corpse. The whole crowd, holding its breath, awaited with anguish.

Bending over as far as possible from the deck, I opened my hands and the corpse fell into the sea. The water splashed loudly, spray flew, and the crowd as one exclaimed, groaned and ran to the side. The women sobbed out loud, and the men also were nearly all weeping, looking at one another with helpless pitiful faces. And in the clear bright emerald depth of the sea, the white bundle could be seen for a long time, gradually turning to blue. It slowly sank lower and lower. Sloping diagonal sun-rays played on it, piercing the clear water, and ran shimmering after it into the mysterious cloudy depth.

But the ship shuddered, the water alongside it splashed, and again the playful waves ran past us, gently splashing against the ship. And again two spreading streams stretched out from the nose of the ship, like two whiskers of some gigantic fish calmly moving on the desert of water. And already the place where little Vladimir was dropped could not be recognized. There the sea was smiling to the sky as calmly as anywhere else, as calmly as if nothing unusual had happened. The crowd quietly broke up.

Only Grigory and his wife remained standing a long time at the very edge, near the flag pole, pressed against one another, mournfully staring at the water along the foaming bubbling stream left by the propeller of our ship.

Mediterranean Sea
December 19, 1898.

It was warm and calm as in the archipelago. Only a gentle breeze freshened the warm air.

Women washed laundry all day. There were troughs and tubs all over the deck, and everywhere merry voices of women could be heard. Towards evening, cables rose to the top of all three masts, with laundry attached for drying.

At mid-ship, a noisy hammering of picks on iron was heard. About a hundred boys were chipping rust from the iron deck surrounding the engine room hatchway. In the evening after work, they gathered on the quarter-deck. Flat cakes were brought from the kitchen and Nurse M. Satz put marmalade on them and gave them to the boys as reward for their work. At such a time, grown-ups are not allowed on the quarter-deck. The children like this ceremony very much! The whole quarter-deck is covered with well-fed boys and girls. One after another they came up to Marie Aleksandrovna, unhesitatingly took their portion, and, swinging their large heavy caps, they bowed.

Snuffling, putting on airs, puffing out their lips they said, "Thank you!" Then each child walked off to one side, put on his cap, and bit into the marmalade, nose and all.

It was noteworthy that during this time there were no quarrels or fights. Also, it never happened that someone finished his portion and came for another. At that time, the eldest was no more than ten years of age, yet all went without jostling and in such manner that on only one occasion did the pleasant routine end in tears.

During the thanking ceremony, the jam from one boy's cake began to slide off and was about to fall on the deck. Of course this could not be permitted. In an effort to catch it, the boy dropped his cap which, caught by the wind, rolled on the deck like a wheel. It disappeared in the waves on the Mediterranean Sea where its appearance produced not a little furor among the fish. The unfortunate boy, spreading the fingers of both hands covered with marmalade, sobbed bitterly jerking his head:

"Oh Nanny! My cap has drowned!"

His companions comforted him as much as they could until his mother arrived.

(Among the Doukhobors, it is not customary for children to call their parents "papa" or "mamma." The father is usually called by name, the mother is always called "Nanny.")

Making the most of the good weather, we again moved coal from the holds to the coal bins and carried garbage from one side of the ship to the other as the ship was not altogether trim. As many people as possible were appointed to this work in order to keep them moving, which in a great measure guarantees good health during shipboard living. All the same, even though unnecessary work was found, there was not enough for everyone and many continued to sit in the bunks. These had to be brought out to the upper deck almost by force. And only upon coming out they naively said:

"How good it is here! Why did we have to sit down there?"

The place especially favoured by young girls was near the funnel on the spar deck, protected on all sides by life boats. They sat in groups like clumps of bright flowers, sewed flags, collected sail thread, or did embroidery, of which Doukhobor women are great masters.

Beside them dallied young men including sailors free from their shift. It should be said they nearly all married during the voyage.

The young people "chattered" as the Doukhobors say, i.e.

conversed. Here and there they broke in to cheerful song. From the other end of the ship came a solemn steady drone: The elders were singing psalms.

Two old men emerged from a cabin set aside for them; they were Ivan Makortoff and Bokov. Ivan Makortoff, father of the delegate Peter Makortoff who had been sent to Canada, was nearly ninety years of age. He was the only Doukhobor wearing a long grey beard. Despite his great age he was still very strong, having kept his teeth all these years. He had a heavy set figure with wide shoulders and a proudly raised head. His stern commanding eyes looked out from beneath grey brows. He walked importantly like a general, firmly and decidedly, as if going somewhere to a battle. He always had a stick in his hand. He seemed to carry it solely to rap with, never leaned on it.

It was very warm outside but since according to the time of the year it was now winter, Makortoff came out fully clothed, wearing a Siberian fur cap with ear-flaps which he brought from exile.

Back at the time of Nicholas I, he was a boatman on the ships of that time, and now when a sailor passes him he raises up his stick as if to strike and throwing his head back he asks:

"Where to?"

At the sight of Makortoff, the sailor wilts at once, as though hit with boiling water and timidly answers,

"To swab the decks!"

For several moments Makortoff examines him sternly, then lowering his stick says:

"Well, well!"

And as if having made friends adds more politely:

"God be with you, go!"

At times he came up to me, shook my shoulder, and said significantly:

"Yes. We are at sea! Different rules. Not on land, my brother, no! Important," he would say suddenly changing his tone, "Important, to hold them well in hand. No fooling around. Strictly!"

And turning sharply to crew members standing here in the room, almost shouting, pounding his stick on the floor and pointing to me with a shaking finger, he would exclaim:

"This person is to be listened to and obeyed. In everything, in full. Understand?"

And the sailors, shifting from one foot to another, would look timidly at the former boatman and not know what to do.

But Makortoff would not wait for an answer. He had already turned and walked away tapping his stick with the look of one who has completed a task; he inspected all the corners of the ship. Sometimes passing a sailor he would slyly wink at him and say:

"Call everyone to the top. Eh?"

When he came to a place where women and girls were sitting, their conversation ceased and many respectfully rose.

"Oh-h- Beauties," he would say, head stretched forward and examining each with his bulging eyes. The girls would become embarrassed and only rarely would anyone say anything to him. Standing a few minutes he would go farther. Even elders in his presence became more sparing of words. At meetings he generally began his speech loudly, authoritatively, as:

"Everything must be done right, in the Christian manner, justly. Without wriggling this way and that. We must be true to our word. What is said, is done!"

In the same cabin with Makortoff there was billeted another man, Grigory Bokov, Grisha as everyone called him. Grisha was a very old man with water eyes, his back bent under the weight of years. Like Makortoff, he was not and probably would never be bald. His face was smooth-shaven, and in his hands he always had a clean, neatly folded handkerchief with which he wiped his tears from time to time.

Grisha did not have even one relative; for a long time he had been living with the community. He has experienced a fearful lot in his life. He has always stood by his convictions with great constancy, and for this he more than once has had to go to jail. His legs still ache from the heavy irons put on him in his youth. But in spite of all the trials which he has had to live through in his one hundred or so years, he has managed to preserve to this day an unusually bright loving relationship with people.

"Brother, love is necessary," he would say in a convincing voice. "Love is everything, all of Christian life. Yes."

Grisha loved everyone including little children. Once in the Caucasus I happened to see two youngsters taking him up a steep hill. One of them pulled him by the hand and the other pushed him from behind.

"Grisha, this way. Put your foot here," said one and Grisha asked in a shaking voice:

"Here, my little dove?"

In his hand he had a bouquet of all kinds of grasses and flowers which he had gathered on this walk.

Young boys gathered around in a circle to listen to the stories about his life, stories that gave one goose pimples more than once. Sometimes laughing they would ask:

"Grisha, will you soon marry?"

Bokov, smiling good-naturedly with his toothless mouth would say: "Soon, dear one! My bride is the raw earth. It must be soon now.

Make me a good white coffin and bury me. Oh-h how it will embrace me!"

"You will not get out then, Grandad!"

"Of course."

"And it's time that you die soon, Grisha?"

"It is time. I wish only to get to Canada," said Grisha, "to bury my bones there, near my brethren. Get me there, dear ones!"

His face was lit up with kindness. It seems no one had seen him dissatisfied, except when someone in his presence said Makortoff was older than he. Then Grisha became angry and in a hurt voice he said:

"Who? Makortoff? He is a youngster compared with me! Yes! I am the oldest one here. No more to be said about it!"

And long after this conversation he wore an injured look.

But in general, he was a person completely devoid of any vanity. It was enough to show him a little attention, some insignificant service, to bring to his face a most moving smile and light up his eyes with ecstasy. He was at his very best when at a meeting it was decided to help someone or to forgive a debt. Then he would melt altogether as if dissolved in an atmosphere of love.

"That's it, brethren, that's it!"

Makortoff protectively looked after Grisha, split lump-sugar into small pieces for him, poured his tea into the saucer, and so on. He did this with a look that said—after all we must look after the old, must help the old man. And from Makortoff's shaking hands it could be seen that not much would have to be added to his age to make them equals. Neither Bokov nor anyone else knew his exact age; judging by talk, he must have been not less than a hundred. After a little while on the deck, Bokov, under the protection of Makortoff, went to his cabin.

Mediterranean Sea
December 20, 1898.

Our ship's doctor, Mercer, a young Englishman, sits on the spar deck, surrounded by youngsters. He indicates with his finger the sea, the funnel, his stomach. He writes down Russian names, using English letters. Frequently the laughter of the youngsters is heard when the Englishman, wanting to pronounce a word correctly, repeats it several times.

"Na-aka," carefully repeats Mercer, putting his stretched out finger on his foot.

"But not Na-aka," the youngsters cry in several voices, "Noga."

"Nooka," says the Englishman.

"Oh what a Nemetz* he is. Now simply: Noga. Understand? Well, Noga!"

"Nuoga," patiently repeats Mercer and finally after many corrections, holding his breath for a moment, he says clearly, "Noga!"

"Correct, that's correct," the youngsters cry approvingly.

"That will be alright!"

All his free time he spent thus amongst the youngsters. The results of these lessons soon showed in his daily morning rounds of the sick. One of the women would get up and complain of a pain in the pit of the stomach. Ordinarily he would wait until someone translates. But now, looking at his little book, he would put his hand on her stomach and looking in her eye ask,

"Your stomach aches?"

The woman would approvingly nod her head.

"And yet how, God! I have no strength. It pains all the time, as if a fire is burning."

And Mercer would be satisfied. A fine, work-loving person, courteous and obliging in the highest degree, he related to people very well, attentively and with respect. Everyone on the ship soon got to like him.

His colleague, another ship's doctor, a red-haired, tall Englishman began, from the first day of the voyage, to behave rudely and haughtily toward the Doukhobors. One day he put out the lamp in the pharmacy when M. Satz was working there, because in his view M. Satz was using up too much medicine. After this it became necessary to ask him not to get involved at all in the medical work on board. From then on he spent whole days in his cabin, lying on the couch and drinking to drunkenness. Rarely, and only at dusk, did he come out on the deck and standing at the side, look out to the sea with half-closed haughty eyes, hands in pockets and gurgling his pipe which he never removed from his teeth.

The least satisfactory part of our ship life was the lack of fresh water. Water obtained by distilling sea water, even on good evaporators, is always unpleasant to taste; to us it was often repulsive.

Our evaporator was really bad. All the same, very much depended on the work of the operator. Yesterday and today the water was so bad that it could not be used in any manner. Unquestionably the operator was responsible, and after a little argument, he admitted it. I had to frighten him a little, saying that if this were repeated he would not receive the reward which had been promised to all the crew at the end of the voyage, and moreover that a Letter of Complaint would be composed.

---

*Nemetz—meaning one who cannot speak, also means "German" in Russian.

Our operator, Mr. Dixon, was a diligent worker who knew his work well. I did not wish to quarrel with him from the start, especially since he could do much harm to the Doukhobors. A good-hearted, stout Scotsman, Mr. Dixon was a happy-go-lucky person, who liked to laugh and to sing but was easily frightened. He was always afraid of something. In order to scare him, I said that the loss of the reward and the Letter of Complaint were not all he could expect if the water remained poor. It wouldn't hurt him to know that the Doukhobors themselves might do "God knows what!" with him for this!

Hearing this warning, Mr. Dixon turned pale and blinked his eyes thoughtfully.

"What are you saying, my friend? Can they be like that? They, who are always so quiet?"

"That's just the point, once they decide to punish someone, nothing can stop them!"

"Who would have thought it," he said with the greatest amazement. "I assumed . . . hm . . . hm . . . I didn't think . . . ?"

And mumbling to himself, visibly disturbed, he went to his machine, looking suspiciously at the Doukhobors standing in groups.

In the evening when the Doukhobor crew gathered on the poop deck for work, Mr. Dixon, together with the captain and other crew members, came up on the deck. Coming up to the (Doukhobor) crew, I told them to seize the one of the English whom I touched on the shoulder and toss him until I told them to let him go.

The good-natured "tubby" was, at that very moment, telling the captain of alleged qualities of the Doukhobors which he had recently discovered. Finishing his cigar and saying several times, "Yes," with a sigh, Mr. Dixon started toward his machine. But I placed my hand on his shoulder, and before he had time to turn around, the soles of his boots flashed through the air and he himself disappeared among the Doukhobors. To the loud laughter of the captain and others, we saw his big round body dive out of the confusion and shoot up with arms outstretched and coattails flying. His face was pale, his mouth grew wide, and in his eyes was not a little fright.

The first time he flew up in silence, but after appearing several times above the laughing faces and seeing that they did not wish to do anything else with him, he howled, making an entreating face.

"Oh! Friends! What's this? What is the matter? That's enough!" he cried, choking, now disappearing in the crowd, now coming up over their heads.

Puffing and blowing hard, he began to call loudly:

"This doesn't matter. But I'm afraid they might drop me into the sea! This is so near to the edge! Oh! Friends!"

In the midst of this laughter, Mr. Dixon was put on his feet.

Quickly running out of the crowd and hiding behind us, he laughed happily, straightening his vest from under his arm pits and pulling down his pant legs.

"What fine young fellows," he said, smiling in all directions. "How cleverly they did it!"

And here he asked to have translated that in future the water would be excellent—like sugar.

"But of course, only insofar as this is possible with our machine!" he added with a sigh, raising his shoulders helplessly.

And to become a friend of the Doukhobors for all time, he laughed and shook the hands that tossed him, showing surprise at their skill and adding:

"How clever they are!"

Mediterranean Sea
December 21, 1898.

We passed the island of Malta today. Our ship's masts carried flags of all colors with which, in the agreed international language, we asked that they advise London and Batum by cable, that all is well with us.

All along we moved within sight of the African shores. From these shores, covered with an orange fog, great heat blazed.

The wind blew directly from the east, at our back, and hence did not freshen the air at all. It carried suffocating smoke ahead. The ventilators did not work; in the holds it was stifling at night, especially in the two front ones.

There was almost no rolling. Only occasionally the top edge of the propeller came out of the water and slapped the water, beating it into a fine spray.

It was time now to prepare for going out into the ocean!

Mediterranean Sea
December 24, 1898.

These past days, the crew puttered around in the holds all day, placing the provisions in such a way that they would not be thrown around if there should be pitching. Barrels were wedged, new supports were nailed where the bunks seemed insecure, side boards were nailed along the bunks from the sides where people climb in, so that in case of need there would be something on which to brace one's feet.

All non-essentials were taken from the top deck to the baggage hold, and whatever remained was tied down most thoroughly. The upper part of the fore-mast was let down so as to reduce resistance to wind. All pump systems were checked. All was put in order as if for battle. We are ready!

In the distance, two huge cliffs were visible, the ancient Pillars of Hercules. Passing them on our second day—that is, today—we saw to our right on the horizon a high grey triangle—this was Cape St. Vincent. From there they watched us as they watch every other ship coming out into the ocean. We signalled the name of our ship and advised that all was in order with us.

Toward evening one could see only the triangular top of the Cape and that only through the most powerful spyglass. Then the last promontory disappeared behind the horizon.

Now we were in the open ocean and subject to its full power. All those sailing on the *Lake Huron* felt strained. All took note of the solemn moment.

How would the old, stern grandfather-ocean receive us?

The Ocean
Atlantic Ocean
January 3, 1899.

The first days passed well enough. From the west a cold breeze blew steadily to meet us; the ship, leaning neither forward nor to the side, smoothly rose and fell together with the huge stretches of wave-tossed water. The waves of this colossal dead swell were so broad and had such gradual slopes that it was difficult to know where one wave ended and another began. This was noticeable only when the ship lowered itself between two watery hills, as if to the bottom of a wide dish, the sides of which shut off the world from us on all sides. It seemed the ocean breathed evenly and heavily as if resting after heavy labour.

It was much fresher here than on the Mediterranean Sea. The air was clear and the line of the horizon unpleasantly sharp. After the Mediterranean Sea we experienced something of what a person feels on coming out of a crowded room into fresh air. The barometer, however, did not promise anything good. Portentously the wind stopped—there was a dead calm. Everything went silent in strained expectancy. Only the ocean continued its measured, lazy rocking, with its silent, hill-like masses.

It turned colder. In the lower sky, at the horizon, right before us appeared a gloomy fog, and its sharp dark line stretched along the sea, the whole length of the horizon. The strip grew rapidly and with a muffled sound, moved toward us. This was the approach of a storm!

Soon the first gust of cold wind struck. It hit the ship with all its might, howled in the rigging, whirled on the deck, tore off a poorly secured tarpaulin and, turning it over in flight, carried it away angrily, into the sea. Sweeping the smoke into fragments, it hooted with delight down the ventilators and whistled in the corridors, as if rejoicing that there was someone to whom it could show its power. The loosely stretched rigging restlessly muttered something, slapping the mast. The ship shuddered and seemed to prick up its ears.

The water lost its gleam at once, as it darkened and wrinkled into thousands of sharp fine folds. Here and there white spots of foam appeared which the wind tore from the tops of the waves and carried in large flecks somewhere further and further past us. Huge breakers could be seen ahead. Heavily and angrily throwing themselves up before one another, they came at us in ordered rows. Not a trace remained of the quiet, restful ocean.

Along the water, as in a snow storm, a white wrack was blown, zig-zagging and bending around the black, blown-up swells. The waves produced a threatening, muffled growl. One after the other they threw themselves hard against the sharp iron breast of the ship striving to reach the deck. Thus far, they did not succeed and, broken and muti-lated by the stiff iron, they fell back to make way for the following waves. Only occasionally one heard the the loud clap of a wave that managed to lick the iron chains bolted to the anchors with the tip of its cold foamy tongue. Then salt spray flew the full length of the ship, with a malicious hissing splash into the sailors' eyes. It rapped the windows of the deck cabin like the roll of a drum. On the front mast a forgotten canvas ventilator braced by a conical top was blown out and bent into a bow. It waved and flapped its outstretched skirts. In the evening twilight it looked like the tall apparition of a monk in a white cassock, waving his arms in despair.

Raising its bowsprit, as if afraid of choking, the ship cut wave after wave. But soon, it lost strength and began to shake. The next day, helplessly, submissively, it rolled from swell to swell and with all its heavy frame, with muffled groans dropped into each chasm which opened before it. A times there was not a soul on deck: it was if all on ship had died. Only wet sailors ran quickly by, and only rarely the tall A. Bakunin walked by, balancing with his hands and covering up his collar. Occasionally, running from corner to corner, M. Satz came from the pharmacy, protecting glasses of medicines from the spray with her apron. For four days the wind increased, until it blew with the strength of a hurricane. And not every hurricane was equal to that which our unfortunate ship came upon!

Then followed drawn out days which brought no hope of a change for the better.

Whole mountains moved upon us. From the stern one could see the ship glide over the top of a swell and then rush down its slope into the deep abyss whose other side stood like a black wall before us. Along this wall, hissing and winding like a snake, lines of foam ran down chased by the wind. The whole wall was furrowed with fine sharp waves; from its howling top, behind which a little sky was visible, whole clouds of white water dust flew.

The ship—which now seemed impossibly tiny, insignificant, with puny protruding masts—slid to the foot of this wall which it seemed was about to fall over and bury it forever. We heard a booming blow. The front part of the ship with the bowsprit buried itself in the water. A moment went by, and another, and by some incomprehensible miracle, its whole body shuddering, the ship dropped off the weight that had descended upon it, tore away from under the water, leveled out, and with a heavy creak again crawled up onto a new swell.

The water that had fallen on the foredeck roared off with noisy cascades to the lower deck, and rushed on, knocking down, turning over and breaking everything that happened to be in its way. It forced its way into narrow corridors, filled them for a moment and flying farther, whirled and foamed on the quarter deck. Seeking an exit, like an infuriated beast in a cage, it rushed with raging streams now to the deck cabin, now to the iron sides, and finally, weakened, flowed from the stern out of the open hatches at the sides.

Most frightful were the moments when, rolling over the top of a wave, the rear half of the ship together with the propeller came out of the water, right to the keel. Then the propeller, without the resistance of the water, span in the air at an insane speed, shaking the ship in all directions. At such times, the whole world turned upside down. The ship shuddered and jumped in all directions with desperate creaking and rattling. It seemed that some unseen giant's hand shook it and pounded the bottom with a huge hammer with such force that in a moment or two the ship would fly into a thousand pieces. This was repeated every 15 to 20 minutes for the last 8 days. Whenever we flew upward with the jumping rear we would take hold of whatever was handy, glance at one another, seized by terror. Those moments seemed endless.

At such times the captain, biting his lips would stare gloomily ahead, as if he saw someone there who was the cause of our troubles. Poor Mr. Dixon became green from fear and painfully frowned, looking at everyone in turn as if seeking help, and in confusion mumbled with pale lips: "Machine, machine, machine." He was afraid that in one of those moments the propeller shaft would break or the propeller would come off the shaft and fall into the sea. Such things have happened.

If this should happen the ship would be deprived of its only means of battling the infuriated elements. It would be converted into an iron box, lost together with its occupants in the middle of the limitless ocean. And what would then happen to the two thousand lives enclosed in this box with only a small reserve of provisions?

No one dared to answer that.

Atlantic Ocean
January 5, 1899.

In the bunks everyone was lying down. Through the dusky raw air, came loud moans, sighs, groans of the unfortunates suffering from sea-sickness. In a dark corner a woman was sitting on the bunk. In a concentrated reverent voice, she was saying a prayer. Occasionally here and there a dishevelled head rose with cloudy eyes and turning somewhere to space, timidly asked:

"Will we get there alive? What terror! See how it pitches!" and closing his eyes pressed himself to the pillow. One could hear from the outside the repulsive oily gurgle of the salt water running. Something overhead, heavy, clumsy, repeatedly rolled from one side to the other with a knock.

Again a wave struck. Everything shuddered, jumped, whirled. The ship buried itself in the waves. The little round windows became dark green. It became darker in the hold, and it was already difficult to find folk in the darkness. Stopping for a moment, indecisively, the ship flew upward faster and faster. The round windows lightened, became light grey. Through them stared a sickly feverish day while the oily water poured over them in tearful streams. It was nauseating to see. Instead of the sound of the sea, the whistle and wail of the raging hurricane was heard.

"Oh, I can't take it anymore," someone groaned with a despairing voice. "My hour has come."

"All my insides are wrenched out," responded someone from another corner.

With a mournful rattle an iron pail rolled on the deck, squeaking from bunk to bunk. A trunk came loose, slid heavily and struck the bunk and braces, now with a corner, now with a side. No one took care of them; they were not up to it.

The windows became completely darkened. It was night. It brought nothing new. Everything was the same. Lanterns in their iron rigging nodded from side to side as if by agreement, then stopped for a moment, as if in thought and impetuously jumped back again together with towels, jackets and other items hung in the bunks. The chilled crew, with bleary tired eyes, wiped the deck with wet swabs, carried out sewage pails, washed them and again tied them to the bunks. It was fearful to get out of the bunks. It took dexterity not to strike the deck as it turned through more than 45 degrees. To fall was a danger because then you would fly, somersaulting in the most wonderful way into a corner somewhere, and if you did not manage to take hold of something there, then you would go back in the same fashion.

The crew alone became so practised that night and day they ran nimbly carrying boiling water in pails, soup, putting bunks in order or working on the deck. It happened of course that some of them slid down the deck but this usually happened when even the most experienced sailors slid together with them in the same direction, shaking their heads in wonder. Along the length of the decks were stretched ropes (lifelines) which people might seize at such times.

After the prolonged spell lying down, everyone was in a gloomy, depressed mood. The sturdy man, Vasya Popoff, a lifeless hulk, pale, with blue spots under the eyes. To all words of encouragement, he waved an arm and looking with cloudy eyes said with conviction:

"Not one will get there—Not one. You will see! Frightful, that's what it is. And when I hear you call, 'All to the top,' I think, well, we are drowning. The end has come!"

Even the cheerful Chernenkoff grinned uncertainly as he cried with a voice still energetic.

"And will there sometime be an end to this? Just look what is happening. We will die to the last man." He waved both arms vigorously. "Is it a fake alarm?" he growled quickly bending over the edge of the bunk and finding a trough. His neck stretched out and reddened from the strain. "Only bile," he said mournfully shaking his head and again hurriedly bent over. "And I didn't take as much as a poppy seed into my mouth. Oh-h-h, what can one say? It looks like death will come!"

Together the Doukhobors fell into despondency. The whole ship grieved. Especially the women. Cheek on hand, shaking her head with sympathy, each whispered, mysteriously closing her eyes with a look which said there was nothing to be done, so we must resign ourselves to our fate. Yes, and the old men lying on the bunks talked about fateful things; when anyone approached they became silent and remained silent with anxious looks. They seemed to be concealing something. Finally after persistent questioning, Nicolai Zeebaroff explained to me that a rumour had spread that the ship was lost and was now sailing without a route through the stormiest parts of the ocean. All attempts to convince them of the opposite had no effect. The old men remained silent or said:

"You know better."

"Of course."

"It is clear."

But by their morose faces one could see that they did not believe it. And the women said plainly:

"Ah, dear man. We all see it! You do not wish to bring sorrow to the people, so you don't tell us. But we all see it clearly!"

And when I asked why they thought the ship had lost its way, one of the women with a knowing and sly look asked:

"Where does the sun come up now? Eh? Tell us. Earlier it came up from this direction. And now it comes up on the opposite side!"

And standing nearby the old man Shamshirin, in a mournful but confident voice added, looking around for approval:

"While we sailed along the land we knew the way. But here, who would not get mixed up? There is no shore, no island of any kind, you can't see the end. Grief, only grief!" and mournfully he lowered his head.

The matter could be righted only with the help of influential elders. Makortoff was especially helpful, appearing in the holds with a guard of two sailors, as always in his fur cap with a stick in his hand. His speech, exceptionally convincing in tone even though not very clear in thought, was said in a firm voice, and he soon convinced all that the route was quite correct, that there was no need to lose heart, for that was unworthy of real Christians. Rapping his stick and looking all around the confused crowd, with his stern, majestic look, he left for his cabin.

All were reassured, and livened up. The women, wiping their mouths with their hands and significantly exchanging glances, spoke:

"Now, sisters, there's someone who knows absolutely everything. He himself has crossed many oceans. In sailing matters, he can do everything." Only Shamshirin, while he did not dare to contradict such an authority, still kept his counsel as he continued to wear the look that said, "All is lost!"

Atlantic Ocean
January 7, 1899.

To fall during such tossing would be anything but safe. Even so people have to go to the top deck. Even for the young it is not easy to get up two flights of slippery steps, now standing almost horizontal and suddenly, quickly rising to a vertical position when one must take hold with both hands so as not to fall backwards. To go up is difficult, but to descend is still more dangerous. At each flight stood guards whose responsibility was to help the weak and aged on their way up, but mainly to look after those coming down. Regardless of precautions there were several unfortunate incidents. Two old men rolled down somehow before the guard could help them and each broke a rib. A boy not waiting for the carriers of hot water, went to the kitchen himself and, returning with hot water, fell and scalded his head and neck. Another fell from the flight and bloodied his face. One grown man, falling, cut his chin to the bone.

Yesterday evening, a thirteen year old girl, coming from the top deck in the dark, got lost, and looking for the entrance to her section, went by mistake to the front part of the ship. At this time a huge wave came on to the forecastle, knocking the girl off her feet and carrying her down the ship, bruising her on the corner of cranes and other protruding parts of the ship. She was thrown into a corner from where she managed to get to the first deck and from there she was taken to the hospital, all covered with blood.

It happened that while covering a hatchway, under the light of which some women and children always lay, one of the sailors dropped a three-cornered hatchway cover. It was heard to strike and then there was a cry; and when they went down into the hatchway, they saw, beside the fallen cover, a little girl lying down with her arms spread out. Fortunately she was only frightened. By good fortune, the hatchway cover landed among the crowd so that it only tore off a lock of hair, slightly scratched her skin, then fell flat, inflicting only slight injury to those around. The sailor who dropped the cover was sufficiently punished by the fright, but he was sent away to shovel coal for the whole shift.

Of course in all these incidents the crew was to blame but if the volume of work they had to do were taken into account, plus the fact that they had no rest by night nor by day, and worked in icy wind that continually splashed the knees in cold water, with clothes wet through (because outside we are splashed almost continously) one cannot be too strict. Sometimes while working on the front deck, they were all swept off their feet. The lighting of this hatchway, and all its ventilators, was in the front part of the ship, and the hatchway itself was isolated from all other spaces. A wave tearing over the side onto the deck would rush with clouds of spray into the opening and into the ventilators of this hatchway. It would then become necessary to close it and to turn the ventilators with the wind.

But this brings another problem. After several hours it becomes so stuffy below, so the lamps go out, and the air is saturated with heavy steam which comes rolling in droplets down the walls. It becomes impossible to breathe and so, whether we want to or not, it becomes necessary to remove several hatchway covers and to turn the ventilators into the wind again. But the first wave again sends a volume of water below—another, then a third and the water below is knee deep. It runs noisily from side to side, sometimes filling the lower bunks, since the drains here are small and the water cannot all run out. The hatchway is again covered and the crew picks up the water in pails and pours it out on the top deck; night and day a close watch must be kept so as to avoid mishaps.

In addition, every two or three days the lower decks must be washed, and sometimes the upper. The washing is done mostly at night as there is no time in the day. It is especially essential that people do not go up then because, after washing, the deck is scattered with carbolic powder. Special attention is paid to the sanitation of the deck, since it was noticeable that two or three days after washing it was covered with a black, oily film from organic waste, which gave off a repulsive smell. If some infectious disease should appear, there would be no way to deal with it among this crowd of people lying around, dejectedly.

The crew became so worn out yesterday evening that, in answer to a whistle calling all crew to the top, only a few people appeared. To the question "Where are the others?" they said, "We don't know." It was apparent they had decided to stop working believing that another 100 would be picked to replace them. The crew had already asked me about this several times. But how would it be possible under these conditions to teach inexperienced people, when even the people accustomed to the work could hardly manage? Those who reported were asked to get the rest of the crew to come to the quarter deck for work in half an hour. And if they failed to do so they would have to face the consequences.

In the gloom of night, amid the spray and noise of the wind, dark figures began to glide over the deck, being tossed in all directions, whispering and conversing with one another. When all had arrived they gathered into a group in the shelter of the spar-deck and quietly talked it over.

"What are we to do now? Eh?" says a concerned voice.

"Who knows?"

"I told you nothing would come of it."

"Yes. But it is true. Who besides us can work now? Nobody!"

"But then again, brother," reasons another, "What about us! All our boots are falling apart from the water; we are never dry."

"If only the community would give us boots when we arrive in America."

"Very simple!"

After a brief explanation, the boys got to work, agreeing on the condition that the community be asked to buy them new boots on arrival in America.

But the poor boys remained in old boots on arrival in America. There were so many other matters to look after that they forgot about their heavy service and their boots.

Atlantic Ocean
January 8, 1899.

The severe prolonged tossing did no little harm. Many people with sea-sickness reached an extremely serious condition. Especially pitiful-looking were some of the women. They had not eaten anything for a long time but kept up their strength with eggs and Nestlé's condensed milk. But of course, such nourishment was not sufficient.

It was fearful to look at them. Pale-faced, thin, blue spots under their eyes, bony hands with blue nails, the forehead perspiring from frequent vomiting. They had long had nothing to vomit, but the empty stomach continued to shrink trying to throw out something. Some-times the convulsions spread through the whole body, then each tossed about the room with wide open eyes, writhing fingers, bending in the strangest ways, wheezing and rolling the eyes as if in agony. In such cases the doctor most often resorted to injecting ether under the skin. This soon produced remarkably good results. There were several days when the doctor literally jumped from one patient to another. Despite all the efforts and strivings of the doctors, however, one young woman died directly from sea-sickness. True, before this she had been run down by fever. The number of sick increased every day. There were several cases of erysipelas, two or three of inflammation of the lungs. The hospital was full.

During morning rounds, the doctors visited 60 to 100 patients. Towards evening the nurse, M. Satz, with the help of the doctors, prepared medicines in the pharmacy, disturbed by attacking waves, and in the evening they distributed these. Fortunately, A. Bakunin, M. Satz, and the Englishman Mercer, managed to win the confidence of the Doukhobors; for this reason the work went very well. All three were young and energetic; and besides, treatments were useful also because, moving among the Doukhobors, they kept them cheerful. And while it seems that A. Bakunin was himself suffering from the rolling, he did not show it and his bold, tall figure moved about the ship all day, together with the good-hearted Mercer, who managed to become firmly attached to the Doukhobors. The women became very close with "sister" as they called M. Satz.

On board the *Lake Huron*.

Atlantic Ocean
January 8, 1899
Evening.

Death does not spare us. Yesterday we made another sacrifice to the stern ocean: that was the ninth death. It was a mournful funeral. I think that no one who was present will forget it.

Again and again, over the empty, wet deck the waves crashed. These waves managed to pack whole piles of salt into the corners. The sailors, bearing the deceased, moved carefully, followed by a procession of relatives. More than once it was necessary to stop the sad procession and take hold of one another, the side, the cranes, or whatever was handy so as not to drop the hatchway covers on which the swaddled corpse lay, and roll together with it down on the slippery deck. The funeral singing was broken by the wild gusts of wind. It covered everyone with clouds of irritating salt spray, wetting the clothes, and rumpling the hair, as if hurrying everyone to the place of burial. And as the corpse was lowered, a black, angrily foaming wave jumped to the top deck, poured over the sailor's feet, angrily tore the body out of their hands, and swallowed it with the same rage. Falling back, the wave appeared with it somewhere far below our feet, opening a deep noisy chasm like an insatiable belly demanding new sacrifices.

And the wind circling in the clouds of foam wailed furiously striving to draw away those standing on the deck. In the portentous solemn howl and whistle it seemed a threatening promise could be heard—"It will be the same for all. Just wait!" Submissively bending their heads, all looked sadly at the relatives of the deceased.

So we sailed days and nights in this chaos, clasped by the enraged elements, unrestrained, implacable, falling on our unfortunate ship which, under the heavy blows of the fierce ocean, continually squealed and groaned in all its joints like a wounded animal. Despondency began to overcome us all. During the day when the ship flew onto the top of a swell where, shuddering, it stopped for a few moments, as if in thought, we saw the endless desert covered with rows of foaming waves. Every wave was a new giant blow in the shaken wounded breast of the old ship. And how many were there beyond the horizon? We felt ourselves to be lost, abandoned, in this frightful waste.

At night the black sky looked at us sternly and implacably, studded with large stars, sparkling with fear. From time to time, the stars were covered by rusty rags of cloud with torn edges. Never catching one another, they flew with unusual speed, low, low and seemed to touch the ends of the masts with their tattered edges. And when the black wall grew before us covering half the sky, and the upper edge of it lit up with a mysterious phosphorescent sheen, it seemed the old ocean laughed angrily, showing his white teeth, growling, and spattering cold salt spittle.

Atlantic Ocean
January 9, 1899
4 o'clock at night.

The wind began to abate at last. Only occasionally did it attain its former force but in these gusts one felt utterly powerless. The swell, following the good example, also began to settle down, though it still surged strongly, put on airs, and once in a while splashed on to the top deck. "Don't get too confident," it seems to say. Today it was incomparably quieter: the sky took on a softer colour, the tops of the waves rounded off, and they became much smaller. No longer did they beat and roar as earlier on the sides of the ship. They only rolled under it smoothly but powerfully from side to side.

The air became warmer. Pale thin people with cloudy eyes came out timidly, shaking, onto the white top deck. Screwing up their eyes from the light, which seemed unusually bright after the semi-darkness of the holds, they gazed upon the surroundings. Shielding their eyes with their hands, many looked ahead with the secret hope of seeing shore, so as more quickly to take leave of this hated floating home. And seeing nothing but water and sky, they turned away, sighing.

Soon both top decks were covered with people lying on fur coats. Clinging to pillows, intoxicated with the warm fresh air, after being deprived of it for so long, the people rested as after a long debilitating illness. For a moment breaking through the grey clouds, as if touched by this sad crowd, the sun smiled caressingly with a ray of warmth, and all faces answered it with smiles of gratitude.

"Sun" weakly whispered more than one pair of lips. But the ray had already slipped from the ship and run as a pale dot over the grey surface of the distant sea.

The first to recover were the children and they immediately raised a racket. Soon they asked for hot porridge. The deck came to life little by little and, among the reclining groups, carriers ran with pails of steaming soup! This was the best sign that things were improving! Towards evening there was lively conversation everywhere. Some tried to sing psalms. People began to stroll about the ship, looking for relatives and acquaintances whom the storm had parted.

Grandfather Bokov came out with the inevitable handkerchief in his hands, joking in response to young people trying to start something with him. The grey beard and deerskin cap of Makortoff appeared and wonder of wonders—Vasya Popoff, pale but deliberate and sturdy as ever, stood on the deck, conversing with the tall, thin Chernenkoff. To them came the good-hearted Melesha (Emelian Kanigan) and, soon after, others came into the group, including the giant figure of modest Nicolai Zeebarev.

The elders were discussing past and future events.

Taking advantage of the calm weather, the crew worked at setting the ship in order. Soon we would come to the shore and we must clean up and bring ourselves to order. All deck cabins, sides, life-boats, ventilators, all were washed with hot water and soda and frequently repainted. Copper parts were energetically rubbed to a blinding brightness, glass was cleaned with chalk and the deck was washed several times, once with sand and finally with hot water and soda. It was as if we were going to a parade.

At night we came into a thick fog and had to slow down. Recent noise was replaced by an ominous strained silence. High in the air a cloudy yellow circle was lighted up by the signal lantern. At the bow, you not only could not see the water, but even nearer objects were completely hidden from the eye; only now and then you saw their dark outlines. Over the ship, clouds were moving silently, running together higher up into long lines of fog. They slid by noiselessly like spectres, now opening, now closing the sinister spaces between them. Where were they coming from, where were they going?

At times it seemed there was no ship of any kind, no sea, no sky, and one could not understand whether we were standing still or moving somewhere among the cold mysterious noiseless spectres. Only an uneven stealthy rustle could be heard as drops of moisture fell from the ropes on to the deck. In the enchanted, strained silence sighs were heard and mysterious whispering on all sides.

And suddenly this bewitched world shivered, trembled, from a wild roar. Our ship was signaling. The enchantment disappeared. We were moving through fog and, about every five minutes, our ship hooted warning of collision with an approaching ship. From time to time the copper throat roared hoarsely as though at first choking on the raw salt fog. "Hoo-oo-oo."

From behind the shaking grey sheet came lower hoarse notes of another monster. "Hoo-oo-oo-oo?"

"Hoo-oo-oo-oo!" we heard from near by.

A sound like broken glass was heard. This was telegraphing from the bridge to the engines.

STOP!

More and more often roared the copper throats, not seeing one another, but fearing a collision. For a long time, the ships struggled, calling one another, decreasing and increasing their speeds.

Then the other ship was heard more and more faintly, and finally from a distance, its last "Hoo-oo-oo-oo," sounded. Again there was silence, the whisper of noiseless spectres and the rustle of drops of water.

Canada
Port of Halifax,
January 12, 1899.

Today at four o'clock in the evening we stood at anchor within sight of the harbour of Halifax. Among the crowded, tall, many-storied buildings along the whole shore, factory chimneys stuck out. From them streamed stripes of heavy smoke which gathered into a dark cloud, and hung motionless over the city like a yellow muddy stain. Sounds of the living earth came from the shore. We heard the exciting noise and rattle of a large populous city. Darting quickly among the buildings came dwarfed, toy-like trains with white smoke. Frequently, the solid hoots of ocean ships were heard, and ducking among them, tug-boats squeaked merrily. All this seemed strange and new after our life of the last thirty-two days.

At the deck rail stood a group of elders. Makortoff, with proudly raised head, examined the city quizzically. "We'll see how you live here," could be read in his stern grey eyes. Misha Bokov peered with his short-sighted eyes and smiling, touchingly cried: "Here is Canada!" Good-hearted Melesha looked affectionately at the land, as if he saw someone there near and dear to him. Vasya Popoff proudly stuck out his chest, as if to say, "Whatever you like there; we, too, will not be found lacking!" And Nicolai Zeebarev clung hard to the rail with his strong hands, as if clinging to the handles of a plow, ready to undertake creative work with the persistence of a work ox.

The women looked at the land questioningly as if asking what awaited their children, their husbands and themselves there.

The crowd stood in deep silence, tense, contemplative, staring at their new land that they had so long and so greedily awaited. The ocean with all its terrors was now forgotten, like a deep dream, as though it had never been. Ahead was the new earth, new life and—who knows?—perhaps new sufferings. On the serious, stern faces of the silent crowd living one life, breathing the same breath, thinking one thought could be read:

"Well what of it? Whatever is to be, we are ready to meet it!"

Blaine Lake Doukhobor Society

First party of Doukhobors on arrival in Halifax.

After several hours, we saw a small tug coming to us from the shore. At the sight of it everyone became excited. This was the first meeting with people of the new land!

"What kind of people are they? Oh! to see them," says one.

81

"Now we shall see," quietly answers Vasya Popoff. But one can see by his eyes that he too is dying of curiosity. Melesha had craned his neck a long time.

"Do you think any of our people are on this tug?"

"What a fine boat. It runs smoothly as a swan," was heard in the crowd.

Now people could be seen in the bow of the tug which was circling us. Hilcoff was there in a big coat with fur on the outside, as is worn in Canada. Beside him in the same kind of coat and caps stood the two delegates sent by the Doukhobors, Ivan Evin and Peter Makortoff, son of the old man. Farther on we could see a group of Englishmen, among whom were two clean-shaven old men in strange long suits and original old-fashioned stove-pipe hats. These were two representatives of the Philadelphia Quakers, sent here especially to meet the Doukhobors.

A deathly silence reigned on board. Nearest to the side stood the elders. Makortoff saw his son and his lips quivered, his eyes losing directness, clouded with tears.

"At last!"

It was so quiet that the sound of the motor of the tug could be heard. But it was already alongside.

Hilcoff and the delegates, taking off their caps bowed low.

"How are you?" was heard, from below, softly.

The crowd shuddered, moved and restrainedly buzzed, as if sighing with a single joint sigh which rolled across the whole ship.

"The Lord be praised. How are you?"

Thousands of hands lifted and waved their caps.

The Englishmen on the ship waved their caps over their heads and vigorously stressing each syllable, called:

"Well-come Doukh-o-bors."

And the Quakers taking off their cylindrical hats, bared their heads, bald as knees, and slowly bowed.

"Are you all living and well?" the delegates asked, bowing even lower with cap in hand. They were pale with excitement, but serious. Soon they must answer to the society. Not for nothing were they chosen, was money spent on them! And feeling so many questioning eyes on them, they bowed still lower as if to say:

"We haven't taken on airs. We remember that we are but those selected from the whole society; tomorrow we will be together with you, and will share with everyone as before."

The crowd buzzed. They wanted to hear of many things, to ask many questions, but the tug did not tie up to the ship. First, we had to pass through quarantine and until then no one could come to us and no one could go from us—not one.

The chief quarantine doctor, Dr. Montizambre, was a Frenchman with a large nose. He asked from below,

"Do we have any that are infectiously ill? Has everyone been vaccinated? How many sick are on the ship?"

Receiving the answer, that no one had been infectiously ill during the whole voyage, that there were only a few chronically ill, and that everyone was vaccinated (those who had not been vaccinated before were vaccinated by Dr. Mercer on board), he ordered us to go to a little island several miles distant. Tomorrow morning there would be a quarantine examination there, and if everything was found to be alright we could go to St. John, where we would board the train.

The tug took off and went once around the ship. The Englishmen quickly waved their caps and shouted:

"Hip-hip-hip-hurra! Hip-hip-hip-hurra!"

"Thank you," called the Doukhobors in reply, bowing low.

A large choir sang a solemn psalm, and it sounded clear and joyful. How much faith it contained! Winged with hope it carried on a light sea breeze, in wide strong waves, to the new land behind the tug. Now the tug disappeared among the boats in the port. Anchor chains rattled. We were moving to the island.

The excited Doukhobors were buzzing like a disturbed bee hive. Soon we were at the wooden dock of the island in a quiet bay, surrounded by a wall of dark green pines. Evening was marked by a bright sunset. And while it was not permitted to walk on the island away from the dock, everyone stepped on the land with pleasure, smiling at the forgotten sensation of the earth firm under one's feet. The Doukhobors admired the wonderful greenery reflected in the water of the quiet bay. Uphill from the bay was a yellow sandy path of pebbles, bordered by fresh grass. High up on the hill among the branches of a spreading spruce a high wooden house looked temptingly out over the land, with the bright red fire of the rays of the setting sun playing on its windows. The wind brought the distant bark of a dog. Land! What joy!

I think that no other view created such a deep impression on the Doukhobors as this little piece of land with the little home at the top. Supper was taken on land on logs lying nearby. The doubts and the weakness were all gone: everyone smiled, chattering gaily, sitting in easy postures around bowls of soup. For the first time it was unnecessary to hold them with both hands for fear that the contents might fall on the head instead of into the stomach.

Canada
Port Halifax
Quarantine Island
January 13, 1899.

Examinations began in the morning. Doctor Montizambre stood with a solemn face beside his helpers at the gang plank, and permitted the Doukhobors to pass before him one by one, from the ship on to the shore. He examined faces and tongues, taking longer with children and the young. The Doukhobors had put on clean clothes and holiday dress. This sedate polite crowd, moving calmly and quietly past the doctor, apparently without confusion, created a good impression on him and on many other Englishmen who had come with him. Letting all the people pass from the ship to the shore, Doctor Montizambre walked around all the decks, and announced that in all the time of immigration never had a ship arrived with so large a number of passengers and in such surprisingly good order.

Once the examination was over we were allowed to go where we wished. In no time, several brisk journalists in redneck ties came on to the ship with free, confident movements. They began writing down all the information they needed. One of them very effectively made drawings—one after another, now drawing unfamiliar types, now whole groups of Doukhobors. He even got to the bunk areas and continued to draw and make notes. Others wrote biographies of Bokov and Makortoff and drew pictures of them.

Two elderly Quakers came on to the deck. They removed their cylindrical hats and with shining heads announced that they wished to pray about the safe arrival of the Doukhobors. They stood side by side opposite the crowded Doukhobors who were also bare-headed. A very old-looking Quaker closed his eyes for several moments, raised his head and meditated. Moving his lips a little he began to recite a prayer with a firm voice. The longer he continued the more feelingly he recited, with a somewhat sing-song tone, emphasizing certain words as if he were pulling them out from somewhere in the depths.

"O Go-o-od!" ever louder and more feelingly he exclaimed, shaking his head. Sometimes he opened his eyes and looked over his glasses, shook his arms in the air and at the end even knelt on one knee. His younger companion imitated his friend, repeating his gestures and facial expressions. Shouting, as if in anger, several closing words, the old man got up from his knee and looked over his glasses with the look of a victor.

"There now. How well it turned out!"

The Doukhobors were dumbfounded though they did not show it. They did not understand a word. All the gesturing and tone of mimicry and the old man himself in his odd costume! They were greatly perplexed. D. Hilcoff translated the prayer and God's blessing which the Quakers asked for the Doukhobors, and explained that these old men had been sent from the Quaker society.

Then Vasya Popoff came to the front.

"God save them for their good wishes, their welcome and their kindness because of their brotherly love, God will not forsake them," he said gravely. Then a Doukhobor woman recited a poem and the choir sang a long psalm to the Quakers by way of reply. The Quakers, all this time holding their bare heads high, patiently froze with eyes closed. But, God be praised, the psalm ended and hats could be put on!

From a distance, I saw a tall energetic Englishman speaking to the Doukhobors and waving his arms. This was a speech by a representative of workers' organizations. Unfortunately I was not able to hear his speech nor the reply of the Doukhobors. Somebody else made a speech and finally something unexpected happened which utterly amazed all the English.

The whole crowd of Doukhobors sighed and suddenly went down on their knees and bowed right down to the ground. People lay prostrate and the majority of the English looked at this picture of people bowing before them with great perplexity. Many apparently were greatly startled, as they stood with open mouths. Even the captain, who continually chewed a wad of tobacco and who had been listening with partly closed eyes, stopped his occupation for a minute and looked at the Doukhobors in amazement. The old Quaker looked over his glasses, stretching out his neck and raising his eyebrows high with a face expressing extreme perplexity. The workers' representative stood with hands in his pockets. On his face could be seen a resigned acceptance tinged with disgust. Poor Doctor Mercer was confused and embarrassed to tears as he had just been telling the correspondents about the dignity of the Doukhobors. The correspondents and some others looked like cocks and even boastfully straightened up as if to say:

"Well, what of it, what did you expect different. After all, we are the English."

Finally, the Doukhobors moved, arose in a deep silence and, it seemed, had more dignity than before. Solemnly stepping forward and bending politely to Hilcoff and pointing to the English, Vasya Popoff said:

"Dmitri Alexandrovich, tell them please that we did not really bow to them even though they may think so. We bowed to that spirit of God which has appeared among them and to God who lives in all hearts which have been moved to accept us as brothers into their home."

And straightening up and looking calmly ahead, in his intelligent eyes could be read:

"Yes, yes. Do not delude yourselves; do not misunderstand us!"

Hilcoff, with a faint smile, translated these words to the English. All roused and began to converse, nodding their heads approvingly, glancing at one another.

"That's excellent, is it not?" the workers' representative said to the captain with a satisfied look, seeking agreement.

"O-o-o yes," unhesitatingly drew out the captain, nodding and now closing his eyes completely with satisfaction at having received an explanation, and he again began working his jaws as if making up for lost time.

The old Quaker, his face wrinkling into a thousand folds from his smile, ran up to Vasya Popoff with outstretched arms and shook his hand saying:

"Very nice! Very nice!" And he shook hands to the right and to the left, giving his old man's look over his glasses.

The Doukhobors smiled broadly taking the white puffy hands of the Quaker in their large hands and bowed awkwardly.

And the women with deeply moved faces kept glancing at him.

"Dear old man."

"Oh-h. What a good heart!"

"How fine," they added.

In a word, all were satisfied.

Then getting off the ship they all went walking on the island. It was a warm bright day and when the groups of Doukhobor men and women appeared like many coloured flowers amongst the greenery, spreading over the island with the hum of bees, together with the sounds of live happy song, all were overcome with a kind of special holiday mood.

For everyone it was light, bright and calm.

First Days in Canada
On the train of the Canadian Pacific Railway
January 15, 1899.

The *Lake Huron* left Halifax on the morning of the 14th of January. With us went Hilcoff, both delegates, the Quaker elders and three journalists. It was turning to dusk when we sighted St. John. From a distance we could see that the shore and squares and streets of the harbour were flooded with people. When the ship came to the dock, the whole crowd waved their hats, caps and umbrellas and a fearful, many-voiced roar reached us. This was Canada welcoming the Doukhobors. The Doukhobors, as always, answered with a psalm.

The unloading began. Trains came to the dock, and we had only to gather our belongings and move from ship to train. The baggage was loaded directly onto a freight train and shipped separately.

Canadians were standing in crowds on both sides of the train. When the first Doukhobor appeared on the gangplank, a marked enthusiasm seized the crowd. All the way to the train they waved to him with their hands and their caps, and roared and exclaimed at the top of their voices. Obviously they were well satisfied with his strong figure, clean clothes, the lightness with which he carried all his baggage, and his clean-shaven beardless face (which Yankees consider to be a mark of barbarity).

"O what a man," could be heard.

"An excellent figure!"

"You can't say he's good for nothing."

"If they are all like that, then we have never seen such immigrants in Canada."

"And he bows, too. Good fellow. Best wishes! Best wishes!"

"How are you?"

"Good fellow! Hip-hip-hurraa!"

And the crowd roared again.

Embarrassed, not expecting anything of the kind, the Doukhobor bowed in all directions with a serious face adding, "Thank you." He must have been glad when at last he got away from the crowd and got into a fine passenger car with leather seats and bronze handles, where an officer of the railway thoughtfully seated him.

"Of course," he thought, "that's how joyfully they are meeting us. For this, God save them! But why shout so much?"

After the first Doukhobor came the second, the third—the appearance of each was met with a fresh burst of welcoming.

But now, a Doukhobor woman came down the gangplank with a pack on her back and two children. The latter looked straight at the large crowd from under their caps. The excitement of the crowd reached a kind of frenzy. There was a steady roar in which nothing could be understood. Even the stout policeman, classic example of imperturbability, tried to smile at the sight of this picture, and puffed out his blood-filled cheeks which had been pulled together by his helmet strap. It was fearful to look at him. What if this black-wool-covered cask should burst! For the greater satisfaction of the crowd, the youngsters began to bow; but as they could not do this while walking, their mother hurried them along. At the entrance to the warehouse stood several open barrels filled with little bags of candy; these had been prepared by Montreal women for the Doukhobor boys and girls. Well-dressed women stood nearby, invited the children to the barrels, and gave them these gifts, smiling pleasantly.

Without expressing the least joy, the children took the tidbits and, bowing sedately, moved on without looking to see exactly what was in the packages. They did not acknowledge the pleasant surprises and accepted the gifts as if it were an old established custom, long known to them, that everyone coming to Canada was met with candy. The Canadian women were non-plussed and apparently uncertain how to take such indifferent and restrained gratitude. "What is this? Ingratitude? or simply wild people unable to appreciate how pleasant these surprises were?"

But since the general mood did not permit criticism of the Doukhobors, it was decided to explain this as a mark of good breeding, in the Spartan spirit. Having accepted such an explanation the women re-acquired their lost confidence and merriment and whispered with renewed liveliness praising the Doukhobor women for giving their children such an upbringing. Some of them, accepting the thanks of a little Doukhobor, looked as if God only knows what they would do with him in their rapture, if it had not been for the heavy barrels which stood between. Fortunately the barrels stood firmly in their places, and the women limited themselves, in the extremity of their delight, to graciously copying the solid manners of the little one, in which they were especially successful when Minister Smart or Hilcoff were nearby.

Nevertheless these were dear women. All through the cold night right till morning they stood behind their barrels. The elders, very well satisfied with the reception, all the same disapprovingly "looked sideways" at the barrels. Of course, we thank them for the reception; only this is altogether superfluous! What is it for—this candy! It's a useless thing! We are not accustomed to this! Too bad, so much money is expended for nothing. But all the same, God save them! It is joyful, very joyful, when they receive us as if they really want to respect us as brothers.

In the warehouse through which the Doukhobors were passing was the Minister of the Interior, Mr. Smart, a handsome man with the firm sympathetic expression of a still-young face; beside him was the administrator of the railroad and some interpreters, mostly Jews or Galicians, who understood the Doukhobors but slightly.

The Minister was very well satisfied with the impression which the Doukhobors made.

"They are noticeably emaciated, it is true," he said, "but look what handsome people they are, how well-grown and strong the women are! See how easily she carries her burden," he said, indicating a woman passing by. "How are you?" he answered to her bow.

The Conservative press had vigorously attacked Smart for his decision to receive the Doukhobors into Canada. And not only Conservatives, but the general attitude was opposed to the reception of the Doukhobors. All feared that the Doukhobors would be sickly and emaciated people, unable to work. They were afraid that it might become necessary to keep them at government expense. Many saw in them fanatical sectarians, unfit for practical life. People laughed at the Minister, calling him "Duckobors"—from the word Doukhobors.

All the same, Mr. Smart, with a peculiar English determination, had continued to gather information about the Doukhobors from the English Consul in Batum, observing and studying the delegates Evin and Makortoff, conversing with Hilcoff and Maude. He quietly did his work without replying to the jeers, and finally gave his agreement to the migration. Of course, it was very pleasant for him to see for himself that not only was his estimate not mistaken, but that the Doukhobors even exceeded his expectations and managed to arouse the enthusiasm of all who saw them and spoke with them.

Now he stood among the sedately moving crowd of Doukhobors and glanced at them with proud satisfaction. He was so well-satisfied with the Doukhobors and the reception given them by the local population that he did not leave the warehouse all night while the disembarkation was in progress. He entered each departing train, smiled pleasantly and bowed to the departing people, or he went on to the ship and watched how some of the Doukhobors quickly took down the bunks and brought the lumber out of the decks and dropped it on the dock, or he looked into the deep hold where the Doukhobors were piling their baggage onto platforms which were unloaded by cranes onto the dock.

About three o'clock in the morning the ship was cleared of all lumber. (This we were obliged to do by the contract with the ship-owners.) Part of the baggage was loaded on to freight cars and the rest was piled into huge piles in the warehouse. The 2,133 people were divided into five trainloads which left one after the other, one or two hours apart. By spring, all Doukhobors were to be settled in immigration halls in Winnipeg (the main centre of immigration) and in other nearby towns. One very sick girl, in the last stages of consumption remained in St. John* as did a woman with a little girl who had German measles while on board ship. All the rest departed for the interior of the country. My work was really completed and, upon leaving the ship I could have gone home. But it was a pity to lose the chance to see Canada first-hand and to see how the Doukhobors would get established. And so I went with them to Winnipeg, an outside observer.

---

*Where she soon died.

On The Train
January 17, 1899.

The heavy train filled with Doukhobors rushed on, roaring past cities, towns, whistle stops, pausing only two or three times a day to take on water, coal and provisions.

It hurried past the hills of Quebec covered with heavy thick forests, past the noisy factory city of Montreal, recognized from a distance by its black high-rising factory stacks from which dark smoke flowed lazily; it passed the beautiful city of Ottawa, the capital of Canada, and tearing out into the open, moved along the shore of the huge sea-like Lake Superior. Ships moved on the silvery surface of the lake and on the shore sail boats rested on their sides with masts unstepped and sails folded.

For fifteen miles the road stretched along the very shore of the lake, and next we rushed through attractive wooded hills.

People stood at the stations, their red hands pushed into their pockets. "Regardless of the cold they are in jackets only or short coats with high collars!" Most had smoking pipes under their hoarfrost-covered moustaches. They had shaven faces, blue cheeks and frequently no moustache at all. On the snow were repulsive yellow spots—spittle of tobacco chewers. Frequently farmers were seen in reddish fur coats with fur turned out and mitts and caps with fur turned in. A red sled flashed, pulled by a pair of large hairy dogs; nearby was their quaint Indian master. Active boys on thin, blue-stockinged legs and wearing light caps called to us, jumping toward the window and laughing heartily, merrily. A moment later they would box one another, but after a few bouts they would run on somewhere else, hands in pockets.

The telegrapher could be seen in the station window. He worked with a strained face, unjacketed but with a hat on his head. On his arms from the wrist to the elbow were black silk bags, to protect his cuffs from dirt. On to the platform a red cheeked buffet-server appeared, a stout ball-like woman divided in two by a tightly stretched apron string. She came out in only a dress to look at "these Doukhobors." Then we saw in the windows a stout, soot-covered mechanic with a huge ox-like head. Then the conductor called, "All aboard," lifting his arm horizontally. Without waiting for bells, the locomotive gave a quick business-like whistle and again we flew farther over the snowy fields.

Puffs of steam and smoke flew past us silently, and clouds of snow rustled by. In the coach it was warm and comfortable. People were resting after the excitement. Some were lying on lowered upper bed shelves; the majority were looking out of the windows at the passing scenery, striving to picture what it would be like in the place selected by their delegates.

"What a lot of people came out to the dock, a regular cloud. As I looked at them, I could not see the end," says Vasya Popoff.

"And how they shouted all together 'E-e-e-e-e,' " takes up Chernenkoff. "Too bad we understood nothing in their language. What is it they were shouting! One seized my arm and began to shake it as if pumping water. And he laughed and talked so quickly. I laughed too and said 'it is very joyful, very pleasant!' I heard only 'Doukhobor, Doukhobor.' 'Yes, I say, I am Doukhobor.' We laughed some more and I said 'Thank you, I must go now' and I went into the train and he disappeared."

"He was giving you his welcome," explained Melesha.

"Of course."

"Very fine people. What can one say? Only speaking confidentially," said Chernenkoff bending over and looking around, "somehow, I didn't take too well to their shouting."

"And the hand waving and one even kicked with his foot. It seemed too exuberant," added Zeebarev.

Vasya Popoff stared straight ahead and with a look of regret, opened his arms.

"That's the custom. It's the people," he said.

"Did you think they would be like us? All stand in an even row and bow quietly: 'How are you,' 'God be praised,' 'How are you,' No, my friends," says Melesha.

The moody Michael Legebokoff entered the conversation. He was a person fanatically devoted to Doukhoborism to the last detail. His face was set firm with overhanging eyebrows.

"When I look at them," he said, "fine, clean people—no argument. Only their customs are far from ours!"

"Of course. There are no customs in the world better than our true Christian ones," took up one of the women.

For a moment there was silence in the coach. All were mentally comparing Doukhobors and Canadians.

"And brethren, it should also be said, much as we have travelled already, many people as we have seen on the shore, yet nowhere was there a gendarme;—not one policeman have I seen. I thought the policemaster himself would be there but to this time I have not seen any of the militia," an elder said, showing surprise.

"You are already lonesome?" asked Melesha.

"But," someone answered, "near the stairway stood a stout one, in a blue jacket and a cap like a fireman's, only black; that was a policeman."

"Yes. I wondered at him," remarked Vasya Popoff, "not a pistol nor a sword; he stood quietly, touched no one."

"It means the people are quiet," answered Melesha. "Why should he need arms when the people are quiet?"

"Only a short stick with a tassel hanging at his side. That's all."

"Probably," Legebokoff added gloomily, "when he taps someone on the top of the head with this stick, there is no need of a pistol."

"In a word one can see it is a Christian country," several voices added in unison.

"We shall see how they will be later."

"We shall see!"

Suddenly there was a disturbance in the coach. There were exclamations and sighing.

"See. See," several voices called, "what kind of country is here? Only bare rock!"

"How awful!"

"Wait, it will change," said the more judicious, "it will change ten times before we get there."

"We still have far to go."

"Can anyone live here? It is a desert."

In fact the whole area through which we were now travelling, was covered with rocks, almost without interruption. The rocks were huge square plates piled one on another in chaotic disorder. It looked as if, a long time ago, the land here had all been covered with an even layer of granite which broke up during an earthquake and the pieces fell permanently into these fantastic positions. From the spaces between the rocks a stunted shrubbery stretched up to the light. It was a deserted, depressing sight.

Supper was brought in and the people became occupied with it. At morning and evening stops, fresh bread, milk and large circles of yellow cheese were brought into the train. In the buffet there was tea and sugar. Boiling water was available all day. This, together with excellent milk, also brought in at the stops, constituted our food on the whole trip. The excellent wheat bread interested the Doukhobors especially. They praised it highly and were already day-dreaming of gathering it in their own fields. All these provisions and all other expenses of the Doukhobors now came from the 'bonus.'

We travelled five days to Winnipeg, moving with express train speed. About half way there, the first train derailed, but the people were only frightened. Our train stuck in the snow in a rocky cut for several hours. A strong wind was blowing that day and it became very frosty. I think it was colder than -30 degrees R*. I tried to go out, but it

---

*About –37 degrees C.

caught my breath. Several Englishmen in leather mitts pounded off the snow iced up under the wheels. The locomotive went ahead to clear the track. Upon returning, it hit the train so hard that it seemed the coaches would fly into pieces. Several times it gathered speed and struck the immovable train, then finally pulled forward. Slowly the wheels squeaked and howled and the train started. Soon we left the defile and again were moving, screeching and rattling, the coaches rocking from side to side. The frost drew on the windows with its icy breath, whined in the wheels, cracked in the dry wooden walls and, when the door was opened, tore into the coach in white steamy clouds. Meanwhile we were well protected from its attacks, and slept peacefully beside the brightly flaming stove filled to the top with hard coal.

Canada
Winnipeg
January 22, 1899.

"Winnipeg, Winnipeg," cried the conductor, quickly running through the coach. The people stirred, gathered their goods and tried to look through the frozen windows at the city where they were to spend the winter. The train stopped and the Doukhobors, one after another, jumped out of the coaches. Here they were met by the head of Canadian Immigration, J. McCreary*, a lively, energetic, good-natured person.

The Immigration Hall was several minutes walk from the station and the Doukhobors, accompanied by McCreary and the interpreters, went there. The snow squeaked and protested under hundreds of feet as the frost was still heavy. From conversations I learned that they had not had such a severe frost here for about eighteen years. And now we were home. Externally "home" was a big, three-storey wooden building with big windows, painted in a dark red color. The doors were fastened open and the crowd, surrounded by wavy clouds of vapour, spread through the corridors and stairways, filling the whole building.

On the first floor was the biggest room, with a very high ceiling and three large windows. Bunks at three levels stretched along the two walls forming the front corner. The centre of the room was occupied by four tables with benches on each side. One door led to the pantry and kitchen, in which were two large kettles for preparing food, and a boiler on a flat stove. Another door opened into the corridor, on the other side of which were the Immigration Office and the office of Mr. McCreary.

*Historical records indicate that the correct name of the Immigration Officer was William F. McCreary—ED.

Friends of the Doukhobors, 1899.
Standing left to right: Sergei L. Tolstoy, Anna de Carousa, Leo A. Sulerzhitsky.
Seated left to right: Sasha Satz, Prince Hilcoff, W.R. McCreary, Mary Robetz.

The second storey consisted of two identical rooms. These rooms were much lower than on the first storey and therefore there were no bunks and the people settled mostly in very small closets which stretched along two walls of the room. Sometimes they settled in the middle of the room right on the floor. During the day the bedding was taken away and the room was clear. There was a table the full length of the room, with benches.

On the third storey there were two rooms but the ceilings were still lower and each room was lit by only one large window so that there was little light in the corners of the room. There were no closets here as there were on the second storey. Along two walls were built single rows of bunks as in barracks. A table with benches stood in the middle of the room.

In the basement of the building there were washrooms, bathrooms and a laundry. The floor there was concrete, the wash basins were covered with a white enamel and, for cleaning the place, a fire hose was used every day. This very quickly washed down the dirt from everything.

That, in general outline, was the plan of the building. There was another building of the same sort located about ten minutes away.

As soon as the people had found places, Mr. McCreary invited them to dinner. The Doukhobors sat at the tables. Before dinner they all exchanged glances, stood up in unison, and bowing their heads, recited to themselves a pre-dinner grace. Only their faint whisper could be heard. The dinner was served by those Doukhobors who had arrived on the first train. The dinner proceeded in silence as the Doukhobors consider it improper to converse at dinner, and even worse to laugh.

The dinner consisted of oat soup with onion and kasha (a grain dish) with cow butter. Then the table was cleared and cheese cut in pieces was served. Milk, syrup in pitchers, and tea pots with prepared tea were brought. Sugar, as is the custom here, was granulated; bread was white. The dinner had been prepared by local women.

Every day from morning till evening, while the Immigration Home was open, Canadians came to look at their new fellow citizens. Apparently this did not embarrass the Doukhobors at all.

"Well then, look and see what we are like."

The curiosity and rudeness with which the English examined the Doukhobors was really astonishing. They looked at them as if the Doukhobors grew wings on their heads or as though they had arrived from Mars. Often one could see an Englishman fix his eyes on one of the Doukhobors with such naive, uncivilized amazement, that it was disgusting. The Doukhobor under observation usually stood grandly, with one foot forward, and looked steadily in a haughty manner at his observer. After standing silently for several minutes opposite one another, the Doukhobor would sigh, turn and walk away and the Englishman would follow him with his amazed, curious stare.

Later I saw that in the United States, in New York for example, the crowd behaved even more preposterously to the outward appearance of a person. There it is enough to have a beard to bring out the supercilious smiles of bystanders. One need only appear somewhere on an important street without a starched collar and bright colored necktie and, even if your costume should be fully becoming, you will soon have someone pointing and calling you "Green." That is like a put-down. "Green" is the name Americans give to any newcomer who has not yet become acclimatized and adopted the outer appearance and manners of the Yankees. Anything can be done to the "green" one, just as sailors do with the newcomer who has not yet sailed. He is rudely deceived, cheated, jeered and scoffed at. People whoop at his appearance, children chase him. Some jovial passer-by suddenly leans toward him and crows like a rooster to the hearty laughter of the bystanders. Someone deliberately steps on his toes, and so on.

Visitors who came to look at the Doukhobors began little by little to converse with them through interpreters. Conversations were mostly about the climate in Russia, how the Russians live, what their clothing is made of, and so on. The Canadians were particularly pleased when, having asked about one or another item of clothing, they were told that the Doukhobors made them all themselves. Their wooden spoons especially interested everyone. And when it was learned that the Doukhobors made them themselves also, someone asked for a spoon as a souvenir. He was given one. And the next day many asked for a spoon and finally, there were not enough spoons so that two or three old men began to make spoons as "gifts" for friends!

Of course, the Doukhobors had nothing to do here. Old men conversed all day among themselves or with the visiting public. Women washed and sewed. Girls embroidered kerchiefs (which, it must be said, they did very artistically) or they sewed one another cockades to wear on their caps. The girls strove for a specially beautiful finish on these cockades. When the cockade is finished the girl gives it to her nearest girl friend. And sometimes one might see it on the cap of some young man! Where these cockades or "flowers" as the Doukhobors call them come from, I was unable to learn, but undoubtedly they are not just an ornament but have also a traditional significance, a symbol distinguishing Doukhobors from other people—in the same way as the "fish" distinguishes ancient Christians. Perhaps, that is why they are given and received so willingly, as presents.

Young people chop wood, clear snow, help the cooks and do chores. The provisions are under the control of two or three elders; they hand them out to the cooks, and when none are left they order a new supply with the help of interpreters. All this comes from the same "bonus" which is now the single source of life of this party until their crops yield earnings. Because of this the elders attempt to start conversations on the theme that it will not do to feed ourselves so richly.

But during the previous three years the people had become so exhausted, had hungered so much, and the emaciation had reached such a serious degree, that the elders, looking at the pale, dry women and children, appeared not to notice the sumptuousness of the board.

The diet was really good. In the morning they drank tea with milk and ate cheese, cow butter, syrup and beautiful white bread. At noon they had soup with cabbage, potatoes, butter and some kind of kasha (grain dish) or beans, which are very popular here for food. So that even after a few days the people had noticeably improved and looked more cheerful. At first not everyone realized that everything was being bought with their own money and many wondered at the sumptuous reception.

"How well they are receiving us, God save them!" many people said, especially women. Those knowing the source of the good reception avoided this question, partly because they did not wish to disturb the general holiday mood, partly for the above-mentioned reason.

Canada
Winnipeg
January 27, 1899.

Then came the first Sunday after the Doukhobors' arrival in Winnipeg. For the first time after the long crossing, the Doukhobors could pray as a whole community, as is their custom.

Now neither the tossing ship nor the shaking, rumbling train would interfere. The prayer meeting was to take place in the large room on the first storey which was cleared of tables and benches the night before.

Before daybreak Doukhobor men and women in holiday dress began to gather here. The women had silk kerchiefs over their caps which they tied in a particular way for prayer meetings. The men stood on one side of the room, the women on the other. It was still dark. Only the windows showed the cold steel light of sky. In the mysterious pre-dawn twilight, stalwart figures of men stood with bowed heads and hands folded on their chests. The women standing opposite had folded white squares of handkerchiefs which they held in hands folded below their breasts.

In the whole group an inspired emotion was felt. The solemn silence before the beginning of the service seemed to be the fulfilment of a special, mysterious idea. Each one in the group, and the whole group itself, was now engrossed with the idea of the soul, of God. Each was absorbed in spiritual contemplation.

In the quiet, undisturbed by a single sigh, one feared to move lest one disturb this deep contemplative mood, when people lose touch with everything earthy and material, and live only in the spirit. Even the dull lilac dawn had stopped its movement, looking through the windows at the stern figures. Time itself seemed to have stood still, since any movement here would be too disturbing.

The first harmonic sounds of the psalm softly, gently disturbed the established calm, often flowing so gently and sincerely that it was difficult to understand where they came from. It seemed that the mood itself had now taken on this form so as to take more firm possession of the souls of the people. Gaining confidence in its power, it now flowed in a mighty broad stream filling the human being. The psalm spoke of the vanity of earthly happiness, knowing that all life is suffering, and it beckoned whither all is calm; where there are no desires, but eternal intelligence and love reign. Sometimes the mighty sweeps of the psalm became threatening—then it spoke of the terrors of sin, and of punishment which sin also brings. And the dark figures continued to stand, as before, with bowed heads seemingly even more motionless and more severe. It was as if they were confessing to being tied to the earth by their weaknesses. But, as if knowing that a person cannot long remain at such spiritual heights, the psalm ended with a broad sigh, as if sorry to be at an end.

The group sighed softly and moved.

Then, translating into a more understandable language what had been experienced in silence at the time of the singing, a woman's voice recited one of the beautiful Doukhobor psalms. When it ended, one of the men recited another psalm, then again a woman recited, and so on. Sometimes during the recitation, someone with voice restrained, corrected an error, or supplied a verse or word forgotten by the reciter. Sometimes several voices did the correcting. The reciter silently listened to the correction, and repeating the corrected part, continued. If someone began reciting a psalm which had already been recited that day by another, the reciter was stopped by one word:

"Recited."

The choir sang again and the Doukhobors came to the last part of their service; it appeared as a visual demonstration of all that was said in the psalms about the body of a person being a shrine of God in which His Spirit lives and therefore, love and respect for the personality of a person constitutes the best means of service to God. During the singing of the psalm, one of the Doukhobors comes out of the group and, approaching another, gives him his hand and they bow to one another three times. After kissing, each of them goes to another and so on until everyone has greeted everyone else. After going around all the men present, he turns to the women and bows to them from the waist, to which all the women reply in kind. All the women do likewise. Each of them, after going around all the women, bows to the men; and they respond to her. When this is finished the psalm ends. The men and women bow to one another very low with the words:

"God be praised!"

The service then ended. The golden rays of the morning sun now pierced the icy flowers of the frozen window and filled the room with a rosy light. It lit up the intent faces of the Doukhobors. The crowd quietly broke up.

It is difficult to say how the Doukhobor psalms were created. In their content they are entirely in agreement with the gospel, and much, especially the words of Jesus Christ, is quoted word for word. All the same, the majority of the Doukhobors are convinced, to this day, that their psalms represent something original, having nothing in common with printed gospel. It seems to them that the unperverted teaching of Jesus Christ can be learned only from their psalms. The Doukhobors call all the psalms "The Book of Life," that is a live book—living, giving life. It "lives in the hearts," as the Doukhobors say. The Doukhobors never wrote down these psalms. They are passed on orally from generation to generation and are preserved only in the memory.

Bonch-Bruevich who accompanied the Doukhobors on the fourth ship which was conducted by A. Konshin wrote down more than 1,000 psalms during his stay in Canada. Despite minute inquiries, additional ones could not be found so that it appears that he managed to collect all of them. At first the Doukhobors did not willingly agree to the writing-down of their psalms, poems and so on; but with the support of certain elders the matter was resolved, and many Doukhobors then helped Bonch-Bruevich collect them.

It must be said that until recent times the majority of the Doukhobors have been hostile to literacy and to school. They saw it only as the means by which orthodoxy could be propagandized among them. For this reason, with minor exceptions, there are almost no literate people among them. Generally in Canada where the teachers, by law, have no right to deal with religion, Doukhobors (chiefly the young) learn willingly.

It seems to the Doukhobors that writing in a book is something dead, unnecessary and uninteresting. When one literate exiled Doukhobor was asked if he would like to have some books sent to him, he replied that it did not interest him very much. He would prefer to receive a living book: that is, someone to visit him. Every soul is a living book. "Our book" the Doukhobors say of the "living book," "cannot be torn nor thrown away nor lost. It lies deep in the human heart."

The Sunday reciting of psalms, besides having an instructive, prayerful significance, is at the same time an ongoing corrective process. If someone reciting a psalm makes an error, not only of a word, but even in the order of words having no significance, he will be sure to be corrected by one or sometimes more voices. According to content, psalms may be divided into several groups. In the main, the base of the Doukhobor dogma—their view of the world—is stated in the psalms. These determine all the attitudes of the Doukhobor to occurrences in the life around him, personal, family, social and political. Psalms state how a person who considers himself a Christian must live. Some of the psalms have a polemic character. In several are described the sufferings and terror of darkness, here many parts are taken from the Apocalypse. The language of the psalms is always surprisingly beautiful, elegant and supremely epic.

Small children, for whom the learning of long psalms is hard, recite special "children's psalms" distinguished by sweet, colourful language.

Besides the psalms the Doukhobors have so-called hymns. Their content for the greater part, consists of allegories from the life of Christ, or tales in poetic form about the adventures of some pious wanderer or apostle. The poems have been made, in all probability, to satisfy the aesthetic needs of man. They are always sung by a choir that wants to sing; they are never sung at prayer services.

According to the Doukhobors, one must never lose serenity of spirit nor self-respect. Every minute one must be prepared for suffering and death. One must always concentrate and be attentive, not only to others, but to oneself, spiritually as well as bodily, since the body is a temple of God, the very form through which God makes himself known. Perhaps this is the source of that fastidiousness and order, the equal of which is very difficult to find anywhere among Russian people.

Musically the poems are very pleasant. Some of them are exceptional for clarity of rhythm and musical life and animation, but they never get to the point of being rollicking. The music of the verses is entirely like the Doukhobors themselves, who rarely are seen to laugh boisterously or to express their joy or grief loudly. With equal restraint and dignity they bear both sorrow and joy. Among Doukhobors it is rare to see a face oppressed or frightened by suffering; great moral strength is shown in their unshakeable tranquility.

The Doukhobors sing often and well, always with unusual clarity. Sometimes they harmonize a complex form especially in psalms, which have almost no conventional melody; and all singing consists of different, often unexpected modulations from one harmonic sequence to another. With a large choir this comes out with a special grandeur. Sometimes in psalms there is a fugue.

Psalms are sung not only at prayer meetings but at other times as well. For the most part, psalm singing is enjoyed by older people; young people mostly sing poems. Wherever a psalm is sung it is considered improper to break it off midway, or to walk from one place to another during singing.

It is singular that with such love of singing and such great ability the Doukhobors have no songs at all for solo singing. Only very rarely will you hear someone in the field or behind his wagon humming to himself, always the same verse or psalm.

Canada
Winnipeg
January 28, 1899.

On Sunday the public began to gather in the Immigration Hall in large numbers. Many apparently expected to see the Doukhobors at religious service, but the fatigued and hungry Doukhobors by this time were sitting at dinner, which they have earlier than usual on Sunday. The public continued to arrive, and it was apparent that they expected something special. About two o'clock Mr. McCreary arrived. He asked the Doukhobors to gather to hear an address from the citizens of Winnipeg.

Nearly all the Doukhobors in the hall gathered in the lower room. Opposite them stood Englishmen in fur coats, wearing sweaters with wide knitted collars, and with pipes in their teeth—"Angliki," as the Doukhobors called them. Many of the Doukhobors also called them "Nemtsi" in spite of numerous explanations on this subject. "It's all the same," they say, "Englishmen or Germans!"

Not a few of the visiting public were ladies. Some of the "Angliki" waiting for the solemnities worked their jaws on their chaw, colouring their moustaches and lips with yellow saliva. This repulsive habit is so widespread here that sometimes children and refined ladies are not free of it. The latter do not chew tobacco but some kind of special mastic or gum. Big and little take up this activity with an enthusiasm deserving a better purpose. The face of the chewer at the time of chewing assumes a special expression of animal satisfaction. Children smack loudly—not a beautiful sight. The custom is highly unhygienic. These gentlemen, wherever they happen to be, in several minutes decorate the floor or the sidewalk etc. with spots. The Tramway Company long conducted a useless war with the chewers, hanging up all kinds of announcements prohibiting spitting on the floor. Nothing helped until someone thought of the following notice:

GENTLEMEN WILL NOT SPIT ON THE FLOOR.
ALL OTHERS ARE NOT PERMITTED TO DO SO.

All, of course, turned out to be gentlemen; during travel the chaw was kept in the pocket and the coaches remained clean.

Now a tall thin gentleman stalked ahead and, in company with McCreary, made his way through the crowd of Englishmen. He stopped in front of the visitors and methodically unfolded his address, long fingers bent back at the ends, the inevitable ring on the little finger. Silence fell in the room.

Glancing at Vasya Popoff, who as always on formal occasions was the president of the Doukhobors, the Englishman asked through an interpreter, "Is this the elder?"

Vasya Popoff, as if caught stealing, looked around at all his brethren as if apologising that he had been asked such a question and answered, "Tell them that we have no elders, as we consider all people to be the same. All people have the spirit of God, and no one can be master of another. For the same reason it is sinful to submit to another, other than to one's soul."

Hearing out the answer, the Englishman nodded vaguely and

announced that he had been authorized by the city of Winnipeg to read an address to the Doukhobors. Holding before him a page typed on the Remington he read loudly and distinctly:

"To the Christians of Universal Brotherhood, to the Doukhobors: The Committee of Citizens of Winnipeg sends hearty greetings to the Doukhobors migrating into this part of the realm of Her Majesty. We hear very good reports of you, of your love of labour, and of your sobriety, and know also by reports that you have had to bear many ordeals for your convictions not to do'that which you consider to be wrong.

"We heard that one of you said sixty years ago that America some day would be your second motherland; and we hope the fulfilment of this undertaking, by the happy providence of God, will be of great benefit to the Doukhobors and to that land to which you have come. You will be convinced that Canada, flourishing under free British institutions, guarantees complete equality and civil and religious freedom to all its citizens.

"Meeting you here today on the threshhold of your future motherland, we welcome you as settlers prepared to work our fertile lands, accepting our laws and promoting the development of the natural wealth of the land. We have a good system of upbringing and education, the advantages of which will become clear to you, and we may be confident that soon you will acquire knowledge of the English language and will be in a position to use all the benefits which are available here to all British subjects and will promote the prosperity of the Canadian nationality under the British flag."

The Englishmen applauded and cried, "Bravo!" The reader bowed to them and handed the page to Vasya Popoff. When the address had been translated for the Doukhobors, Popoff said on behalf of all:

"We have already seen much of your brotherly attitude to us. Only God knows how joyful it is to us, to our hearts, that you accept us in the Christian manner as brothers and give us refuge. There is nothing further we can say. Only one thing—with all our strength we will strive as much as possible to justify your confidence. God willing, we will continue to live as brothers. Meanwhile, we bow to you for your love and your welcome to our whole society. May God save you."

"God save (thank) you," repeated the crowd earnestly, bowing in the direction of the English. All the same, Vasya Popoff, thrifty of words, politically aware, had mentioned not a word about the English flag, prosperity of the British Empire, the Queen, and so on (at which the speech of the English was, in the main, directed). McCreary and the reader of the address apparently noticed the omission of those important subjects and exchanged significant glances. But what could be done? The speech of the Doukhobors could not be altered.

A worker with a pipe in his teeth, flashing his eyes and waving his arm with each sentence, made a brief impromptu address:

"We have long talked of a social commune as something unrealizable. Dear as this idea is to us, we rarely dare talk of it as something possible. Nevertheless, now it seems possible without fear to defend the feasibility of such an ideal, because such a commune already exists in reality. The commune is here before you. There it is." He ended sharply, waving his arm in the direction of the Doukhobors and stepped aside.

A burst of applause awarded the orator. From all sides could be heard the expression beloved of the English: "That's right." Then the reader of the address shook Popoff's hand, bowed to the rest, and departed with McCreary.

But the English men and women continued to stand and watch the Doukhobors, trying to start a conversation with them. An elegantly dressed woman approached one of the elders and, smiling sweetly and leaning forward with half-closed eyes, asked him, "Do you believe our Lord Jesus Christ atoned for us with his blood and blessed us, my friend?" She continued smiling even more sweetly, touching him with her hand covered in a kidskin glove. "I am asking because if you believe this, I am your sister in Christ," she concluded, looking expectantly into his face.

The stern figure of the old man stood firmly and apparently did not yield in any way to the sweet smile nor to the gentle touch. He continued to look serious and there was not a trace of a smile on his face.

"Madam," he began, "this is unknown to us. We think little about this. We think the important thing is what Christ passed on to us. This is the legacy of brotherly love, that people will live as brothers. And when swords are beaten into ploughshares and the lion lies down with the lamb, then the Kingdom of God will begin on earth. Therefore all people are our brothers and sisters."

"But you know that He suffered for us on the Cross and thereby atoned for us for all time?"

"Who knows? Somehow I cannot sort out how He atoned. Everything can be; only this is unknown to us," he continued calmly.

Upon hearing Legebokoff, the lady decided that she was not being understood and, as it was time for the Doukhobors' supper, she went away promising to come in again sometime and converse some more. Supper was brought and little by little the remaining English departed.

Canada
City of Brandon
February 3, 1899.

Brandon is a very small city lying a few hours travel by rail from Winnipeg. Here a substantial number of the Doukhobors are wintering, more than three hundred persons, and I wanted to see how they have become established. The two-storey Immigration Hall seems to be the largest building here. The hall with bunks and kettles, is of the same type as that in Winnipeg, except that it is much smaller in size. For this reason, in the yard near the hall there is a large tent in which is piled the baggage, for which there was no room in the hall.

Here the life of the Doukhobors is more simple, quiet and more businesslike. There is less solemnity than in Winnipeg, where people live in a show window; though here too the local residents met the Doukhobors very cordially, and occasionally come to look at them and try to make new acquaintances. Looking at the life of the Doukhobors here, one feels that they are living in temporary circumstances, strange in their enforced idleness. It is clear that the Doukhobors are pining for spring, when they will be free to undertake joyful, creative labour. Nicolai Zeebarev, wintering here, had managed to find day labour, and other Doukhboors are keen to be hired to saw wood and do other work. They get fifty cents to one dollar per day, sometimes more. Women take in laundry. Some have found work in tanning.

Since they do not know the language, the Doukhobors reach agreement on price with employers by gesture. As they already have their living quarters and board, they do not seek high pay. Besides, they do not know local rates; in comparison with Russian labour rates, the Canadian ones seem very high. Canadians, of course, took advantage of this situation and more and more often have hired Doukhobors, paying them less and less. The result is that the Doukhobors have significantly lowered the wage rates in Brandon, and this produced justified dissatisfaction among the English workers who presume that the Doukhobors are deliberately competing with them and lowering the wages for labour.

The workers called a meeting at which it was said that the government had made a mistake in accepting the Doukhobors, since they were turning out to be dangerous competitors of local workers, like the Chinese, and that they apparently do not wish to know about any interests other than their own; and so on. The workers were especially indignant that the Doukhobors received monetary assistance (bonuses) from the government when neither English nor any other immigrants ever received the same. The workers did not know that the "bonus" was nothing more than the reward which the Canadian government pays to every immigration agent for attracting settlers to Canada and that in this instance the agents (Mr. Maude and others) turned over their rights to the Doukhobors. After the meeting proclamations appeared on the fences of Brandon, headed "Away with the Doukhobors." In these proclamations, the workers expressed their hostile attitude to the Doukhobors and forecast all kinds of calamities to Canadians if they did not defend their interests from these "new Chinese" who were encouraged by the government.

For a long time the Doukhobors themselves knew nothing about this hostile movement among Brandon's workers. Once they appreciated the reason for it they became more demanding of pay and they did not go to work in the city as often. And while there were no explanations between the workers and the Doukhobors, relations between them soon improved as the workers saw that the Doukhobors had lowered the wages only through ignorance, and that they had no intention of taking work away from local workers in this manner. Such misunderstandings occurred to a smaller degree in two or three places where the Doukhobors wintered, and these were resolved locally.

Unfortunately, the Canadian workers in the main remained uninformed on the question of what the money was which the Canadian government gave to the Doukhobors; this was the cause of many later misunderstandings as well.

To return to where I broke off! The food eaten here is unusually simple. In the morning there is tea with bread; at noon, soup, sometimes kasha (a grain dish); and for supper, bread and tea or kasha remaining from dinner. Very little cheese is eaten and only on Sundays.

Nicolai Zeebarev, together with other workers, stays busy shovelling snow away from the hall, banking it high around the hall and tent or buildings and space for provisions, etc.

There are no speeches or ceremonies here, which is explained in part by the fact that there is no one here to conduct such ceremonies. Zeebarev, despite his wisdom, is the least fitted for such activity. All kinds of solemnities such as public speeches embarrass him—a simple, strong person—and obviously fatigue him. On such occasions, as if embarrassed by the high tone of the orator, he smiles confusedly, reddens and replies with but two or three words of thanks. It seems to him superfluous to "pronounce" words; as he says, "It will be better seen in practice!" His powerful, able hands are helplessly folded during the speech and one feels he does not know what to do with them.

At dinner Zeebarev started a discussion about provisions.

"Tell me, please, why do they eat so richly in Winnipeg? Good grief! Is that acceptable? Cheese, honey, some kind of milk—they eat four times daily! Why are they fattening up? Like little children! What happens to me if I taste honey? Will I be better? What are the elders thinking of? There's Vasya Popoff, Chernenkoff, Legebokoff—do they not know that it all comes out of the money we have for getting started? If we spend it all, then how will we plough? How will we live through the summer?"

"And again," added another elder, Michael Baulin, "what about other places? In Portage la Prairie, or Dauphin, or at our place we all eat thriftily; we save so as not to spend too much; but they eat luxuriously! This makes for differences; that will not do!"

"This must end altogether," was heard from the other end of the table, "so the food will be the same everywhere, in all places."

"Three meals is enough, entirely enough," continued Zeebarev. "So all elders have decided—in the morning, tea; at noon, soup; and for supper, kasha or beans or noodles may be prepared. But this foolishness—honey and cheese—is altogether unnecessary!"

"Milk is also unnecessary," said one of the elders.

"Except only for the sick," confirmed Zeebarev.

"We must come to agreement so that all will be in accord," adds Melesha, nodding.

The conversation ended in a decision to write a notice in which will be given the above-mentioned standard of nourishment. The notice is to be sent to all places where Doukhobors are wintering, and in Winnipeg I am asked to give the content of it by word of mouth.

Canada
Winnipeg
February 7, 1899.

When I arrived back in Winnipeg I told the Doukhobors what the Brandon brethren thought about expenditures on food; everyone felt extremely confused. Chernenkoff, with a guilty smile, sadly smacked his lips and with a glance seeking confirmation from Vasya Popoff, mumbled with a sigh, "Who knows? How has it turned out that way—this food? H-m-m—is it a sin?!"

Vasya Popoff's face was covered with fine droplets of perspiration; he turned red and confusedly handled the edge of his jacket, looking mostly upwards as if watching a mouse running on the moulding. Finally gathering strength, he said, helplessly raising his eyebrows, that people needed to get strengthened, and he added, "And again, we did not know that they were eating differently from us. We thought that, as we were fed, so were they in other places."

"Well, yes. The important thing is we didn't know about it," Chernenkoff said a little more cheerfully. "All the same, Vasya," he said rapidly in a business-like tone, "in that case we must change so that there will not be—God forbid!—disagreements." By "disagreements" the Doukhobors mean all kinds of anger, judgements and dissatisfaction in the society.

All were uncomfortable. But no one was as confused as Vasya Popoff, the same Popoff who was able to hold himself so grandly that he would not wink an eye, and in the most difficult situations might only grunt sometimes.

The point was that Vasya Popoff is one of the most devoted proponents of communism, which he has shown in deed more than once. In a time most difficult for the Doukhobors, the last years in exile in Tiflis province, the elders together with Vasya decided that every Doukhobor must bring all his money to the common treasury. As managers of this treasury the society selected several trustworthy people. From that day private property disappeared. Not only money on hand at the time, but all earnings had to be brought to the treasury. The managers of the treasury gave to the heads of families a monthly sum according to the size of the family. The sum per person was decided by a meeting of elders. Equipment and horses were divided equally also.

When the first common capital was being gathered, Vasya Popoff was one of the first to bring all his money (something more than ten thousand), not concealing a penny for himself. Not all acted so sincerely and open-heartedly; many left themselves a little for emergency, for a rainy day and so on. It turned out that along the way and in Canada, first one, then another, striving to remain unnoticed, went to the Immigration Office and there changed his reserve of Russian roubles unknown to the society—one, ten roubles, another twenty, one, a hundred and more. Of course, such matters could not be concealed from a watchful society and the secret soon became obvious; but no one criticized such thrifty elders. This was left to the conscience of each. Only, if at a meeting some such elder talked a lot about the need to live a communal life, an awkward silence ensued and some one looking calmly at the speaker said, "Yes, of course, that would be better," and the orator would stumble, mumble two or three words more, and stop. But Vasya Popoff gave away all his capital and savings so completely that he turned out later to be poorer than others, who previously had been poor compared to him. And suddenly this Vasya Popoff had overlooked this prime question of nourishment!

In the evening when all had gathered, Vasya Popoff gave to the meeting the proposal of the Brandon people about changing the community food rule.

"Well, then, elders, how will it be?" he asked in conclusion, "Do you agree to that; or will you decide something else."

The elders sat silently, breathing heavily in their tight jackets.

There was silence. Each waited to see if another would begin.

"Well, how about it then?"

"Well, there is nothing to talk about," said an elder with an eagle nose and overhanging eyebrows. "Of course we agree."

"The matter is obvious," confirmed a little old man in a high tenor with a good face and intelligent eyes. He put his hands on the table and handled a string with his fingers.

"That's what the community is for, to do as brothers."

"As for one, so to another," voices were heard.

"How else can it be? Are we to eat a little better and others not? No! Of course, we were uninformed about this. Since it is so, it must be ended," said one of the elders.

"An end to it; no more!" supported another.

"Then all are agreed?" asked Popoff.

"All, all of course," the elders droned like bees.

"Very well; but what food is to be used?" asked Chernenkoff. "As they write here, or perhaps to add or to reduce? How will it be?"

There was a silence again, except for two men in the back rows who had not had all their say on the first question and who were conversing in low tones and nodding at one another, looking into each others' eyes. The first to break the silence was Michael Legebokoff.

"As is written, that is good. There is no need to wish for better. Only perhaps butter is unnecessary." The favourite thought of Legebokoff was pure vegetarianism, the principle of not killing living beings, interested him little.

(Doukhobors are all vegetarians. But some of them are guided in this matter by the ethical side; some look upon vegetarianism as does Legebokoff. This explains how many, never using meat, find it possible to eat fish.) But many expressed opposition to Legebokoff's suggestion.

"It would be difficult, difficult," they shook their heads. "There is risk of the people weakening by spring."

"What of it? I will go along with the society. I mentioned it only because it is very expensive. Again, we have lived without butter," continued Legebokoff.

"We have been without eyes," the high tenor continued, plucking his string.*

"Let the people build up their strength a bit," uncertainly said an elder with a pale sickly face. "In a word, it is to be as is written."

"No need to discuss further."

"It is well-written."

"To this we are agreed," several voices spoke in competition.

---

*Once in Tiflis Province, from a shortage of butter in the diet, the Doukhobors all suffered from night blindness.

Shamshirin standing sideways to the table, hands behind his back, looked at the elders from under his brows, awaiting silence. He said in a decided voice, "And what has been ordered for the old diet—there is honey and other things—those are to be eaten up?" He turned his head and quickly disappeared behind others in the back rows. The crowd moaned.

"It's not to be thrown out," several elders said, smiling. Chernenkoff smiled broadly, looked at the others and said, "Well, what can you tell him?"

"The old man likes honey," said Vasya Popoff somewhat mockingly, wrinkling his upper lip.

The elders departed. In this manner one norm was established for all, and what had been ordered before was eaten up—to Shamshirin's satisfaction!

On the Prairies, Canada
On the train of the Manitoba Northwest Railroad
En route from Winnipeg to Cowan
February 12, 1899.

In two or three months the Doukhobors would have to vacate the Immigration Hall to make place for the next group. They had to hurry with construction of temporary living quarters on the lands selected for the Doukhobors by their delegates. But while heavy frosts continued it was useless to think of sending workers to the bare prairie, where they would have to live in tents, thirty or forty miles from the nearest little town.

In the first days of February it turned significantly warmer; frost in the morning did not exceed five degrees Reamur (six degrees C). Two parties of English workers were sent to the district. One of them went to the Northern Settlement and the other to the Southern. In both districts the English workers contracted to build several block houses, each for about thirty persons. As soon as each block house was ready, Doukhobor carpenters would move in and build bunks in two levels.

The expense of hiring the Englishmen and the purchase of stock and equipment were covered out of the bonuses. On the proposal of the Minister of the Interior, a commission was set up to decide business questions and control of expenditures; it consisted of Mr. McCreary, D. Hilcoff and one of the respected citizens of Winnipeg. Soon information was received that one block house had been completed in each settlement.

Today the first party of fifty Doukhobors set off for the Northern Settlement. I went with them. Before departing for Russia, I wished to see the places where the Doukhobors would settle. The railroad on

One of the communal "barracks" houses built in 1899.

which we were travelling (Manitoba and Northwestern Railroad), a branch of the Canadian Pacific Railway which crosses all of Canada, was still under construction. We would travel on it to the last station, Cowan. From there to the settlement the distance was sixty versts. We would have to travel by horse through the empty prairie, without a road, along the track left by the English workers.

All our party got into one coach. In it sat several English squatters and one ever-smiling half-breed. At first the Doukhobors sang, which the English liked very much, and chatted; but with the coming of evening, fatigue took over; conversation ceased. Each tried to settle into the most comfortable position and soon the whole coach went into a deep sleep.

Canada
Cowan Station
In the boarding house
February 13, 1899.

At two o'clock in the morning we arrived at Cowan. The brakes squealed, buffers bumped, the train stopped. The drowsy Doukhobors moved lazily, gathered their belongings and looked out of the windows. But from there, only the black night looked back at them. Apart from the reflections of their own faces and the coach lamps, nothing could be seen. Somewhere the bright yellow point of a lantern flickered; it jumped strangely and lurched in all directions, as if flying in the air. It seemed as if the person carrying it was running over uneven ground. The light came nearer and nearer and in a few minutes an interpreter, Galician Ivan Ivanovich, came into the coach and with him was N. Zeebarev, who had come here with the English workers. Brisk, active, like all local pioneers, the interpreter energetically moved the lantern in all directions and called in his broken Russian language, "Well, get ready! Quickly, quickly! You're sleepy! Well. Fine, boys, one must work quickly here." The Doukhobors, indulgently looking at his bustling, hurried to leave, hardly taking time to greet Zeebarev, smiling happily at his brethren.

Leaving the coach, we came into pitch darkness. After the brightly lit coach, we could not see where to step. It seemed we were falling into an abyss. Besides, the bustling interpreter blinded our eyes with his lantern, which lit nothing but his hand and his white hairy moustache.

"Why is he confusing everything?" someone said.

"Well, is everyone here, or are there more?" cried the interpreter in the direction of the dark group of people.

"Yes, everyone, everyone; lead us on," someone replied impatiently.

The spasmodic light moved forward and after it, in a single file, the Doukhobors moved. We walked through a snowy waste lost in night darkness so dense that one could hardly see the dark back of the person in front of one. From the dark chasm, dark silhouettes of giant sleeping trees came right before our eyes. Majestically, calmly, they stood, spreading widely their furry, heavy branches covered with a thick layer of snow. Under their huge shadows, here and there, great trunks shadowed the snow, bare of branches, levelled by the destructive hand of man. Threatening silence reigned here. Timidly, in single file, the people got through this wild place, not daring to exchange a word that might disturb the sleep of these venerable giants. The only sounds were of dry snow creaking under soft steps and the heavy restrained breathing of the winded people.

Ahead we felt a dark wall of forest. After climbing a little hill, blood-red lights flashed like the eyes of some unseen monster frisking alone in the forest; guarding its rest.

"And here is the boarding house," the interpreter cried merrily, waving his lantern, glad that finally the awesome silence of the party could be interrupted.

The people, roused, hurried up and began to talk. Near the boarding house stood a tent with wide spreading skirts, pitched here by an enterprising Englishman. There, the weak light of a lamp hardly piercing the stream, could be seen several horses and oxen. The animals were lazily chewing their night rations; vapour from their breathing filled the tent; it was hot and stifling.

The boarding house itself was a low building made of heavy logs, chinked with clay for warmth; earth was piled on the plank roof. It was very hot inside and quite dark. On the floor about twenty Englishmen and several Indians were sleeping, together with their furry dogs. None of them paid any attention to us, although to get to the next room we had to step over their feet. Only one Indian mumbled something, sitting in the corner with a hand bandaged in a cloth, on which he blew from time to time to ease the pain. The whites of his eyes flashed at us out of the dark.

In the next room, beside a red-hot stove, a young blonde Englishman with his sleeves rolled up was handily drying pewter dishes. With him was a red-faced Galician woman. Without stopping his work, laughing merrily, he busily assigned us to tables and managed to joke with his co-workers—not an easy matter, as he joked as much with his hands as with his voice. Somehow we got settled on the floor and benches and those who had no other space sat at the table; so we whiled away the rest of the night. Waking, I saw the restless Englishman, covered with perspiration, passing out hot porridge* in the next room; the Galician woman poured tea, hardly moving her sleepy eyes.

It was time to prepare for the road. For the Northern Settlement five pairs of good large horses and three pairs of oxen had been bought with the bonus money. The oxen were left at the settlement where they were used to skid logs from the forest for construction, and the horses were hitched in pairs to sleighs to haul provisions and other baggage from Cowan to the settlement. Mr. McCreary was most insistent that as much flour and other provisions as possible be hauled to the Northern Settlement while the snow road held, because between Cowan and the Northern Settlement there were swampy marshes, and with the coming of spring it would be very difficult to cross these. Of course, five teams of horses were hardly enough for this purpose, so about ten English teams were hired as well.

Zeebarev complained about this hired draying. "It would have been better to buy horses and sleighs for this money and then they would remain with us. We could use them for ploughing. Now look and see—oats, hay, flow like a river because they have no feed bags. They pour the oats onto a blanket or right on the snow. What can you do about it? One's heart bleeds. You tell one to put more on the load and he does not want to listen. 'You did not hire me,' he says. 'The

---

*Oatmeal porridge is the usual breakfast of the English.

government pays me.' What can you say to him? The only thing would be to reject them altogether."

Discussing the question in Winnipeg, Hilcoff showed McCreary that it was much more advantageous to buy one's own horses than to hire them, but McCreary did not agree.

"If that is done," he said, "it will end thus; the money will be gone and there will be no livestock and the baggage will be stuck in Cowan and Yorkton (the nearest railway station to the Southern Settlement.) The Doukhobors, I have noticed, are stubborn people. They do not wish to look after horses, as is the custom here, and with improper care the Percheron soon dies. Perhaps in the Caucasus their care was good, but it won't do here!"

Canada
En route between Cowan and the Northern Settlement
February 13, 1899.

By general agreement, several Doukhobors remained in Cowan to build blockhouses. This was necessary to offset boarding house fees.

After breakfast our team was hitched up. They loaded as much as possible from the coach that we came on, and set off. It was warm; the beautiful big horses walked easily through the loose snow, monotonously rattling the single trees. The Doukhobors, crowding in disorder, walked beside the high-loaded sleigh on which sat one or two people. Young men who had been sailors on the ship became playful and kept pushing one another into the deep snow; several times they came after me, dragged me off the sleigh and piled on top of me all together until the older ones freed me from their so-called "little group."

"That won't do," the elders reproved the young men. "Be easier!"

"Why easier?" they answered. "You know how he drilled us on the boat. He kept saying, 'When we get to shore, then you can have your way.' Now we should bully him a little!"

"Bully him!" said the old men. "You will wet your sheepskin coats in the snow and they will burst open. Then the frost will bully you!"

"What of the coats? We will start using sweaters like the Germans."

"Look at the Indian I have become! Ho! Ho! Ho!" roared a big young man, lying on his back and raising his feet clothed in thick socks and yellow Indian moccasins.

The elders grumbled that such fooling would not do, but the frolicsome youths were difficult to control.

Again and again they started wrestling and then ran to catch up to the sleigh ahead, sinking in the soft snow to their knees, every minute stumbling and falling over one another. The elders apparently did not like to see the youths taking so easily to Indian moccasins, English sweaters, kepis with ear muffs and other foreign clothing. Even though many elders by necessity dressed the same, such unfaithfulness to Doukhobor custom could not be accepted without a struggle.

Soon after we left Cowan we also left the forest behind; now we were travelling over smooth prairie. Now and then small stands of lonely poplars would stick their bare brooms up to the sad grey sky. In places under the sloping snow a branch of wild peas, beloved food of Indian horses both in summer and winter, stubbornly pushed out. Here and there, lone moose tracks could be seen; intertwined like a chain was the sly, tangled track of the fox; we saw scattered tracks of the timid rabbit. In one place we came upon a print of snowshoes of an Indian hunting here.

Towards dinner we came again to a big forest consisting of poplars, pines and other species. There among big trunks blown down by the wind, a camp fire burned merrily and a kettle boiled. Around the camp fire sat about ten Englishmen; these were our draymen. We stopped beside them.

The English horsed, unhitched, were eating oats poured right onto the snow. This once more caused Zeebarev to become distressed. At the same time, when the Doukhobors, without giving their horses rest, poured them oats without measure, the Englishmen began to talk.

"How many times have we said that these horses must not be given heavy food while they are hot."

"These are not Indian horses," said another.

"They like to be fed regularly, three times a day, one measure of oats each time, not more," a stout Englishman with red veins on his cheeks and nose said with emphasis.

The Doukhobors paid no attention at all to the instructions. One of them, Sherstobitoff, with a stubborn smile, as if for spite, added a handful of oats to his horses and looking at them lovingly, said, "There, there! The Nemtsi [Germans] are talking total nonsense. After any ride in the mountains, driving the Governor or for some other reason, no matter how tired the horses may have been, we never waited. We gave them all the food they could eat and it was good to see what fat, sleek, clean horses they were! Very hair-splitting people, these English. No need to fear food; you cannot spoil kasha with butter,* and every animal has its own understanding. It will eat as much as necessary and that's the end. What if he himself were fed by portions? I'll bet he wouldn't be so fat!" Sherstobitoff laughed, pointing to the

*A Russian proverb.

preaching Englishman who at this time was downing a huge sandwich of cold meat and jam.

The English, (seeing that they were not being listened to), went to their own camp fire.

"Oh, that's alright. They'll soon learn," said the stout one. "We have seen what happens when settlers want to do things their own way!"

"Yes, it always ends very unhappily," said others. "Their pocket books will teach them!"

After eating, we went on together with the English. In one of the little fields a squatter's simple home suddenly appeared, the first abode we had seen. His land was surrounded by a barbed wire fence. the road went right past the little house, near which we saw the owner, a thin old man in a red tuque with his hands in his pockets. It appeared he was waiting for us, for as soon as the sleigh on which the interpreter sat came up, he went to him.

"Good day," he said, looking hastily at the Doukhobors with anger in his eyes. "What happened to the coupling bolt from my wagon? Tell me, please, eh?" he began, demandingly turning his head questioningly to one side.

"What coupling bolt?"

"What do you mean—what coupling bolt? Why do you ask that about which you know? My coupling bolt, an ordinary coupling bolt which lay here all winter until these people began to sneak by here," cried the old man, insistently knocking his pipe on the wagon; the end of his tuque shook with indignation.

"I do not know of any coupling bolt; you probably lost it and now nag us about it. And why would we need your coupling bolt?"

"Ask them—your young men. It lay here, I tell you, in this exact place, may lightning strike me!"*

"I have nothing to talk to you about, you are babbling nonsense. If you do not like the fact that the government gives them money and not you, then be angry at the government. You have no reason to smear honourable people. Good-bye!" The sleigh moved on.

"Yes," cried the old man, spraying saliva, "we used to lynch such honourable people in California and here we should tie their neckties until we teach them to respect the property of others. We shall see, yes, we shall see these honourable ones! Damn them, and damn you, too!" the old man called after us, holding his pipe in his hand.

"Strange old man," said one of the Doukhobors when we told them what the trouble was.

---

*Meaning "may lightning strike me if what I say is not true."

"Why must he prattle nonsense? Probably knows that we would never take anything and is envious of us—nothing else."

"And what did we do? Are we hurting anyone?"

Everyone looked for and examined reasons why the old Irishman should take offense. The accusation did not hurt anyone or touch anybody's vanity. Doukhobors are ideally honourable in relation to the property of others. They were so used to being trusted by others that it did not enter their heads that such an accusation could be serious. The incident showed them that not all were as glad of their coming to Canada as might have been concluded from the reception given them.

The road through the woods was sheltered. It became quite warm. Doukhobors who had gone far ahead of the sleighs took off their coats and hung them on nearby trees.

"When our people come they will pick them up."

"See if they don't leave them on the trees. You know it is said, 'do not touch what lies on the road.' "

"Well," Zeebarev said scornfully, "it's plain to see that it's our clothing. Who else wears it here? They'll have to bring it!"

The point is that on the prairie it is taken as a rule never to pick up an article found on the road if you do not know its owner for sure. So one does not "find" things here. This rule—the so-called law of the prairie—was worked out here a long time ago, when white people first began to settle. The law has been enforced by very stern measures; every breaker of this rule was hanged from the nearest tree. But since on the prairie it is often hard to find a tree, this enforcement of justice was carried out by other means. The horse was unhitched from the two-wheeled cart and the wrongdoer was tied to the end of the shaft. Then they got into the cart and raised the shafts with the wrongdoer hanged on the tips until the needs of justice were satisfied. Then the horse was hitched and the travellers proceeded on their way. It is understandable that in this way the rule became very much a part of every prairie dweller. Therefore, no matter how much your property might be left about, you could remain at ease about its safety.

Canada
Thirty miles from Cowan "Land Office"
Evening, February 13, 1899.

The day has ended; winter twilight has come. The forest had become sparse and more and more frequently there were large glades. One after another, the sleighs suddenly disappeared in a steep valley, at the bottom of which was a river, and on the other side of it appeared new buildings against the background of the darkening sky. Here was the Land Office, in a small settlement that had sprung up here in the past few weeks.

This was considered to be halfway between Cowan and the Northern Settlement. The village here consisted of about ten buildings; one was even two-storey, but they were all built of thin white boards and the roofs were covered in black tar paper. On one of the canvas signs was painted in red paint, "Home of Pioneers." On the wall of another building a Chinaman with sleeves rolled up was writing with chalk, "Laundry." In some windows, saws, huge Canadian axes and other tools could be seen hung out for sale.

As soon as we entered this Bret Harte village, we were surrounded by a crowd of Englishmen with rolled-up sleeves, pipes in their teeth, and axes or saws in their hands. They dropped their work to meet us, all smiling welcomingly and waving their broad brimmed hats.

"Welcome, Doukhobors!" could be heard from all sides. Children scrabbling underfoot squealed loudly. Furry dogs disturbed by such unusual noise barked violently, looking into their masters' faces.

From open doors, women with red faces, skirts tucked in and sleeves rolled up, looked out nodding their heads to us in welcome. Even the Chinese laundryman left his sign for a time and, baring his teeth, tried to wrinkle his face to resemble a smile. He had the appearance of one who any moment might burst into bitterest tears.

In the middle of the village, on the square, covered with mounds of hay, barrels, logs and other goods, we were met by a tall man with a wide-brimmed hat and the face of Napoleon III. This was Mr. Harley, an officer of the Immigration Department. He stood up on a pile of hay and gave a short welcoming speech for which he was rewarded with loud applause from the citizens of the new village, the barking of dogs and the deafening yell of children.

The Doukhobors answered for the hundredth time, "God save you" (thank you) for the reception. Then the orator got down from his rostrum and led us all to the big blockhouse which the government had built here for all settlers needing a roof. The blockhouse was not yet finished and the floor was covered with a thick layer of sawdust instead of planks. In the middle of the blockhouse stood two iron stoves, heated red hot as is the custom in Canada.

The blockhouse already had occupants, a typical vigorous English farmer with an equally sturdy wife and three children. All of them looked at the Doukhobors with hostility. The mother—watching her son to see that he did not come too close to the Doukhobors—called, "Bob!" several times, but he was preoccupied. Finally leaving her place, with decisive steps she ran to him, pulled his free arm with all her might, threw him up in the air turning him over in flight, and took him to her table. During the evening meal she started weeping several times, apparently annoyed by the presence in the blockhouse of such a large number of strange people.

"I don't understand why you are crying," said her husband. "You understand, the blockhouse was built not only for us, but also for them! They have as much right to it as we!"

Canada
Land Office
Early morning, February 14, 1899.

In the evening when it became completely dark and lamps had been lighted, nearly all the inhabitants of the village came to visit us. Three of the Englishmen brought violins under the folds of their coats and soon the blockhouse was filled with wild enough sounds. Dancing began. Even the stern farmer's wife decided to dance something in the nature of a waltz with one of the gentlemen. The gentleman desperately threw up his heels and succeeded in throwing sawdust in many eyes, which did not interfere with the general merriment, since those blinded, wiped their eyes and resumed their places.

"Yes, Joe is a master of the dance. Nobody here can compete with him," could be heard.

The encouraged Joe, after complete exhaustion of the one woman, seized an Indian who was there and together in a very short time they so dug up the floor that it looked like a rough sea.

The public, sitting on one another and emitting unheard-of quantities of smoke from under wide-brimmed hats, called for a jig in which as many gentlemen took part as could be squeezed into the available space. The musicians were losing their energy. They had long ago removed their neckerchiefs and hats, and in a frenzy pressed their small instruments with their strong hands, producing from them unexpectedly deafening sounds. The dancers at this time, with frenzied speed, stamped their feet, jostling one another in one place and completely destroying our floor. Finally, worn out, they rolled over onto the floor to the loud approval of the visitors.

Then began competitions; gymnastics and wrestling. During the competitions, Bob, together with his sisters, sat on the table and after every victory clapped his hands. But this day apparently was fated to bring tears. Two competitors, hugging one another, lost their balance and on the run sat in the lap of the farmer's wife, who was sitting on the only chair. A sinister crack was heard, the chair did not hold out and the wrestlers, together with the squealing farmer's wife, flopped on the floor and in some manner squeezed Bob's feet. He made this known with a deafening roar! There was a commotion; everybody exclaimed; the farmer's wife was given cold water; they comforted Bob as well as they could. The games were soon resumed, except that the farmer's wife now sat on the other side of the table, and a big Englishman took Bob onto his back, where he was completely safe.

The Doukhobors looked at these diabolical pranks disapprovingly, like people who had outgrown such a stage of development.

"It apparently seems to them to be very good, to perform such tricks."

"This is altogether senseless," noted the elders decisively.

All the same, approving remarks could be heard as well.

"See how strong he is!"

When the tug-o-war began, many clearly became interested, though they tried to conceal it.

"What do you think—could our Feduke pull this champion of theirs?" asked someone, comparing Feduke and Joe, who turned out to be the strongest competitor in the rope pulling.

Feduke, a huge phlegmatic boy with a round, good-natured face and small smiling eyes, himself answered in a thin voice, "This one in the blue jacket?"

"Yes, this one."

"I could pull three like that," quietly noted Feduke.

"You watch, lest he alone ties you up like a sheep!"

"Don't just consider that you are stronger than he."

"In that case I shall pull him right away. If that is possible—or will they get angry? Who knows?"

I explained to the Doukhobors that the English would not get angry but would be very glad if they would take part in the games.

"Completely senseless!" someone noted, but Feduke had already risen to his full height and, squeezing through the crowd, stood among the English, smiling confusedly and stretching his square hand to the end of the rope.

"You wish to pull?" he was asked.

"What are they saying?" asked Feduke. It was translated for him.

"Well, yes!"

The Doukhobors craned their necks to see better. Opinions were heard that Feduke could not do it. But it was clear that all now wished only one thing, to see Feduke the victor. The English surrounding Feduke asked him whom he wished to pull. Feduke pushed his finger at the blue jacket of Joe.

"By himself?"

"Let him take two young men for helpers."

Joe, confidently smiling, said that he already had two good friends, showing his hands, but Feduke insisted that two more men should take Joe's side.

"Or I don't wish to pull," he announced stubbornly, prepared to drop the rope.

After some loud talk the English agreed. Now Joe and Feduke sat on the floor opposite one another and stretched out their feet, each pressing his feet against the soles of his competitor and in their hands they held a thick rope. Behind Joe sat two young men grasping the rope.

"Well now, hold on, Russia!" someone of the English exclaimed.

Joe began to pull the rope carefully at first, with his arm muscles; then, pressing more securely against the feet of Feduke, with his whole body. Feduke became serious; only his eyes smiled as usual. He pulled in the rope lightly. Then it seemed that the competitors for a time sat motionless. All the same, Feduke's neck swelled up, his face filled with blood and in Joe's eyes appeared a fire of anger. A few more moments they sat in apparent calm, gluing their eyes into each other's. Suddenly Feduke bent his back in a bow and at once straightened up and threw his head back; showing his neck with blood-filled veins, he at once lifted Joe and his comrades who immediately fell to the sides except for Joe, who fell right on Feduke's feet.

The English and Joe roared with laughter, crying out in many ways and praising Feduke's strength. They surrounded him on all sides, touching his shoulders his hands, feeling his steel muscles and shaking their heads in wonder. But Feduke coiled the rope in neat rings and quietly went to his place.

"What's there to it?" he answered scornfully to questions of how strong the English were.

"What a fine thing you did!" the elders noted ironically.

"Do you feel better now?"

The Doukhobors smiled with restraint but apparently were very pleased. It was very late and the visitors left after this competition, wishing us good night.

It was time to sleep. The farmer put the table between him and us and lay down to sleep. We busied ourselves a long time on the dug-up floor, putting our felt cloaks under us.

In the darkness the red-hot stove showed up as a red spot. It was stifling. Outside the wall, the wind sighed loudly. A horse snorted occasionally. And then something cracked in the iron stove pipe and seemed to run with light steps over the roof. There was no sleep. One could hear the people turning from side to side. Someone sighed loudly.

"You are not sleeping," I heard somebody's careful voice from one side.

"No."

"Nor I. Why is it?"

"It's very hot. That's why there is no sleep," someone answered.

"But all the same—strange people, these 'angliki'. As I watched them, they seem to have a completely Christian side. See how they received us with understanding."

"But they exhibit such customs as will not do at all."

"That's their way," countered a sleepy voice.

"That's what I'm talking about. What kind of a custom is it to exhibit such things?"

"It has been said each city has its own customs, each village its habits—and so it turns out," someone added, yawning.

"No, this is not so here. In the Christian way, all must share some customs. Yes," continued the first voice, and went silent, apparently thinking. No one disagreed and there was a weary silence full of strange unexplainable night noises. And through the little window could be seen the restlessly flaming Northern Lights.

Canada
At the Northern Settlement
Evening, February 14, 1899.

Early in the morning we proceeded further. Crossing a river, we again went through forest. Here apparently there had been a big fire! As far as the eye could see stood huge smooth trunks shining with a bluish light. The bark had fallen off a long time ago. Rain and wind had washed and dried them many times. Charred at the bottom, deformed broken branches at the sides, these stumps stood shining with their dark-colored bodies, and among them lay those comrades unable to withstand the all-consuming flame. It is said the forest was burned by the Indians during a war with the whites. It is horrible here! These corpses rock dismally, crashing, rattling their deformed branches as skeletons do their bones.

The greater part of the day we passed among these sad corpses, telling us of people's ingratitude, their senseless enmity and greed for self-destruction. And a strong native prairie wind sang, taking hold of the dried-cut branches, and it seemed to persuade them that there was no need to grieve. The winds go everywhere through the whole world and everywhere they see the same; and so it will be always as long as the world exists. And the naked giants, hearing this, groaned, shaking their bare tops in horror, so as to escape from the depressing loneliness which, because of the wind's stories, became unbearable.

At the feet of the giants our caravan snaked in a quiet narrow ribbon. Looking at us they seemed to call, "Where are you going? Do you see how we have been deformed here? It is frightful, frightful!"

"Frightful!" It was hooted everywhere.

"Frightful!" angrily cried a single crow who flapped his black wings over our heads and disappeared.

"Frightful!" screamed the gloating wind, attacking the people and covering their eyes with snow, sweeping drift after drift on to the road and covering their tracks.

"It is fearful, brethren; it is a wild place," someone said.

No one answered.

Then the forest thinned out; it grew brighter; ahead the prairie lay wide. Pressing gently, a steady breath of south wind came upon us, dishevelling the tails and manes of the horses. And while the winter sky hung in a leaden curve over the land, everyone sighed easily as if they had come out of prison to freedom. And soon on the horizon among the fields could be seen a single hill: "Pennecci-vootchioong" (Thunder Mountain), as the Indians have named it. There the Doukhobor lands begin.

"Now we will be there soon," sighed the fatigued Doukhobors with relief.

The mountain is so called by the Indians because at times of thunder, lightning strikes almost exclusively on its top. And if you ask an Indian where the rolls of thunder come from he will point to the top of this hill and will repeat the legend of his people, that now a baby eagle is coming out of its shell. And the thunder is nothing more than the strike of the eagle's beak on the shell of the gigantic egg. Twilight arrived but the blue hill could still be seen in the distance as if we had stood still all this time.

And, true, we were moving very slowly. The road from the land office had barely been travelled. The heavy horses bogged down in knee-deep drifts of loose snow. The tired animals were all in a sweat. They had faithfully pulled the heavy sleigh, shaking their heads and looking sideways at the people with good-natured eyes. It was not easy for the people either; step after step the melancholy Doukhobors went on, spread out in a long line after the sleigh. The road seemed endless.

Then Zeebarev, walking ahead, turned and said, "Now it is our land. Right from here!"

Soon we descended into a little valley at the bottom of which flowed the Swan River, or Wobisto-Ossisipi, as the Indians called it.

It had become altogether dark and horses and people had lost their strength, when coming around a turn we saw a large pile of building timber, and on one of the bare hills stood two blockhouses, one completely ready but the other unroofed. From the brightly lit tent, which from a distance looked like a huge paper lantern, English carpenters came out to meet us. They helped us unhitch the horses, and took us to the finished blockhouse. It was dark and there was the smell of fresh wood; in the darkness white bunks could be seen and on the raw earthen floor shone white chips which had not been removed.

We were home!

Canada
En route from Northern Settlement to Yorkton
Fort Pelly
February 15, 1899.

Today I began to say good-bye to the Doukhobors, as I thought, for all time.

The kind Mr. McCreary had gone to some trouble over me, and a horse was waiting for me for distant travel. I was to go through Fort Pelly, to the Southern Settlement; from there to Yorkton, the last station on the railroad; and from there to Winnipeg—and thence to Russia.

But what a driver this was, what a sleigh and horse! Before me stood a little horse like our Cossack horses. It was hitched to an unusually strange vehicle consisting of one thin board about a yard wide; the front end of this board was bent upwards and in the middle attached to it was a box, well-padded with hay with a covering of canvas. This was an Indian sled. Below, instead of runners, were attached two thin narrow wooden strips. The driver matched the vehicle, a full-blooded Indian with dark red face and brightly shining teeth, black eyes with yellowish whites. From under his black-and-yellow striped tuque hung black hair right to his shoulders, in braids. A short jacket of yellow deerskin, decorated at the seams with numerous beads, and red woolen pants with the same thick beads on all exterior seams reminded me of the pictures in the books of Gustov Emar which, like others, I had read repeatedly in childhood. On his feet were moccasins decorated quite beautifully with colored beads.

"Astom,* sir," said he, half in Indian, half in English, and smiling merrily, indicated the box with a dark hand. I crawled submissively into the long cradle and stretched out my legs. The Indian bent down and, enveloping me with pleasant-smelling smoke from his pipe, covered my feet with fur and carefully laced up the canvas. To tell the

---

*Astom is Indian for "come here."

truth, it was especially comfortable to sit in this strange looking sleigh.

One more "thank you" and we started on our way. The Doukhobors in blue jackets and bare heads bowed and wished me a good trip. Once more I looked back from the hill at the little group of people with serious faces. So deserted, so alone this little handful of people seemed pitiful, tightly gathered in a bunch among the bare stumps of the wild forest, surrounded on all sides by a snowy desert that cut them off from all the world.

First party of Doukhobors, a day's journey from Yorkton, 1899.

It was sad and painful to look at their serious and motionless figures. A whole series of distant pictures of the past arose in the memory.

The Doukhobors were already invisible behind the thick high skirting of brush. But like dark clouds hanging over the land, heavy persistent thoughts, thoughts with which the Russian is born, under the yoke of which he lives and dies, importunate, dreary, took form one after another.

All around, like the sea, stretched the endless prairie—empty, bare, nothing to hold the eye. Dead silence. Only the light rustle of the sleigh and the puffing of the horse could be heard. In such unusual silence the ears begin to ring, and sometimes it seems that some hardly audible, almost transparent, glass sounds brought by the light breeze, stretch through the air like gentle sighs of unseen beings flying through this boundless, empty kingdom of snow. On the endless, deserted perspective, the monotonous background of the prairie, the weary eye draws shimmering patterns from the light twinkling points.

You close your eyes and again come gentle, harmonic sighs. All this seems unusual, like a fairytale, and you surrender yourself to the power of caressing nature; oppressive thoughts go away one by one and mental pain abates; rocking gently with the steps of the horse, you forget yourself in some kind of sweet drowsiness.

"Oh, hey!" cried the Indian over my head, but his voice sounded unusually gentle, as though from somewhere far away. This son of the prairie continued to run behind me at the side of the sleigh, holding the rope reins in his hands. Several times I proposed to him that he sit behind the cradle (since no more than one could be placed in the cradle) but each time in reply he would bare his teeth, in which he continually held a pipe, and with a merry smile would say in his language, "Nishi-shin,"* and for greater clarity, would repeat in English, "Arright."

True, a great part of the road we walked, but wherever the road was packed, the horse started a fine trot, and the driver with unusual lightness ran in the deep snow as if it were nothing unusual. This apparently did not cause him any exertion. Fine lungs!

Rapping his whip on the sleigh, he started some improbable song consisting of a repetition of one and the same phrase. It started on a very loud, high note, when the voice came out of the throat like a cork out of a bottle; then the song proceeded more and more softly till it became unclear mumbling. Then, loudly stopping his breath, he began the same phrase with fresh enthusiasm and so endlessly, always rattling a stick on the sleigh.

At first I liked it very much; then the monotonous wild wail began to bore me, especially when I understood that there was no foreseeable end. And awkward as it was to break musical inspiration, but fearing for the safety of my ear drums, I had to do it, and tried to ask what were the words of the song. The Indian spoke so little English that from his brief explanation I could not understand whether these were words in the song or whether it was a song without words. All the same, my question achieved its end; the singing stopped.

Before us was a long descent into a valley on the bottom of which snaked a river. Its shores were thickly overgrown with trees and low brush. My driver stretched out his neck, straining to see, and waved his hand in a leather glove; smiling joyfully, he announced, "There's a white man!"

---

*I'm alright.

I tried to see some signs of a white man yet I saw none for a long time. But the Indian turned out to be right. Right on the shore, between the trees, a tent flashed. Around it lay discarded boxes, all from conserves. It must be they liked to eat here! This was appropriate as it was already dinner time and besides, a piece of bread was all I had. My Indian companion did not have even this. As people who know told me, not to eat for a day or two does not constitute a deprivation for the Indian. He makes up for it afterwards at one sitting.

After studying the tent, the Indian finally told me this must be the government surveyor's cook who had arrived before his master at the place of work. Nearby stood a sleigh like the one that I was riding on, but without a cradle. In its place there was a big pack of some kind of goods, carefully covered with canvas and laced from all sides. A thin white horse was eating hay.

"We shall dine here," categorically announced the Indian with delight, looking at the tent and eagerly breathing in the smoke from its tin pipe.

I tried to object that I did not know the surveyor nor his cook and did not wish to stop. But the Indian hastened to reassure me.

"Oh, sir, do not worry. He cooks beautifully!" he announced, and swallowing his saliva he turned to the tent. Before we came up, several dogs approached, barking loudly, and at the door of the tent appeared a red-haired young man in a black vest and a long white apron.

"How do you do?" the man welcomed us. We responded. After a few sentences about the bad road, he asked what we would like to eat. "I now have a varied selection—whatever you wish!" and he went over a list of edibles. I said if he were so kind we would be satisfied with what he had ready. My driver did not appear to like the answer very well, but he did not announce his preference.

At last I was unlaced and, still shaken up from the ride, I entered the tent. The hot air surrounded me, filled with the tasty odours of different foods. At the wooden table sat an older Indian with long tousled hair and a little beard. His serious face had a stony expression. He arose at my entrance, bowed and sat down again with his hot tea.

"You are not a Frenchman?" the cook asked me. I told him I was a Russian.

"You possibly came with these new immigrants; what do you call them? I cannot remember—devilishly difficult name. But I am a Frenchman, French Canadian; my name is Maurice." And he began to chatter endlessly while busily seating me at the table. At this time, not looking at the Indian, he moved his tea and biscuits to the very end of the table.

The Frenchman chattered endlessly while he dried the dishes rapidly.

In half an hour he managed to tell his biography, countless stories in which he was always the victor. He told how he was wounded in hunting and showed a red stub of a finger. He managed to ask about the Doukhobors and he sang some songs. At the same time his able hands were mixing something, shaking, straining. On the flat stove different dishes were cooking, despite my requests that he not do this.

While the merry host was treating me, the Indians did not lose time. They quietly downed everything there was on the table. As soon as the reserve of served biscuits decreased, the Frenchman, without a word, brought another handful out of the bag and put them in front of the men. Finally, under the continuous chattering of the Frenchman, everyone had had enough. However, the irrepressible cook did not calm down, but asked that we wait another minute.

"In three minutes I will make you such pies as you will not find in Europe!" he cried and was already mixing something in a pot.

I protested that it would be late to travel.

"This will take just a moment; it will not delay you!"

"Oh, yes, this will not detain us," joined in my driver. "No, this will not hold us up at all, sir," he argued, moving his full mouth with difficulty.

The Indians, sitting side by side at the end of the table, with concentrated faces strove to fill their thin stomachs as tightly as possible. Perspiration rolled from them; occasionally they exchanged comments in low voices.

"Mai-aiten miskino (it's a bad road)," they both sometimes mumbled, shaking their heads and continuously working their jaws.

After eating some sweet pies—which indeed were very good!—we began our good-byes. The Frenchman would not take any money and was really offended that I offered it to him. I had already left the tent when the Frenchman slapped his forehead.

"The devil take it! I forgot to show you something. Here, please— one minute; I will show it."

From under the mattress he pulled out a mirror framed with leather.

"Look at it," he turned it in front of my nose. "No, look, see what a remarkable flower is embroidered on the back. It's poetry. Beautiful! I bought it about two weeks ago in Montreal. And this quilt, there too. Is it not a fine thing also?" I hastened to approve both items and got out of the tent hastily.

It was already late. The Indians stood near the sleigh and talked sadly about something. The old man was examining his thin horse, consulting with my driver.

"Matchee (it is bad)," disapprovingly he turned his head.

"You think it will not get there? Too far? Swan Lake? That's another fifty miles."

The old man was hauling skins and nets to fishermen on Swan

Lake, to sell some and exchange some for fish. Both looked sadly at the old horse. Holding its head low, with sunken sides and half-crossed eyes, it was dozing, rocking on its twisted knotty legs. And its hanging lower lip under which could be seen yellow, worn teeth whispered something in sleep.

"Tomaku statim, tomaku indien (poor horse, poor Indian)," the old man said quietly and took his lines. The horse turned its ears, strained, and with an uncertain step pulled its load; beside it stumbled its pitiful master in old worn-out breeches and a jacket over his bare body. We silently looked at them until they disappeared around a turn.

This scene of oppression and submission to one's fate brought me a lively reminder of our peasants, a thousand times looking at lean animals, stomachs thinned out during the winter food shortage, a thousand times convinced that they could not work in the spring. But just the same, they hitched them to the plough because it was necessary; what must be, must be. We, too, set off.

Canada

Fort Pelly

Same day, February 15, 1899.

"Fort Pelly, sir!" cried the Indian, bending down to my ear.

For all that, five or ten minutes passed and in the surrounding twilight not a single light, no sign of habitation could be seen. For more than an hour after darkness fell we were still on the way. Thanks to the sweet pies we were very late! And the Indian, who had overeaten or was over-tired, or both, continued to walk. Suddenly, as if coming out of the ground, dark figures of dogs appeared and came upon us with angry barking.

"Match (bad)!" roared the driver, chasing them away with a whip.

Against the dark background of the sky several triangles of Indian tepees appeared. In the nearest of them was a small dark opening. Someone asked a question from inside and the driver answered. The same voice spoke to the dogs and they went away from us to their pen, growling, save for a small pup which continued to bark loudly.

In a minute we came to some kind of building with lighted windows.

"Here is the hotel. It will be very comfortable for us here. Mrs. MacDonald is a beautiful housekeeper," said the Indian while unlacing me.

"And who is Mrs. MacDonald?" I asked.

"Oh, she is an Indian, but her husband was an Englishman. She's a widow."

We entered. In the overheated low room several people were having supper.

"Good evening," they replied to my greeting.

"Beautiful evening, isn't it?" several voices asked me while I was taking off my coat.

I hastened to reply that it was excellent, although there was nothing excellent in the fact that a warm wind was blowing and the snow, falling in large flakes, covered the whole face and rolled melting down one's collar. For some reason it is the custom here in greeting to praise the weather regardless of what it is really like. This does not prevent one from speaking of it as it really is, after a few minutes of conversation.

Before I could remove my winter clothing, a girl with a typical English face, pleasant-looking, well-proportioned, in a white dress and apron, came out of the next room.

"May I offer you supper?" she asked.

I expressed agreement and the thoughtful girl, daughter of the mistress, as I learned, put me at a table. Here sat an Indian in warm European clothing, two husky Englishmen with neckerchiefs and a tall young policeman in black breeches with yellow stripes at the sides, and a short red jacket. On the window sill lay his wide-brimmed hat. Behind the policeman, leaning on the back of his chair, stood an older gentleman in a wide hat, with a pipe in his teeth, down the stem of which his saliva flowed and dropped on his vest, producing a bright spot.

A lively conversation was being carried on. The older gentleman, Mr. MacKenzie, a local fur trader, was seeking to buy a new herd of wild horses, and was discussing this with the policeman and herders.

"Why do you need such a large number of horses?" asked the policeman.

"I have an idea, I have an idea," said MacKenzie, smiling slyly, twisting his finger in front of his eyes. "I'll take them to the wild peas on the White Sand River and you'll see how fat they become, and in the fall, you'll see, I'll lose nothing."

There was a pause.

"And what will you do for the skin of a big, of a very big bear?" said someone from behind, in broken English speech. Turning around, I saw a half-breed Indian in half-European clothing, lazily stretched out on the counter with a pipe in his teeth. Mr. MacKenzie looked at the Indian for some moments and turned back without saying a word. In the next pause, the same voice was heard.

"I have seen a very big, an unusually big bear as lately as this morning. Very huge," drawled the Indian through his teeth.

Mr. MacKenzie turned with annoyance in his direction and pointing his finger at the floor said in an angry voice, "When you bring the very big bear here, then we will speak of the price."

And saying this, he turned back to one side. "I am tired of giving you food and powder and money on credit. What have you brought me lately? Foxes and foxes! I have them by the hundred! Nobody wants these foxes!" cried MacKenzie. He turned to him once more, spraying saliva. "You have long been saying you saw a black fox. Where is it?"

The chocolate face of the Indian did not move a muscle. He smoked as lazily as before. But after a few minutes he quietly said, "But to kill a black fox one needs powder and I haven't had any powder for two days, none at all, not even one loading."

"I knew it, I knew it!" cried MacKenzie. "That is the only problem, powder." And here, completely losing his control, MacKenzie, knowing the Indian language very well, began to say something in this language to the Indian.

But the latter continued to lie as quietly as ever, as if this did not concern him. He did not reply with a single word even afterwards when MacKenzie turned to me.

"These are ghastly people, I tell you. They eat up everything. And do you think the 'gentleman' Indian will eat just anything? No, he takes everything of the best. He eats California preserves in the winter. They will soon eat me up, these 'gentlemen,' I assure you, or my name's not MacKenzie," he concluded, knocking his pipe on the policeman's chair.

"All the same, in twenty-three years here you have not been eaten much," laughed the policeman, exchanging glances significantly with one of the Englishmen. MacKenzie wanted to protest but restrained himself and, energetically packing his pipe, merely puffed with an injured look.

"From the time the 'gentlemen' Indians adopted this civilization— that is, the demoralization I'm telling you about—there is no working with them. They're an altogether different people. Oh, I tell you, if their red skin turned white, this would be a smaller change than that which has already taken place," he continued, addressing me.

"I came here when an Indian village of one hundred tepees stood, in place of Winnipeg. All travel was on horseback and the only way to sleep was to tie the horse to your leg so as to hear if someone was getting to you. A camp fire couldn't be lit. And before riding up a hill you crawled close up and saw whether or not there was an enemy tribe of Indians in sight. At that time if a herd of bison came across your path, it was necessary to stop and wait sometimes for two days while they passed. You would lie and watch how they moved in a black stripe, south to north away from the heat. And now where are they? In the museum in New York!"

"And what did you do here?" I asked.

"I? I was still a boy then. My master brought whiskey to the Indians and for this he took skins from them and everything else. So the master would serve whiskey to the Indians and we would hold the horses saddled ready so that if something happened we could get away more quickly. From drinking whiskey the Indian becomes completely insane.

"Sometimes at night when the whole village had had too much, they would start firing. They would recall some old feud and begin to fight one another, and when one of them won he would run to the relatives of the beaten one to kill them and to cut up their tepees. And the relatives of the beaten one would take vengeance on the killer and his relatives. Yes, blood would run in the creek as in a war. At night this would take place around camp fires and you would wonder whether you had happened to come to hell. If they got very rough we would jump on our horses and go as fast as we could. At that time they kept their word strictly. If one said something, you could believe it. And what hunters they were!"

The Englishmen, putting their feet on the backs of their chairs, chewed their cuds to the conversation of the old man, spitting to the side, and the Indians, as if we were not speaking of them, lay in lazy poses and dozed with impenetrable calm.

"Yes, that's so," said the old man, seeing that apart from me no one was listening to him. "All the same, it is time for me to go," he said getting up. "Good-bye, gentlemen."

After him went the English and the policeman. The Indians continued to lie motionless; occasionally fire flamed up in pipes. It was time to retire.

Marie cleared the table. Her mother, a stout Indian with a good-natured, welcoming face, came out to help her. Marie several times urged her to go to bed and she accepted her advice.

On examining pictures in the newspapers with which the room was papered, I came to the table and there saw to my surprise *The Odyssey* of Homer in Greek. Another book was a volume from a large English encyclopedia, both in excellent leather bindings.

"Whose books are these?" I asked Marie.

"These books belong to Mr. Williams, sir, both of them."

To the question of who Mr. Williams was, Marie blushed and said that that was the name of the policeman.

"He reads *The Odyssey* in Greek beautifully, and is teaching me now," she added with pride. "I am now translating the tenth chapter."

How do you like that? A policeman is reading *The Odyssey* in the original and a Metis is translating it.

I said good night shortly and went behind a thin board partition to my bed. There was no need to light candles, as it was light, there were cracks in the partition separating the room from the sitting room. I lay in a wide double bed at the head of which hung a frame with a broken mirror in which remained only a small unpleasant shining triangle in a corner. For several minutes I watched the light and smoke coming to me through the cracks. The Indians were still sucking their pipes, not moving from their places. Soon I fell asleep.

I was awakened by a strong shove in the side.

"It's alright, sir; do not stir," said a dark face bending down to my face. "Everything is alright now."

I was completely at sea. There was a ringing in my ears from a fearful boom of a drum, a screech of fiddles and a stamping of dozens of feet; the bed trembled and shook, as did I and two swarthy boys, whom an Indian woman was putting to bed with me. On the floor, as well, lay some unexpected dark bodies.

"A little merriment, sir—it's so pleasant, I trust I did not disturb you?" she asked mincingly, and went away.

"Oh, not at all," I hurried to reply, rubbing my hurt side. "Not at all."

"Well, good night."

Putting my face to one of the cracks I enjoyed the unusual picture. The whole room was filled with Indians in all kinds of costume. Many were in wide red breeches with large beads and many-coloured Indian belts, with jackets on bare bodies regardless of the winter. Several sported real European suits. All had long hair, sometimes braided, sometimes loose. The women generally were in dresses of a European pattern. But what happy faces! How much joy and boundless merriment was in these copper-red faces! Like spirits their thin, well-proportioned figures whirled.

My driver, leaping in furious excitement in one place, jumped off the floor lightly like a ball in his moccasins; his coal-black hair, flying up in time to the furious jumping, surrounded his head with a large black ring. His teeth shone brilliantly from his continuous smile of bliss. At times he would howl, apparently unable to restrain his joy. Then he quickly bent over and embraced his partner, a fifteen-year-old Indian girl with a strikingly beautiful straight profile, with unusually large black eyes; together they whirled with such dizzying speed, laughing loudly at collisions with other pairs. All this colourful bright life whirled, flickered in the eyes, giving one no chance to look at any specific individual.

Laughter, yelling, merry exclamations came continuously, accompanied by the deafening boom of the drum, which enveloped the crowd with its exciting rolls, drowning out the fiddle which screeched with all its might. Teeth flashed as did the whites of eyes. Loose strands of hair, scarves—all these flew through the air in fearful disorder, mixing one with another.

The dark-faced boys, in friendly embrace, slept on my bed peacefully through this infernal cacophony and, spreading out, squeezed me into a corner. But fatigue took its toll and I followed their example and slept.

Canada
Fort Pelly
February 16, 1899.

In the morning I walked out with a heavy head and awaited my transport for further travel. To my amazement I saw that, rather than a small town, Fort Pelly consisted of three buildings not counting a little house on chicken legs in which the policeman lived. One building, our hotel, was a blockhouse, plastered on the outside with light clay. A little distance away was the home and store of Mr. MacKenzie, of the same rough construction; and then the Fort itself.

The Fort was built a very long time ago by (the trading firm) The Hudson's Bay Company. This firm was the first to begin dealings with the Indians, and kept moving deeper and deeper into the interior of the land. It built forts for its buyers in which they could defend themselves from attacks from the Indians. Today, of course, they did not need this kind of defense, but the forts have remained in these places, reminding the Whites of different times, and the Indians of the time of their power and authority.

Nearby were several tepees that we had passed yesterday, set up on the snow. Smoke came from the open tops of the tepees now. Apparently the "gentlemen Indians" were cooking food. Around the tepees children, dressed only in shirts, ran barefoot on the snow, chasing one another with merry shouts.

"Oh, they are happy!" I remembered yesterday's expression of Mr. MacKenzie.

"They are always happy," he had said to me yesterday, not quite with scorn, not exactly with envy, but in any case with annoyance, in answer to the question: "How do the Indians feel now?"

As I approached a crying child near MacKenzie's store I saw a curious picture. Several suckling children were tied to boards in the Indian manner and had been stood as on exhibition, side by side, leaning against the wall in the verandah. The considerate mothers entering the store stood their babies there so as not to produce unnecessary noise inside.

A hairy yellow dog came up to one of them in a friendly way, closed her eyes and gently licked the chocolate cheeks of the little one from all sides. Apparently he did not like this very much for he desperately turned his head and poured all his strength into a hoarse cry.

An Indian woman came out of the store with some purchases in her hand. Her face was sad. She wept silently, as people cry when they realize the inevitability of their sorrow. And the sorrow must have originated in the store of Mr. MacKenzie, whom the "gentleman Indians" were eating. Lifting to her shoulders one of the exhibited youngsters, she wandered with a defeated look towards the tepees.

Poor Redskins! What pitiful lives they must now accept! On the wild prairies, where previously their rights were disputed only by herds of bison and wild horses, there are now surveyors' posts, signs of a boundary they dare not cross. Bravery, strength, endurance—all that of which they were proud and by which they lived—are not needed by anyone. They are scorned because they are coloured. Strength and ability are now replaced by dollars, so difficult to secure, and for which they must become slaves of the white immigrants. They cannot adjust to this order of life and tribe after tribe is quickly subjected.

Now there are about one hundred thousand Redskins in Canada. Of these, about seventy thousand live a settled life, occupied with trades and agriculture. Most of the settled Indians are engaged in hunting and fishing. Many others engage in hunting and fishing and sometimes, though unwillingly, hire out to farmers for agricultural work. The remaining twenty-five thousand continue their nomadic way of life, hunting moose, deer, bear and other animals.

At the time of peacemaking between the whites and the Indians, the Canadian government concluded treaties with separate tribes, under which each tribe had a particular area of land allotted to them which was considered their property. Of course, the Indians could not hunt so successfully on their limited area of land and therefore, as compensation for freedom of movement, they received from the Canadian government a monetary payment. Sometimes this payment was made in products. From that time the government took upon itself the responsibility for these wards and does much for the Indians. For that very reason there cannot be a being more deprived of human rights than the so-called settled Indian. No Indian may move out of the boundary of the land set aside for his tribe without written permission of a special officer, the "Indian Officer" responsible for that district.

The Indian can sell no livestock or produce raised on his land. And what's more, he is not responsible for breaches of these rules. Every autumn, in all public places, announcements are hung out under the signature of the Minister of the Interior, in which it is said:

> Everyone buying from an Indian any products of the land, like potatoes, wheat, etc. is subject to a fine of three hundred dollars or to a jail term of one month.

The same goes for whiskey. Every white man driving with a bottle of whiskey in his pocket through an Indian Reserve is subject to a very heavy fine or to a jail sentence.

The government, wishing to improve the life of Indians and to train them to agricultural labour, supplies them with agricultural equipment, seed, livestock etc.; but all such change is very slow. If now the majority of the Indians are living a settled existence, they achieved this at the cost of human lives.

On Indian Reserves the government has started many schools in which about ten thousand children of both sexes are being educated. Raising a new generation from childhood in cultured conditions, the government expects the best results. But here too Indian blood tells. Children who have spent their lives in rags under the open sky summer and winter, when put into hygienic, cultured conditions, are sick for a long time with different ailments. These most often turn into consumption.

As everything indicates, a slow death is in prospect for the Redskin tribes who have been masters of the prairies. The white man with his civilization is slowly but surely killing them.

Island of Cyprus
London, March 26, 1899.

On April 18, I returned to Winnipeg from travels in the Doukhobor lands and began preparations to go to Russia. At this time a letter came from England in which the Committee of Quakers asked me to come to London. They wished me to find a suitable ship and go with it to Cyprus so as to bring to Canada from there about one thousand Doukhobors who had migrated to Cyprus in August, 1898. I immediately telegraphed the Quakers my agreement to undertake this work and in two days left Winnipeg for London.

At the time of my arrival in London, the Quaker Committee, represented by a very likeable old man, W. Belows, had begun negotiations about hiring a ship. It was proposed to hire the *Lake Superior*, on which the second party of Doukhobors had sailed from the Caucasus. The ship was to be hired by Quaker Brooks. It remained only to examine it.

I told the Quakers of the conditions on which I would undertake to move the Cyprus Doukhobors. The job carried some responsibility and risk. I demanded first that the ship should be fully answerable to me, and second that I should have, as on the *Lake Huron*, full control of the ship and its passengers, from whom I would have to organize the necessary crews as on the first voyage.

On examining the ship, I found that it required certain repairs and cleaning. All my requirements in this regard were very quickly and suitably carried out, due to the energetic demands of the Quaker Committee. As a result I was able to go at once to Liverpool and the *Lake Superior* and to set off the next day on the voyage to Cyprus.

Island of Cyprus
Larnaka, April 15, 1899
(day of leaving Cyprus to go to sea).

From Liverpool to Gibraltar and beyond, our voyage enjoyed good weather. As a result, the *Lake Superior* sailed at good speed, making ten to twelve knots. On April 11, Friday morning, a rosy stripe appeared on the horizon: This was Cyprus. Coming nearer, we saw that the whole island consisted of bare sandy cliffs of an orange colour, covered with a brightly sparkling white sand.

The sun burned here as in the tropics. The sea near the island was of a bright blue colour. All nature, the dark blue sky and the lazy blue sea and the painfully sparkling island, all this was saturated with the fiery burning rays of the sun. There was not a breath of wind. This heap of blazing rocks covered with hot sand gave off intense heat which increased as we approached the island. Half a verst from the island the ship dropped anchor. On the shore we saw palms and some kind of strange shrubbery.

Soon a small boat brought Mr. Sterch, an old Quaker looking after Doukhobor affairs here. With him was an Englishman, St. John, who had been selflessly working among the Doukhobors all through their stay in Cyprus. He himself had nearly died here from debilitating diarrhea, a sickness from which many Doukhobors had died. The Doukhobors, 1,126 persons, arrived on the Island of Cyprus in August and, in seven months, more than a hundred of them died there. They died mostly from the terrible local yellow fever and from diarrhea. It attacks not only people but also horses, dogs, chickens and other animals. All life here is subject to this terrible scourge.

The central part of Cyprus, Atlassa, where the Doukhobors settled, is unusually fertile. The crops there are luxurious but the hot tropical climate and yellow fever which had killed such a large number of people in a short time, and which has ruined the health of a great many of the remaining, compelled the people to flee from this ruinous, terrible island, kingdom of the fatal yellow fever. Medical help was provided for the Doukhobors by two medical assistants, (feldshers): Anna Pabetz and Elizabeth Markova. Another woman, who together with St. John had previously looked after Armenians moving to

Cyprus, helped them look after the sick. Now the Doukhobors had come to Larnaka and settled, partly in empty buildings, partly under the open sky in the shade of large trees.

Mr. Sterch, who had come on deck, announced that tomorrow he wished all the Doukhobors to move to the ship. But I did not agree to this. The ship had not been sufficiently prepared, baggage had not been loaded and the people would be stumbling around in this turmoil, in coal dust and unbearable oppressive heat. While the ship was standing, the ventilation system did not work. To stay three extra days in this overheated iron box would be far from harmless for famished people. But Mr. Sterch did not pay attention to my arguments and insisted on his own way.

What was I to do? I had to announce categorically that if passengers arrived in boats tomorrow, I would lift the gangplank and admit no one until the ship was completely ready for the reception of passengers. Mr. Sterch, a very old man who had been especially helpful to the Doukhobors during all their time on the island, this time was in error. He was troubled that the Doukhobors would spent these two nights on the street. How? The Quakers had taken on themselves the responsibility for the people and suddenly these people must spend two days "on the street." This he could not permit. All the same, when next morning a number of sloops came with passengers and were returned to shore he saw that he had to give in.*

During the time the ship stood by, the Doukhobor crew managed to learn a little about ship work. They washed the ship and, in two days, brought it into exemplary condition. Only then, finally, to Mr. Sterch's great satisfaction, a row of feluccas began to move from the shore to the ship with sharp lateen sails, laden with Doukhobors and their belongings.

Before loading the people, a large part of the baggage which the Doukhobors wished to have with them had to be taken away and loaded into the hold. I was amazed at the passive attitude of the Doukhobors to this operation. There were no attempts to keep some trunk or pack. All that I marked for taking to the hold was handed over to the sailors. One felt some kind of flabbiness, a letdown, in this crowd of people worn out by illness.

Before beginning the loading of the people, a medical examination was carried out. To tell the truth, this examination produced a bad enough impression, and concern for a successful voyage increased. Although there were relatively few really sick, the completely well were also few. All had brownish-green faces, and in answer to the question,

*This able old man who had done so much for the Doukhobors remained in Cyprus after their departure to market a fine crop of wheat sown by the Doukhobors.

137

"What is your illness?" you heard only two words—diarrhea and fever. I was very loath to take one Doukhobor who had been ill with severe diarrhea for eight months. I proposed he stay in Larnaka till recovery and afterwards be sent to Canada by another ship. But he implored me so sadly not to leave him to die among strangers that I had to accept him.

The Doukhobors settled very comfortably on the ship, with lots of room. Yesterday evening, the day of loading, tea was served on the ship; and at noon today the ship weighed anchor to start the long voyage.

Atlantic Ocean
May 9, 1899.

The crew of young Doukhobors was organized exactly as on the *Lake Huron* and even though on the *Lake Superior* there were only half as many passengers, the crew consisted of the same number as on the *Lake Huron*. I decided this because it was necessary, in view of the passengers' poor state of health, to maintain strict order and cleanliness, so as to protect the ship from epidemic illness.

Even without that, the medical personnel had to work hard enough, receiving forty to sixty people every day. On the ship six people now worked among the Doukhobors: Mercer, Anna Pabetz, Elizabeth Markova, Alexandra Satz,* the Englishman St. John, and the Englishwoman who had helped the Doukhobors on the island.

Fortunately, on this voyage the weather was mostly excellent. There was almost no pitching. The angry Atlantic Ocean, which met the first party so roughly, for several days now tried to start a rocking, but then apparently took pity, quietened down and let us get to Canada safely. But in those few days of relatively little tossing, the weakness of the Cyprus Doukhobors showed. In many the illness resulted in a stoppage of the pulse; in some, even the breathing stopped and extremities began to get cold. Again, injections of ether were used with great success. Hot compresses were put on the chest and extremities; a little cognac was poured into the mouth and in a while the sick recovered.

Some had to be given artificial respiration. And the very sick Doukhobor that I had urged to stay in Cyprus, despite the efforts of the doctors, died at the time of the storm and was buried in the Atlantic Ocean. This was the only death during twenty-eight days of sailing. We arrived in Canada with the same number as when we left Cyprus, as a baby girl was born at sea. The Doukhobors called her Hope.

---

*Sister of Maria Satz who remained with the first party in Canada.

Winnipeg, Canada
May 15, 1899.

The weather in general was excellent all the time, except for several days of storm on the Atlantic Ocean. Near Newfoundland we were somewhat agitated when a stiff cold wind began to blow from the north. We feared ice. At this time of year large icebergs come down from the north which, crowded in a narrow strait, block the way for ships sometimes for a week or more. In the evening, on entering the strait, we saw several colossal masses of ice sparkling with pale green spots against the twilight background of the sky. They passed us by slowly and majestically.

At night I woke up aware of rough bumping—the ship trembled; from outside could be heard noise and scratching; it seemed as if thousands of teeth and claws scratched at the iron sides of the ship.

Running out onto the deck I saw that the sea was covered with ice all around us as far as the eye could see. The propeller was turning slowly and the ship, breaking ice with the sharp prow, hardly moved getting into the depth of the ice field. Sharp pieces of ice, piling up onto one another with a roar, seemed about to climb on the deck. Sometimes the propeller stopped when immovable masses of ice were encountered. But in a little while the open sea appeared ahead and we went at full speed through the clear space.

We met no other impediments and entered the mouth of the St. Lawrence where our ship had to stop for a quarantine examination. We were examined by the same Dr. Montezambre. He was very well satisfied with the health of the passengers and the order on the ship.

The examination lasted three hours and as soon as it was over we started up the wide St. Lawrence, arriving in Quebec at night. There, trains had already been prepared for us. Not waiting for morning, we began to change to the coaches. At eight a.m. the last trainload of Doukhobors left Quebec for Winnipeg.

Personally I suffered much on this voyage. In Cyprus, despite the fact that I went ashore only a few times, I caught the local fever. In a day it forced me into bed and on days free of fever I had to work twice as hard as I would have if I had had no fever. Due to this I became so weak toward the end of the voyage that I moved with difficulty. And when the last Doukhobors left the ship and got on the train I went into the compartment assigned to me and lay down in a half conscious state. In this condition I tossed the whole trip to Winnipeg. I had to stay in Winnipeg because of my extreme illness, and the trains with the Doukhobors went on to Yorkton.

Lands of the Doukhobors
Township of 36 square miles.

So that the reader may more easily understand which lands the Doukhobors had, and under what conditions they occupied them, I shall tell briefly how Canada grants land to settlers.

All lands in Canada are surveyed into true squares of thirty-six square miles. These squares result from strips six miles wide which stretch from North to South to the United States and the same lines from East to West from the Atlantic to the Pacific Ocean.* The first lines are called ranges and the second townships; the squares themselves are called townships.

The ranges and townships are numbered, the ranges from East to West, and the townships from South to North. In this way each square of thirty-six square miles may be readily identified, knowing only two figures, the number of the township and the number of the range in which the township is found.

The township itself is divided into thirty-six square pieces of one square mile each, called sections. Sections are numbered in the same manner in all townships: specifically, the count begins at the south-east section which is numbered one, and the following higher numbers go to the west to number six. In the next row the count runs from west to east, beginning with number seven at the west side of the township to number twelve on the east side. In the third row, numbering again runs from east to west and so on.

Each section has four allotments, or homesteads, as they are called in Canada. They are identified by their location with relation to the directions; that is, north-east, south-east, north-west and south-west. The allotment, or homestead, consists of one quarter of a square mile, which is equal to one hundred and sixty acres, or by our measure, fifty-nine desiatin. At first the Doukhobors called these homesteads "smoke" and later farms.

Lines dividing the land into townships and sections, besides being on maps, are marked on the land itself. Government surveyors, with parties of workers, work summer and winter laying this network onto once virgin land. If such a line goes through the woods a cut several feet wide is made; if over prairie, a furrow is ploughed. At the corner of each section, a little hill is built up, atop of which is put down a steel peg. On one side of this peg three Roman Numerals are cut, separated with hyphens: the number of the section, the number of the township and the number of the range. In such a survey of land, the settler can very easily identify the homestead he wants to take. He needs only to

---

*This is not true of the whole country but only of the prairies—TRANS.

look at the post which is in the corner of the section in which he wishes to settle and read the number. His quarter of the section he can describe by compass directions. Besides, in any office of the Immigration Department anyone may see approximately what kind of land is in one or another township, as there are maps of all townships showing sloughs, mountains, rivers, woods and so on.

Anyone wishing to may take a homestead if he is eighteen years of age. The conditions of purchase are very simple. The buyer announces in an office which homestead he wishes to secure and if it turns out to be free, on the payment of ten dollars, he becomes the owner of fifty-nine desiatin (one hundred and sixty acres) of land. However, in the first half year he is required to plough a part of the land and even build a very small home; that is, in one way or another to begin development of his land. If he does not do this, he loses his right to the land and the money he paid is not returned.

In any township, any land may be taken except townships eleven, twenty-nine, eight and twenty-six. Sections eleven and twenty-nine are set aside for schools, while eight and twenty-six are the property of the Hudson's Bay Company, which was the first to begin trade with the Indians and, moving farther and farther into the land, built forts for its traders and established trading centres. Money received from the sale of school lands goes into the school fund. Of course, the Hudson's Bay Company and school sections are also sold but under different conditions. The price is determined by agreement and fluctuates between ten and twenty roubles per desiatin and higher.

Besides this, in many parts of Canada the government gave to railroads, by way of subsidy, substantial quantities of land. The land was given not in one piece but sixteen sections in each township lying within a stated distance from the railway line. The following sections were so given: 1, 3, 5, 7, 9, 13, 15, 17, 19, 21, 23, 25, 27, 31, 33 and 35. The railroads sell their lands at relatively high prices, although they sometimes reduce their price by half if the farmer in the first four years cultivates half of the land.

As a result of such a system of distributing lands to farmers, the government, doing all possible to settle empty lands stretching thousands of miles, has preserved itself from the greatest evil—large landowners. Here every owner actually works his land. If the farmer cultivates his land it belongs to him. Buying for resale is impossible. It is impossible also because only one allotment of one hundred and sixty acres is available to any one person. If the farmer has a son more than eighteen years of age, he too may apply for a homestead.

These are the general conditions of securing land for private ownership in Canada.

For Doukhobors these conditions were made significantly easier.

The Canadian government looked upon the Doukhobors as a valuable acquisition for the country and behaved very attentively to them, and did everything possible to ease for them the difficult time of getting started. They were permitted to take lands for every man not younger than seventeen (not eighteen as for all other settlers). Money for the lands was not taken from them in advance as the land laws required; the due date was not even established.

"We will take it when it will be easier for the Doukhobors to pay the money," said the Minister of the Interior.

In Canada there are no agricultural communes. There is not what we call a hamlet village. There, every farmer works his homestead, cultivates it, takes responsibility for it before the government, and has not and cannot have any relation with another farmer, not even a neighbour. He becomes an agricultural unit, fully independent master of his allotment. Therefore, for an English farmer, the fact that the land in the next section belongs to a railroad company presents no inconvenience.

— For the Doukhobors living in communes, in villages, such an allocation of lands turned out to be very inconvenient. Let us imagine, for example, that some village has sixty-four homesteads according to the number of men having the right to take a homestead. The land of this village would be found to be scattered over an area of eighty-one square versts in pieces of two and a quarter square versts each, mixed with other lands belonging to the railway company, Hudson's Bay Company and schools. From the village they would have to travel nine versts* (6 miles) to get to the end of their land.

To travel six miles every day would have been quite impossible.

Considering all this, the Canadian Pacific Railway, at the request of the government, agreed to give up its lands in the areas taken by the Doukhobors for settlement. The railroad received the same number of sections elsewhere in Canada. The Hudson's Bay Company and the school authorities refused to give up their lands to the Doukhobors, expecting to sell their sections at high prices when the Doukhobors developed their lands and the population increased.

The lands selected by the Doukhobor delegates and Hilcoff were at once declared to be reserves and no one could then get a homestead in the area until the final decision on this question. In the same way, even before the arrival of the Doukhobors in America, two reserves were set aside for them: one, the northern, bordering on the south with the Indian Reserve of Chief Keeseekoose and the southern one bordering on the north with the Indian Reserve of Chief Cote. This did not

---

*1 verst=3500 feet.   1 mile=5280 feet.

obligate the Doukhobors to settle in these reserves. They could pick lands wherever they wished, regardless of the reserves.

In this chapter I shall jump ahead and tell what lands the Doukhobors selected and on which they are living at this time.

The first shipload, 2140 so-called "Cold Mountains people," occupied the northern district. They built their villages on the banks of the Swan River. Two villages went beyond Thunder Hill in Saskatchewan. At that time, when they began to build the villages, the nearest railroad station was Cowan. Cowan was about eighty versts (55 miles) from the nearest village, Michailovka, former centre to which the Doukhobors settled from the immigration halls. The road passed through impossible places and often there was no way to travel from the colony to Cowan. But the first summer the railroad was built to the northern settlement and went even farther to the north-west. The nearest station, Swan River, was ten versts (8 miles) from Michailovka. Beside the station of Swan River, a little Canadian town was quickly constructed. All the residents of the Land Office settled here and in its former place remained nothing but a few broken pieces of the buildings.

In Swan River the Doukhobors of the northern settlement soon built large barns, warehouses for provisions and room for visiting Doukhobors. The road to Swan River from Michailovka was cut almost straight except for a part that joined an old Indian Road from Swan Lake to Fort Pelly. Clearing right of way for the railroad line, clearing land, and other preparatory work was carried out almost exclusively by Doukhobors. They also continued to work in this manner.

A small group, about ten of the "Cold Mountains people," settled in the southern district near the Stone River; they preferred the land there.

The second shipload—Elizabetpol Doukhobors and some from Kars—settled in the southern district. The third shipload—"Cold Mountains" and Cyprus people also settled in the southern district in the area of the Stone and Dead Horse Rivers. In the southern district, the nearest town, Yorkton, was twenty-five versts (17 miles) from the nearest village. The road for the whole distance was good, even and well-beaten. There were no problems on this road, even in spring, in getting to Yorkton.

Twenty-three Kars Doukhobors arrived with the fourth shipload. This party was conducted by A. Konshin and V. Bonch-Bruevich, E.D. Chiriakova and V.M. Velichkina. The majority of the Kars people settled in the southern district along the Rivers Assiniboine and White Sand. And only about one hundred of them, for different reasons, took lands along the Saskatchewan River some three hundred versts (200 miles) from the southern settlement in the Province of Prince Albert*.

To describe the climate of Canada, or more particularly the north-west areas in which the Doukhobors settled, I shall get the help of Mr. Kriukoff. N.A. Kriukoff, who studied agriculture in Canada, wrote an interesting and instructive book on this question, from which I shall excerpt some data. My personal observations in this regard, even though brief, agree fully with those stated by Kriukoff about the climate of Canada.

As I said above, in January (1898-99) for over a week there was a frost attaining thirty-five degrees Reamur. It was said that it had been eighteen years since there had been something similar. One must say however that, due to the exceptional dryness of the air, the cold here is felt much less than in other parts of the world. The same dryness of atmosphere renders the summer heat less oppressive.

The following winter (1899-1900), according to Canadian reports, was warmer than usual. The first snow came only in the middle of November and the whole winter saw only a few days when the frost reached minus twenty degrees Reamur (-25 degrees C). For the rest of the time, the temperature fluctuated between thirty and ten degrees below zero Reamur. Frequently there were long thaws, continuing for a week or more. In January there was rain.

That the climate is not extremely severe may be judged from the fact that cattle pasture all winter on surface feed and peripatetic Indians spend summer and winter in canvas tents.

In Fort Pelly in the centre of the Doukhobor villages, trader MacKenzie kept herds of thousands of horses and many cattle. All this stock pastures the year round on the prairie surrounding the Fort.

Mr. Kriukoff says:

With regard to the climate of the north-western regions, it should be noted first of all that the annual isotherm here takes a significant turn to the north, especially in the area between the one hundredth and one hundred and twentieth meridians, so that places located at certain degrees of latitude here are warmer than in all the rest of Canada. Because of this, cultivation of wheat rises from the Mississippi Valley almost to sixty degrees latitude and a huge area of land of the north-western region becomes available to farmers. In the area of Fort Vermilion, located at 58 degrees 24" latitude and 116 degrees 30" longitude, wheat ripens, as well as barley and other grains, in the first half of August.

Earlier, herds of wild bison wintered on the Athabaska River, as well as on the Mississippi near St. Paul. Meteorological observations in Winnipeg and in Fort McLeod, located at a distance of nine hundred versts one from the other at the same latitude, show one and the same temperature, but at Fort Simpson, situated 1,155

---

*This is an error. He meant the district of Prince Albert—ED.

versts north of Fort McLeod, it is warmer than in the latter. American researchers explain this as follows:

In the United States, to the east of the Rocky Mountains and west of the Mississippi, lies a huge waterless territory more than one million square versts, with an elevation above sea level of about six thousand feet. This is called the Great American Desert. Moist warm wind, blowing from the Bay of Mexico and reaching the Great American Desert, cools, giving up a significant part of its moisture and, dried out in this manner, flows at higher levels to Canada, bringing warmth.

The lands of the Doukhobors on the eastern side, bordering on the province of Manitoba, located between 102 degrees and 108 degrees longitude and between 52 degrees and 55 degrees northern latitude, are exactly in the region of influence of this beneficial wind, making possible the growing of wheat at extreme degrees of latitude. There is no doubt that wheat in time will become the chief product of the agriculture of the Doukhobors.

I have personally had occasion to see beautiful wheat grown by farmers in those places where the Doukhobors have settled. At a distance of no more than half a mile from Michailovka, right in the corner where the borders of Manitoba, Assiniboia and Saskatchewan come together, lives a farmer. In August his whole land was covered with a heavy growth of wheat. A mile from him lives an Irishman whose land has been cultivated for wheat for several years. The farmer who is in charge of the Post Office in Kamsack, located among the Doukhobor villages of the south district, hired Doukhobors to harvest his wheat, as did Wallace and Mulock, whose farms lie among Doukhobor villages, and other farmers whose names I do not remember.

Other crops and gardens here also produce excellent harvests. Oats, which I saw at the farm of Jacob Wurtz, who lives half way between Yorkton and the Doukhobor villages, for size of spike, weight, dryness and other grain qualities, was as good as one ever sees. This remarkable productivity of the soil of the north-western regions of Manitoba came about, it is thought, as a result of an accumulation of droppings of many animals inhabiting these areas. These accumulations also come from ashes from prairie fires and from decaying plants and animal remains. The general character of these soils is dark grey loam (black earth) with clay subsoil; the depth of the fertile soil is sixteen to twenty inches.* According to the researches of Louis and Gilbert, in three samples of dried out black earth in Manitoba and the north-west regions, the nitrogen content was as follows:

Sample from Portage la Prairie (Manitoba)   .2471%

---

*Kriukoff, *Canada.*

Sample from Saskatchewan North West Region   .3027%
Sample from Fort Ellice (North West Region)   .25%

According to the conclusions of the above-mentioned chemists, these soils are twice as rich in nitrogen as the cultivated lands of England.

As for harvesting crops, better conditions than in places settled by the Doukhobors are difficult to find. Rains so necessary for plant growth in May and June come in large quantities at this very time of the year. In July they come rarely, and in August, September and December there is beautiful dry weather. Heavy dew at nights also helps good growth and, thanks to the unusual dryness of the Canadian air, the grain becomes hard, dry and unusually healthy.

In the first summer (of the year 1900), due to a shortage of livestock and equipment and to various disorders such as moving from place to place and so on, the Doukhobors sowed relatively little land and, worse, sowed late. Nevertheless, regardless of such unfavourable conditions, rye and barley turned out very well and in places (village of Terpenie and on the Assiniboine River) yielded excellent crops. According to the Doukhobors they had not seen such crops in Russia. In two villages (of so-called Tambov Doukhobors) in Tambovka and Smirionovka, wheat was sown and also turned out excellently.

It should be noted that while wheat is the main product in Manitoba and the above-mentioned places in the north-west region, all the same it cannot be sown at once. The soil here is virgin and therefore requires very good preparatory working for several years. Usually, for the first three or four years, potatoes and other garden produce are raised on these lands. They sow barley, oats, rye and only then, in the fourth or fifth year, sow wheat on lands so worked.

Peculiarities of the climate and of the soil require, of course, particular methods of working the land. These methods are developed mainly on so-called experimental farms, set up in different parts of Canada. These farms are established by the government under the direction of the Ministry of Agriculture. Through long experience they find the best practices of working the land in every given area, they find the best practices of working the land in every given area, find the sort of seed which yields the best in these places and so on. Experimental Farms carry on a wide correspondence with farmers, send them free samples of seed, make use of their experience and so on. At the same time, Experimental Farms readily reply to all kinds of questions concerning agriculture. The office side of the work is so set up that answers are received promptly. Ordinarily, these answers are composed very thoroughly, clearly and quickly. It is understandable that under such conditions farmers make good use of information developed on the

Experimental Farms, carrying on a lively correspondence, informing them on their observations and results of applications of certain practices and so on.

To acquaint the Doukhobors with the existence of these farms and their purpose, the Director of Experimental Farms paid a visit to all Doukhobor villages, suggesting to them that they make use of the information developed on his farms. At the same time, he promised the Doukhobors that he would get in touch with the Minister of the Interior about giving them the necessary amount of seed for sowing in 1900 on credit. Through the efforts of Minister Sanders, seed was delivered to the Doukhobors, though he refused to give wheat saying they should not begin with it. A good crop of wheat could be expected only after three or four years, when the land had been well enough worked for it.

The greatest disadvantage of the climate of the north-west regions, as in Manitoba, must be the not infrequent falling of the temperature at the beginning of August. Sometimes, at this time, for two or three nights the temperature falls below zero Reamur, after which warm weather returns; here this is called 'Indian Summer!' In such years the wheat grains are wrinkled. These frosts, however, have no great significance since wheat harvested in Assiniboia, Saskatchewan and Manitoba is still considered to be the best in Canada.

Crop grades are established each autumn by government inspectors. The first grade in this classification ordinarily is wheat harvested in Manitoba and the north-west regions. A series of lower grade wheats are produced in other parts of Canada. It should be noted, however, that with the increase in the area of cultivated land, the frosts become rarer, weaker and finally almost disappear.

Mennonites who came from southern Russia have been living in Manitoba for about thirty years. There are about twenty thousand of them. Now these are among the wealthiest settlers of Canada, owing their wealth entirely to wheat. At the time of their coming to Manitoba, they were much afraid of these frosts. But with the cultivation of land and increase of the cultivated acreage, the frosts began to lessen and now they are considered there to be a rare occurrence. Many of the Mennonites still speak Russian and very eagerly hired Doukhobors as workers, paying usually from fifteen to thirty dollars per month, plus keep.

To the Doukhobors, such frosts are not new. On the wet mountains of the Caucasus, where they were settled at an altitude of six thousand feet above sea level, their first crops of barley and rye were completely destroyed by those early frosts. Later, with the increased areas of fields, the frosts became less and did not prevent the Doukhobor settlements from becoming the wealthiest in the Caucasus.

On The Settlements
Canada Assiniboia Southern Settlements or
Colony of Doukhobors
May 21, 1899.

Thanks to the dry, healthful Canadian climate, the fever finally left me. When I became a little stronger I prepared to go to the settlements. D. Hilcoff had invited me several times to come. At the same time the medical personnel left Winnipeg with me, wishing to work among the Doukhobors on the prairies. Among these was the already mentioned Doctor Mercer, the Englishman who had taken time off from his Marine Service to help the Doukhobors. He became attached to them and did not wish to leave them without medical help in at least the early part of their life on the wild prairie. There were also M.A. Satz, who had arrived with the first ship and had been living all this time with the Doukhobors; A.A. Satz, her sister; then among the Kars Doukhobors the energetic V. Velichkina worked busily, and finally Anna Rabetz and E. Markova, who had arrived with the third ship from Cyprus.

None of these persons, of course, received any reward of any kind. All of them had their return fare to Russia covered. Their keep, with minor exceptions, was not provided and sometimes their living conditions were worse than those of the Doukhobors in all respects. Any personal funds they had were expended on medicines, as the money available from the bonus was insufficient to cover all the costs of the clinic. True, sometimes there were donations for this purpose—but in general the work was always held up for lack of funds.

Together with us also was a Herbert Archer, an Englishman who worked continually in Canada to help the Doukhobors communicate with the Canadian government. He was now going to see D. Hilcoff.

The Cyprus people were living in Yorkton. From a distance their establishment looked like a camp; around the Immigration Hall stood pointed tents among which camp fires burned surrounded by Doukhobor men and women. The Cyprus people had begun to move out to their land but for the time being this move was going only very slowly. Rabetz and Markova decided to remain here with the Doukhobors among whom they had worked so much in Cyprus. They settled in a tent which was soon pitched for them.

We drew near to the Southern Settlement by evening. Huge blockhouses could be seen from a distance, scattered about a cleared space in the poplar forest. Behind the village was a thick forest. These awkward buildings, without windows and with earth piled on the roofs, surrounded with glistening cut-off stumps, gave the impression of something primitive, strong and stubborn. Among the stumps lay many branches left frðm trees cut down for building logs. Here and there were two or three remaining birches. Behind the buildings there were holes from which clay was taken for sealing the cracks between the logs. Several wagons were scattered, here and there, among the buildings. On one of them a harness had been dropped. Everywhere there were girders, chips, different household articles. Here was an untidy pile of hay. Everywhere one felt a disorder, the absence of a master's hand, and the whole settlement appeared uncomfortable, scattered. Among the buildings, Doukhobor men and women wandered, children warmed themselves in the sun and elders, gathered here and there, conversed. The Kars and Elizabetpol people settled here. They had arrived on the second ship. When they learned that we were looking for Hilcoff, several people ran for him and soon he came to us, surrounded by a group of elders.

In his first words Hilcoff made it known that he wished to go to Europe as soon as possible. It would soon be a year since he had had a rest from work, endlessly travelling between the settlements and Winnipeg, Quebec, Ottawa and so on. Now he was preparing to go to Prince Albert to inspect the lands for the Doukhobors coming on the fourth ship. Returning from there, he would turn over all matters to me and go to Europe, as he felt extremely wearied.

Meanwhile he suggested that I go to the North Settlement. No one had been there since spring and information from there was very meagre. One had to see if there were sufficient provisions; and, if not, to arrange delivery, arrange medical help and try to organize employment on the railroad being built near there. More important, one must try to improve the earth road to Cowan, since it would be easier to deliver provisions from there than from Yorkton, to which it took four days to travel (one way) with the horses. The Doukhobors of the North Settlement once had to remain three weeks without salt because of this poor road.

Medical help was allotted as follows: in the South Settlement would be M.A. Satz; in the North Settlement, A.A. Satz; and Dr. Mercer would travel from one to the other helping in the more difficult cases.

Canada
Assiniboia
Southern Settlement
May 23, 1899.

It was nearly the end of May and because of the shortage of oxen they were just beginning to plow and dig the earth for sowing crops and gardens. The oxen and wagons which they had were busy hauling baggage and people from Yorkton to the settlements. Using these, too, they delivered provisions; that is, flour, salt, rice, butter, sugar and tea. With them they also skidded logs from the forest for building homes, and delivered seed for sowing.

It was obvious that with such a small number of oxen it was impossible to serve some two and one half thousand people. It had been concluded that baggage would have to be delivered on hired teams so as to free the oxen for plowing. They had no money for additional cattle. The small remainder of the bonus had to be conserved for flour so that they would not be hungry in the autumn.

The main problem nevertheless was that of the land. The elders wandered whole days over the Southern District picking places for villages, trying to locate them so that it would be convenient for each village to get to its land. They considered how many villages the Kars people should break up into, and the same for the Elizabetpol people and the Cyprus people. They also considered how many should be in each village, etc.

The most difficult problem to resolve, of course, was the question of how to organize Community Life. So far, all those in the Southern Settlement constituted one Community. The use of cattle, equipment and the division of flour was now equal for each, because these things were all bought with money belonging to all, the bonus.

But even now separate groups had been initiated, living their own life independently of the whole Community. These were the more prosperous villages of the Elizabetpol people, and often the Kars people. They already had their own cattle, wagons and their own food. So far they all lived together in common barracks. These better-off communities gave their cattle and wagons for the use of all in the Southern Settlement, but it seemed entirely possible that as soon as they set up their own villages, their lives would be entirely independent of the remaining villages.

In certain newly formed groups, which would in future form separate villages, the members were already living a non-community life, strictly separating "mine" and "yours" with other co-villagers.

All this, of course, would be finally determined only when each village was established on its chosen land and no longer connected with the bonus or the common life in crowded barracks. Meanwhile, despite its good sides, this community structure, necessitated by circumstances, was frequently the source of difficulties and misunderstandings. It was especially difficult with regard to horses and oxen. No one wanted to be a driver for long and for this reason horses frequently passed from hand to hand, which in itself is bad for livestock. During these transfers it sometimes happened that the animals remained unfed, unwatered or without enough rest, as the new driver frequently did not know how much work the animals had done. As a result, the livestock of the Doukhobors, in particular the horses, frequently perished.

Canada
Assiniboia
Northern Settlement
May 26, 1899.

In external appearances, the settlement of the Northern Region, compared to the Southern, seemed much more integrated and comfortable. The barns were set in a regular order near a hill on the shore of the picturesque Swan River which was overgrown here and there with high reeds. Further away was a tall forest of great spreading spruces and large pines. In all the passages between the buildings long strings of fish were hung out to dry in the sun. There was so much that it looked like a fishing village.

A heavy cable was secured across the fast, turbulent river and on it moved an unbelievably puny ferry made of several timbers and boards. I had to cross on this ferry. The water splashed over the side and only by standing on logs piled on top was I able to preserve myself from a cold bath.

Horses were taken over swimming. To each was tied a long rope, one end of which the ferryman took over to the other side of the river. Then the horses were pushed into the water and pulled by the rope from the other side, helping them to overcome the strong current.

The whole village met us as if we were long-expected guests. Everywhere complaints were heard about being abandoned; there were sighs and lamentations. The same evening, the capable Zeebarev established us in tents pitched on a hill above the village. We sat a long time in our living quarters conversing with Zeebarev about the state of affairs. We heard much that was sad and difficult to correct: flour was in short supply. There was no butter or sugar at all. Only the fish supported the starving people. But not everyone ate fish; for them it was especially difficult. There were no greens of any kind, and to make up for this deficiency in the food, the Doukhobors gathered some kind of grass in the fields, boiled it into soup, putting in as a special tidbit several part-frozen potatoes. They seasoned it with several handfuls of flour. As a substitute for bread there was kvass.*

Certain other provisions—several kegs of butter, sugar, tea and, most important, a carload of flour of six hundred and twenty large

---

*A drink made of fermented bread.

bags—were in Cowan. But there was no way of delivering all this. After a rainy spring, the sloughs lying between the Land Office (Swan River) and Cowan had become impassable lakes. The Settlement of the Land Office, not having time to gather enough reserves, was also suffering from shortage of provisions.

"That's what we have got into here," said Zeebarev. "When the salt was gone to the last grain—I can hardly talk about it. We grieved so! Several times we sent a team to the Land Office. They got to Swan River, sat there awhile, and returned empty handed. Finally they brought some from Yorkton. And there, as you know, by the time you get there, ten or twelve days passes. And how much can you bring from Yorkton? There are five teams in all. They don't have time to bring sugar and butter. It is well if they can bring the seed that is needed and some flour. The same animals must skid the trees for building and plough a little, the people can't do everything!"

"How do you mean—people?" I expressed surprise.

"Well," laughed Zeebarev, "Twenty-four women hitch themselves to the plough and pull. You will see tomorrow! They tried to dig with shovels, but got too tired. This way the work is lighter and it goes faster. Yes, it is very serious, very difficult for our people. What can one say? Only we don't grieve. We trust in God. This trial will pass too! Important thing is, we don't have the livestock—without livestock you can do nothing! We began to build new villages, but here too livestock was needed to skid the logs for the buildings. By autumn we must get the buildings done. And flour must be moved to the villages and the stock must rest too, or we will kill them altogether. And so it turns out that we must do the ploughing ourselves."

As if justifying himself before someone, Zeebarev ended his recital.

Early in the spring, the Doukhobors of the North Settlement had taken work on the railroad being constructed from Cowan. Some came from the Southern District too. On this work they earned $4,076.21, of which $2,468.99 was for the Northern District. With this money they bought footwear and various small agricultural tools; the English teams were paid for hauling provisions and baggage; and part of the money was handed out for minor needs and provisions.

The bonus was now reaching the end; it could not be depended upon. It must provide some help to the Cyprus people. Therefore, only one thing remained: to look for work so as to provide bread for the Northern District and acquire some livestock, without which, as Zeebarev said, the Doukhobors can never get on their feet. On explaining this state of affairs to the gathered elders, particularly that the bonus, which had seemed to all to be the source of life, was coming to an end, I pointed to employment as the only means of existence. Here I suggested to the meeting that they look for work and, with this in mind, that they go first to Cowan to the chief engineers of the railroad under construction. The elders fully approved this plan. After a day of more detailed information about the state of affairs of the Northern Community, it was agreed that Zeebarev and I would go to the Land Office where the chief engineer resides, and would try to get work on the railroad.

Canada
Assiniboia
Northern Settlement
May 27, 1899.

Early this morning I hurried out to the field to see the ploughing Zeebarev spoke of yesterday. Somehow I could not believe that affairs stood as poorly as it had seemed to me after spending a few hours on the settlement. When I came to a narrow strip of ploughed field I saw at the far end of it a colourful crowd of people slowly moving in my direction in a long file. These people were hitched in tandem pairs to an iron plough. It became quite awesome when, stepping heavily on the wet grass, this sombre procession began to approach me. There was something solemn, deeply moving, in the figures of these straining women pulling the heavy plough. The heavy sticks to which the rope was tied cut into their breasts and stomachs. With sunburnt hands the women pushed the plough trying to reduce the pain.

In the lead an older tall woman with a stern face moved with measured but heavy steps, looking at the earth. She knows what life is like and even this work does not surprise her. She knows this is necessary.

"He who takes the plough and looks back is not a ploughman."

And she, strong in spirit and in body, is prepared to go around the earth's sphere in this harness with the same quiet stern face, seeing this work as her duty.

Beside her were similar calm, sometimes troubled, faces, with sadness in the eyes. Here was the pale face of a girl with fine features, with drawn folded lips. She walked with upraised head and her thin neck was marked by two tensely swollen veins. With her melancholy wide-open eyes she looked into the depth of the clear spring sky as if looking for something that would reconcile her to this coarse unfair life. In her eyes filled with sadness could be seen a child's perplexity and sadness and thirst for love and happiness. Paired with her was an older woman. Industriously leaning her whole body at each step, her features were contorted with pain. Now and then she turned her good-natured face to two little girls walking after their mother across the field and

153

said something to them. At such a moment her face lit up with some kind of inner light, as if she was happy that she and not they must pull this strap. One of the little girls, tangling her feet in the tall grass, gave her mother some branches of wild strawberries.

Pair after pair of these women passed me as in a dream; then came the last pair with faces apathetic from weariness, with distracted eyes looking straight ahead. The plough rustled, turning over the furrow from under which the tops of partly-covered field flowers waved sadly—and the ploughers passed by as in a dream. From a distance I heard their song. It was a song of weeping; it was more a groan escaping at last from chests exhausted and over-strained by long suffering, the groan of reproach, the wail calling for righteousness, for all that is human in man distinguishing him from animals.

And the brilliant river laughed in the sun, sparkling through the leaves with its fast running streams. It laughed at the two-legged creatures calling themselves with the proud name of humans, able till now to do nothing to deserve the name, nothing; otherwise they would not be witnesses to such a scene. And the frightened aspen trembled with fear from head to foot, trembled with all its new spring leaves unused to life, muttering something senseless from the terror which had overtaken it. Several birds shook their heads in bewilderment as they looked with curiosity at the sight never seen before and which they could not explain to themselves.

And over all this spread the clear innocent sky. The last drop of dew shone with emeralds in the marvellous thick grass, and the untamed breeze shook the tall feather grass. And from a distance poured and poured the soul-searing groan—song of the unheard-of, coarse injustice, and terrible grief.

There, all were pulling, pulling, pulling. . . .

Canada
Assiniboia
Northern Settlement
May 28, 1899.

In the tent considered to be the out-patient clinic, work went on feverishly from first thing in the morning. It was full of people. Everyone was there. The old and little ones, men and women, all awaited a turn to use the services of a doctor who in a day or two would leave for the South District.

The majority of the sick were those who had caught yellow fever in the Caucasus and could not get free of it, even here. All were overdosed with quinine. One of the results of this was that quinine taken in large doses had no effect. Another was that among the sick coming to the doctor were very many having clear indications of quinine poisoning. The doctor was horrified at the "per person" division of the quinine which was being practised by the Doukhobors and in every way tried to persuade people to return all the quinine they had on hand to the medical assistant.

"There is a mass poisoning here. This is simply impossible," he complained. "They eat quinine like bread."

"We have become so addicted to it," explained the Doukhobors.

Part of the quinine was returned to the pharmacy, although I was convinced that more than half was still with the Doukhobors.

There were various sicknesses here but two were particularly noticeable: yellow fever, with its many complications; and internal troubles, appeared as all kinds of catarrh and diarrhea. Not a few patients were simply exhausted people. The children had an especially sad appearance, with large stomachs, thin legs, puffy grey faces and arms thin as whips. Many suffered from rashes, sores and eye afflictions, resulting from undernourishment. The doctor prescribed fish oil for all, and all medicines were distributed from the supply brought here. I was seized with fear at the sight of this large crowd of sick people. All day and late into the night the doctor and assistants worked, and still did not see half of those who came for help. Yet more than a hundred sick had been seen. and this out of a population of 1,400.

Here, indeed, was the final totalling of all that the Doukhobors had suffered in the last while. This was what their spiritual freedom had cost them. In these famished grey, earth-coloured faces, in these shaking hands, in these misty lifeless eyes which it was strange to see in bodies once richly endowed with health, the history of the Doukhobors could best be read. This was an excellent illustration, explaining much that is hidden deep in the lives of human societies.

Unfortunately, the Doukhobors in relation to medical science are at the same stage of development as are all Russian people. They have no healers of their own, not even some who are a little knowledgeable. All medical help is provided to them by "old women," who use the same treatment among the Doukhobors as in other parts of the Russian Empire. They treat with corrosive sublimate, blood letting, manure, and all kinds of infusions, often harmless, often poisonous, and only rarely beneficial and—something that really surprised me— even with "whisperings."* These "whisperings," the crudest of superstitions, do not sit well with one's concept of the Doukhobors, who in their religion and general spiritual development show little superstition.

---

*Charms or spells. .

In the big collection of Doukhobor psalms, poems and other Doukhobor literature, compiled thanks to the strenuous efforts of V. Bonch-Bruevich, a whole section is devoted to all kinds of incantations, exorcism, whisperings, etc. Its content is laughably senseless and full of childish efforts to create something terrifying and mysterious. It must be said, however, that a doctor or assistant need only appear among the Doukhobors and they drop their "old women" and hurry to consult him. In general, I noticed that the Doukhobors behave very trustfully to doctors and their treatment. And women actually like to have treatments. Once there is a doctor nearby, not one Doukhobor will go for treatment to an "old woman" and I do not remember an occasion when one of them would compare the effectiveness of a doctor with the treatments of an "old woman."

Not a few curiosities could be heard and observed in the out-patient clinic tent. Men complaining of pain in the back claimed that their main tendon had burst and one woman with a sad face confidentially said that her fertility sinew had dried up, as a result of which she was infertile. One of the patients suffering from catarrh of the bowel, before explaining her illness, asked everyone for silence.

"Sh! Sh! Do you hear?" she said to the doctor, and placing his hand on her stomach, looked with frightened eyes and listened attentively to the growling.

"There, there! Do you hear?" she said, raising her pointed finger. "That is it, hernia gnawing itself. And so it gnaws and gnaws day and night. It gnaws, simply does not let me live."

In her imagination there was some kind of evil animal which got into the person and gnawed away at the insides, inflicting unbearable suffering until it got to the heart. Then death would come. Some took the beating of the aorta which could be heard because of the emaciation of the stomach walls for the same "gnawing" which thumped so, wishing to get out of the person.

For treatment of yellow fever they sometimes took heroic measures, wishing to starve the fever. Before the medical assistant stood a broad-shouldered woman with a fairly good moustache and a stern look. Beside her a timid, puny man took shelter. This was a wife who had brought her husband to the doctor. The yellow fever which she had cured had returned to the man.

"And how much it tortured him," the portly woman said in a deep voice, lovingly glancing at her lesser half. "How much it tortured! Horrors! I gave him white quinine and red; I rubbed him with turpentine; I made him drink kerosene, and what didn't I do. Nothing takes it away, do what you will."

"Yes, that's it exactly. Nothing helps. That's true," confirmed the man with his weak tenor.

"Once I thought of a cure. I said to him one evening, 'Simion,' I said, 'get dressed.' 'Where to, my dear?' he asked. 'Get dressed,' I said, 'I know my plan!'

"At that time he was lying at the chimney, dear man; there it pushed him this way and that, throwing him in all directions."

"It did everything but turn me inside out," laughed the little tenor.

"We walked out into the street. It was frosty, there was even a ring around the moon—there was such a frost! The dear man held on to me; it was so cold and still he shook. We came to the cut (in the ice) and I said to him, 'Undress now, Simion, completely.' At first he didn't want to. But I sternly ordered him to hurry up."

"It was very fearful. It's easy to say—in winter, on the snow. And it continued to throw me and shake me."

"Here I took him under the arms and began to bathe him in the ice cut. Can you believe it? The fever shook him at that time and twisted him into a knot, poor man."

"After that he became all blue, almost black. Now, I thought, now all fever must have jumped out. And true, from that time until now it was as if he hadn't had it."

"That's entirely true what she is saying. Until now, from almost three years ago, it didn't return. Only when I went on the railway right of way, it twisted me up again."

Even on the Doukhobors, accustomed to such methods, this created an impression.

Among the sick were several people almost poisoned with corrosive sublimate, with which they had tried to kill the hernia or fever.

But most of all I was amazed at a scene I came upon in one of the warehouses. Quite a few people were crowding there and outside, by the wall, stood a young man leaning on the log wall, pale as a corpse, looking ahead strangely with a fixed stare. His face smiled blissfully. In the barn, it seems, the gathered Doukhobors were "letting blood" for one another.

"It is May," one of them explained to me, "And it is essential to let out the spoiled blood."

"During the winter it stagnates," explained another. "This is a hindrance to a person."

"From where do you let the blood?" I asked.

"From wherever anybody wishes. If one has a headache, then the blood must be drained from the head. But, simply, as now in the spring, we all let it. Few do not wish it. It helps a great deal because during the winter it stagnates and so on."

"And do you let out much blood?" I asked.

"No. What are you afraid of? Just a little. About this cupful." He showed me a blood-covered cup having a capacity of a good glass full.

For a long time I discussed with them the circulation of the blood and pointed out the fearful harm they are bringing upon themselves by this bloodletting, at a time when strength is so necessary and there is not enough nourishment; but all my explanations had little influence on the Doukhobors. For many years they have been letting stagnated blood for themselves, and it was not for me to convince them.

The "Little Town"
Canada
Land Office or "Little Town"
June 3, 1899.

We did not find the engineer in the "little town," as the Doukhobors had named the Land Office. All the inhabitants of the "little town," made up partly of railroad workers and a few farmers, were awaiting him impatiently from day to day. With his arrival, land workers and others were to begin work on the line under construction. All the Englishmen living here would go, with the exception of two or three storekeepers and restaurant operators. Now, with nothing to do, the majority spend their time playing football and crowding into the two boarding houses, not knowing where to go, bored and idle.

In a prominent place in the village there was a large tent. This was the Land Office. Its manager, Mr. Harley, who was also the immigration officer, told us that Engineer Turnbull could not come here until the dry weather arrived. Even if he were able to come, work could not begin now as there was water on the whole line, which prevents any kind of work.

"Of course," he concluded, "it might be better near Cowan—that I cannot say. And it could be that today we will see the engineer. Only I warn you, that if you want to take the earth work, you must be on guard and catch Turnbull as soon as he appears here. There is an Englishman here," he continued confidentially, "who wants to take a contract out for the earth work on the whole line. And if he succeeds, there will be nothing left for your people, as he wishes to bring in Italians for the work."

Apparently it would be necessary to make every effort to get some of this work and counter the English contractor. As we discovered, this energetic fellow tried to get to the engineer in Cowan, but to our good fortune he was forced to turn back mid way, as the flooded rivers did not permit him to continue. When we heard stories of impossible floods, and learned that the horse of one farmer had drowned, Zeebarev and I knew we could do nothing but sit at the Land Office and await the arrival of the engineer.

In the "little town" Zeebarev and I found about fifteen more Doukhobors. These were part Elizabetpol and part Northern Settlement Doukhobors, also awaiting the opening of the work on the rail line. Some of them were now earning a little. Some were able to get work sawing wood here in the "little town" while others worked for nearby farmers. But this was so little it was not worth considering.

We were all still living in the blockhouse where the first party of workers stopped on the way to the prairie. Now there were two rows of bunks and through the full length of the room stood a long table. We had to accept nourishment that was just so-so, the same as in the villages. In the morning, several of the Doukhobors would go out to the prairie and soon return with large quantities of strawberries. This was the main condiment to go with bread. There are many of these berries here compared with other places. Of course they were eaten in large quantities on many farms, and some Doukhobors—more conserving types—dry out flat cakes of strawberries for winter.

A large part of each day passed in discussions of what the Doukhobors had seen here, and their views about labour earnings and the need for livestock. Sometimes the Doukhobors would start a psalm. On entering the blockhouse, the Englishmen would settle down on the benches in the most comfortable poses, putting their feet on the benches and, not removing caps, continue to smoke their pipes, occasionally spitting a yellow stream to one side. Soon the whole building would be filled with smoke and coarse jokes were heard, rewarded with loud laughter from the listeners. The Doukhobors disliked all this very much but they calmly continued their singing and when finished kept a dignified silence.

The Englishmen would try to start conversations but the Doukhobors brushed them aside.

"What is it? We don't understand what you are saying. That is all there is to it."

"Why are they loafing around?"

"If only they came with a good attitude, but they come and fill the room with stench, and look around for a way to make a laughing stock of someone, cackling like ganders, not knowing why."

The Doukhobors complained that the English youths bothered them by picking on them in various ways. The other evening one of our people went out but they saw him and began throwing chips at him and when our people went into the warehouse they began to pound the door with rocks. And they threw stone after stone that sounded like pistol shots, laughing loudly as they did so.

From conversations with the English I learned that such pursuit is a form of testing. The English, hearing that the Doukhobors consider all kinds of force over a person as evil, learning that they are guided in their behaviour by the principle of non-resistance to evil, decided from boredom to research this question in practice. It was a situation full of temptation. On one side there was complete idleness and boredom; on the other, a group of people who permit anything to be done to them without resistance. Understanding "non-resistance to evil" was impossible for admirers of boxing.

"How is this," said Tommy and Johnny, "that someone, devil take him, should beat me and I remain silent? Is this what these Douks are saying?" They say this, staring and raising eyebrows.

"And what is boxing for them? May lightning strike him. This is utter nonsense. Cursed be my own life. This cannot be."

The question begins to occupy the idle village more and more.

"Perhaps this is what they profess, but actually just touch them; they will show you such non-resistance that—oh! oh!" They speculate.

Finally some young men turn up to whom such uncertainty is unbearable. They try to nudge those robust fellows. But to their surprise, the fellows move away. First efforts provoked, these self-appointed researchers become less and less satisfied with little things. They blow smoke in the faces of the Doukhobors, throw chips at them, press into their home and behave there as if in a pig pen. All this, however, is borne patiently without resistance; the Doukhobors simply say something and shake their heads disapprovingly.

The jokes and jibes take on the usual characteristics. Almost everywhere in Canada where Doukhobors have lived they have experienced this attitude of the English. Finally, however, the Doukhobors are left alone and treated with respect, which is engendered by the firmness of their convictions. The principle of non-resistance continues to produce sometimes irritation, sometimes bewilderment; more often, the most ironical mockery and merry laughter.

Yesterday evening, the following incident took place. Elders and young men were sitting at the long table and drinking tea. There was calm conversation. Suddenly the door opened wide and into the building tumbled two young Englishmen. Both had apparently been drinking and were now in excellent spirits—the best condition for learning about the religious views of the Doukhobors. One of them, pushing his hands into his front pockets and setting his feet wide apart, apparently not fully sure of them, stopped at the entrance. His cap slid on to the back of his head. With merry insolent eyes he looked around the room. His comrade stumbled at the entrance and, to balance, put his arms around a post. He stood this way for a time, bending forward and hugging the post with one arm to keep his balance. He lowered his head and morosely stared at the ground.

The Doukhobors remained silent and studied their guests.

"How nice!" said someone quietly.

"Hey you, good evening!" cried the merry young man.

"Good day, good day, good guest!" answered the Doukhobors with laughter.

"What are they saying?" asked the more serious young man, hiccoughing, still looking at the ground.

"How would I know? I think, thanking us for the visit."

"True," agreed his comrade.

Then the action began. At first the merry one tugged at the sleeves of the Doukhobors, pushed their elbows, so that they spilled their tea on the table, cried 'cock-a-doodle-doo' and so on. The Doukhobors remained silent, looking soberly at the jovial one.

"What will they do, what will they do!" sighed someone, stroking his head.

A crowd of Englishmen at the entrance looked on.

"Oh, these fellows will show them non-resistance," came a merry exclamation from among them.

"Billy, listen, Billy," the serious one addressed the other, "are you not a little too kind, my friend? Try putting sand into the tea. Try it!"

"That's an idea!" cackled the experimenter, and picking up a handful of ashes near the stove, poured it into the cup of one of the elders.

"Good gracious!" exclaimed the injured elder, "What is that for, eh? Tell me, what is that for? Is this permissible?"

"What people!" is heard from among the Doukhobors. "Worse than the Asiatics! God forbid!"

"To people who do not understand, who are in darkness, how can you explain?" voices are heard saying.

"There is nothing to do but keep the door locked, that's all."

"Worse than the Tartars!" said someone from the elders.

"Look! Look!" cackled the Englishmen, baring their teeth. "They are sitting as if they had been served sugar!"

"No, these are entirely barbarous."

"This is positively worse than the negroes. May we be cursed if this is not worse."

"What fools! Savages!" the English cackled in many different ways, enjoying the scene, egging Billy on to new tricks.

This continued a long time. Then Billy came up to an old man and snapping him on the head spat into his tea, to the general amusement of the public. He turned to the people and began a disconnected speech about this group being complete dunderheads, saying that they should be taught a few things.

The Doukhobors shook their heads, sighed and expressed surprise on their part about the rude, ignorant individuals. At this time a stalwart, awkward figure of a young Elizabetpol Doukhobor rose from the table, having looked on in silence till now. Leaving the table, he somewhat undecidedly, as if confused by his large figure, straightened up his jacket and, timidly coughing, moved over to the voluble Billy. With a calm face, saying not a word, he seized poor Billy by the scruff of the neck with one hand, and with the other hauled off and hit him on the ear so that he hiccoughed and rolled out unconscious. After a few moments gaze at Billy lying at his feet, the young man turned red from restrained excitement and returned to his place.

All this happened so unexpectedly that both the English and the Doukhobors were benumbed for a minute. A silence ensued. Only the heavy puffing of the young Elizabetpol man was heard.

"That's alright," said the drunken voice of Billy's gloomy comrade.

"Now, that was unnecessary," argued the Doukhobors, rising from their places and preparing to help the injured Englishman.

"Now what is this for? Why did you injure an ignorant person who, through his ignorance, his blindness—oh, you're a fine one!" said an old man with a tragic agitated voice to the young Elizabetpol man, looking into his eyes with mournful reproach. "Surely it is not our business to fight, eh?"

"This won't do. This won't do," came reproaches from all sides.

The young man, red from shame to the tips of his ears, stood with hands at his sides among the scolding elders, confusedly looking straight ahead, apparently unable to understand how such a sin could have occurred. The Englishman was brought to consciousness and he left with his comrades, approving of the fine fellow who was able to stand up for his people.

In explanation of this behaviour, completely inconceivable and impossible even for the most ordinary Doukhobor, it must be said that the Elizabetpol man belonged to a group of Doukhobors in the Caucasus who took no active part in the movement of 1894-95. They did not have to defend their principles with the price of blood as did the rest. Their convictions had not been tempered in the hearth of practical tests and therefore, among the youths especially, one could meet people insufficiently imbued with the idea of non-resistance to evil by force. The extent to which this occurrence was unusual and violent may be judged by the fact that the news of it flew through all the villages and agitated Doukhobor society profoundly.

To give a complete account of the consistency of the Doukhobors in putting into practice the idea of non-resistance would constitute an assignment in itself, but I cannot help mentioning one unusually striking occurrence when one of the English farmers kicked and killed a Doukhobor boy who was playing with his children.

The boy's father did everything he could to free the farmer from pursuit of the law and, despite his deep sorrow, forgave him and was able to speak with him in full friendliness as with a brother. This occurrence is far from exceptional or unusual. A Doukhobor cannot behave otherwise in such circumstances. For a Doukhobor a different reaction in a similar situation would be criminal.

Canada
Village of Cowan
June 5, 1899.

After waiting for Turnbull for over a week, we decided at last to go to Cowan. What we suffered by the time we got to the town it is difficult to convey. It was a continuous struggle! My poor little horses, Gee and Jay, splashed up to their bellies in sticky mud, stumbled and fell every minute. Countless times they had to be unhitched and the traces tied to the back axle of the buggy to pull it back out. Then we set off on foot to find a way by which the flooded place could be by-passed. Now we were convinced that delivery of provisions from Cowan to the North Settlement was out of the question.

All along the road, here and there, lay articles dropped from loads. Everything was there! In places there were mountains of flour, rice and other provisions. They were carefully covered with canvas to protect them from the rain. Nearby, a migrating farmer had dropped all his property, protecting it to some extent by an old tent. Further on, leaning against the trunk of a tree, stood a chest of drawers, from the lowest drawer of which hung a rag; the wind shook and tore it in all directions. Here too, under slanting streams of rain, stood a table and under it a child's cradle. All this was left with the firm conviction that not a single article would be lost, that upon returning for his property, the owner would find all. At the sight of this picture, best illustrating the morals of the land, I was forced to remember my distant native land, and I thought: would many of these goods be preserved if they lay so unprotected at home?

On the way to Cowan we saw numerous broken wagons stuck in impassable swamps. Our light buggy suffered the same fate. In one of the valleys where it was especially bad, the coupling bolt snapped and the buggy, broken in two parts, had to be left. We unhitched the horses and led them. We didn't have the heart to ride them—they were so exhausted. Spattered with mud from head to foot, cold, they were barely able to plod along behind us. Dense twilight covered the dark forest and we continued to weave, plunging to the knees in mud. And behind us the tired horses groaned and sighed, enveloping us with the warm steam of their breath.

About two versts before Cowan a new struggle began. From here right to Cowan the road was paved with wooden logs. It was built in a special way: thick smooth trunks laid side by side across the road, and to keep them from rolling away, posts were put down between them. At first we were overjoyed at the comfort, but soon we became disillusioned. The earth between the logs had been converted into thin mud and in places there was none of it. Most of the posts pounded in between the logs broke and the logs spread and left gaps. Thanks to the rain which had watered us generously along the whole road, the logs became very slippery and it was very difficult to walk on them. There was a risk of breaking a leg or of falling on a sharp post. The unfortunate horses jumped from log to log as in a circus. Several times we tried to walk at one side of this improvised pavement, but here it was so deep that for fear of drowning the horses we clambered back on and continued our balancing exercises, risking breaking our legs and those of our horses.

Wounded, beaten, covered from head to foot in thin mud, we finally saw the lights of Cowan through a clump of trees and, there we found rest for ourselves and for our four-footed friends.

Canada
Village of Cowan
July 6, 1899.

Instead of the unapproachable, pompous figure of the Chief Engineer such as we have them in Russia, where they imagine themselves to be "King and God" along the whole line in their charge, we saw a plain little man in a grey jacket, high, thick stockings and worker's shoes. Mr. Turnbull's office was as small and plain as himself. Hurriedly constructed from simple boards, it looked like a house of cards. Inside, in the middle, stood an iron stove. On the walls were hung plans of the road, and here also stood two cots on which the draughtsman and the engineer's assistant slept.

The whole day we argued with the intractable Englishman, and only in the evening managed to compose a contract for work, which then and there, without formalities, was signed by me and Zeebarev. Both of us were considered contractors and the persons responsible.

According to this contract the Doukhobors were to be paid fourteen cents per cubic yard on the roadbed of the railroad. Wheelbarrows, boards, shovels and other tools needed for the work were to be provided by the railroad company. Delivery of these tools from the warehouses to the place of work was our job. But at the close of work the Doukhobors were to leave them at the place where the work stopped, except for shovels which the Doukhobors had to deliver to the nearest warehouse.

The Doukhobors would not be responsible for breakage of tools; they would be repaired by the Company. Broken tools or their parts had to be presented. The Company agreed to keep in its warehouses along the line, food products for the Doukhobors, but the Doukhobors would take these to the place of work. The Doukhobors might have a free pass to Winnipeg for necessary purchases for the work party. The Doukhobors must work everywhere that the engineer asked. There was no limit to the number of workers. The warehouses would supply goods on credit to workers.

This contract was closed on June 5, 1899.

"Now, if only some more people would come out to work," concluded Zeebarev, sighing, "we would all be provided for."

"And what do you think?" I asked him, "Will many people come out?"

"About two hundred should come out, or even more. But who knows how it will be with our people! Sometimes you can't tell them anything that should be done. We shall see!"

Nevertheless, N. Zeebarev was apparently very well satisfied. And how could he be otherwise? These earnings for the Doukhobors of the Northern Settlement were the only means of escape from their desperate situation.

In the best of spirits we set off on the return trip to cheer up the Northern Settlement and to urge workers to go "to the line." All the way Zeebarev thought about how the Northern Settlement would acquire reserves of food for all winter and summer from this work, and how they would buy livestock, ploughs and how they would plough and plough.

"And as soon as we start on the land, nothing can then frighten us because our beloved work is land work," he said. "We have become so used to it."

About two hundred persons did come out from the Northern Settlement to work on the railroad.

Conferences on the Northern and Southern Settlements
Canada
Assiniboia
South Settlement
June 27, 1899.

At the beginning of June the Doukhobors began to move from their settlements to their own newly formed villages. From that moment each village began to live its own particular life. Most of them at first were set up on a community basis; "communally," as the

Doukhobors said. These communities were not constructed according to any single plan, and their community life did not always take the same form.

This was a time of construction among the Doukhobors; life was just beginning to take shape, and agitation and discord took root and flourished. Between the supporters of community life and its opponents there was an intense silent struggle. It was the more fierce because the social ideal and approved way had always been on the side of community life, as every Doukhobor in the depth of his soul, even the most ardent supporter of private property, considered community life essential for genuine Christians, which they considered themselves to be.

At the same time, material conditions were such that only a very few people could live by themselves; that is, independently outside the community. Whether they liked it or not, those who dreamt of a separate farm or even of private property within a village, with their own money, had to harden their hearts and support at meetings the proposal to live a community life. Even those families which were rich or strong (in numbers of men available for work), who could begin independent life, did not venture to raise this question before its time. It would be too apparent that they were simply running away from the poor so as to save their own money and their strength for themselves, and that they feared the poor's nearness as they would be forced to help them and to share their goods with them.

"Not to share is impossible, and if you share you will become the same yourself."

And to go away was impossible, impossible because there were only a few people of such wealth. They could not form a large group, and a Doukhobor who could not live without "brethren" who could repudiate him for such behaviour. For him it was everything, the whole world. The risk was a little too frightening.

Understandably, in the presence of these factions the community could be neither single-minded nor durable. Understandably, strain was felt in its inner life. There was restrained dissatisfaction between the people. Under such conditions, life for members was heavy and wearisome; it affected everyone's nerves and deprived people of strength and energy, which were exactly the most necessary things for them now.

Among the Elizabetpol and Kars peoples things were different. They came to Canada with means—and some families with large means. True, there were enough poor among them, but at the same time, power here was on the side of the rich and the well-to-do. These, with few exceptions, at once set up a different life. "Each for himself" was their guiding principle. It must be said that the Kars and Elizabetpol peoples stand much lower in their moral development than do the Wet Mountain Doukhobors, who may be considered the best group of all. For example, in quarantine the Kars Doukhobors always tried to avoid settling near the Wet Mountain people, as they knew that the latter were poor and that they would have to use their money to help them. They looked for lands in Quebec or spoke of the United States and ended by settling three hundred miles from the Wet Mountain people in the region of Prince Albert, where they would be out of reach.

They took with them a small number of the poor who had been in their party and whom they exploited as far as possible; and the poor went because "near the rich you can live from a new beginning, and then we shall see!"

Still those communities which had been formed by the Kars and Elizabetpol peoples immediately stood out and still represent the most cooperative villages, strong in community life.

The Kars and Elizabetpol peoples, with the exception of the just mentioned communities, live by families. Neither have common treasuries. Livestock and equipment are often personal property; only a part belongs to the villages. But in hauling baggage and provisions the rich help the poor, giving them livestock for the purpose. Those of the poor who wish to, go out to work. Their earnings become their personal property. Among the Elizabetpol people, there are poor people indebted to the rich. The Cyprus (Wet Mountain) people live in communities. Each village is a commune. Earned money is expended for the needs of the whole village. All the Wet Mountain people of the Northern Settlement also live in village communes.

Canada
Assiniboia
Northern Settlement
July 2, 1899.

The following paper came to the North Settlement on one of the loads which arrived from Yorkton today.

June 25, '99.

Very Important

We ask that this not be held but passed on from village to village in order so that not one village will be left but all will have heard.

We wish to have a discussion with all the brethren: 1) On what we are to subsist? 2) As we are all brethren as one, so we should eat as one. It is important that their should be no grumbling about each other. 3) Also to consult about everything else.

For this purpose, we, all the Cyprus people, ask that from each village two respected elders should come on the sixth day of July; that is, on Thursday.

We are writing to the Wet Mountain (North Settlement) people and to the Kars and Elizabetpol peoples to arrive without delay on the above-mentioned date.

The place for the meeting is where the Tambov people are now; that is, on the South Settlement.

This is to be passed on in order on the North Settlement. Each village must sign that it has heard and give the name of the village on this page.

Vasili Potapoff

On the back of the well-soiled paper were the signatures of those villages which had read it.

Vasili Potapoff was one of the most respected of Doukhobors elders. He was still very young, no more than thirty or thirty-five years of age, but his distinguished mind, unusually gentle character, the purity marking his personal life and his modesty make him one of the notable people not only among Doukhobors but in any place in any group of people. He was one of those rare people who attract to themselves the love of everyone. A stranger to all kinds of Pharisaism, he acknowledged perfectly well the shortcomings of his fellow believers. Thanks to this, his great love for the whole "brotherhood" and to its separate members was devoid of any kind of unjust partiality, that particular narrow sectarian worship of it, which is often seen in the mass of Doukhobors. He was continually absorbed in concerns for improving the material life of the brethren and, most important, in anxieties about their moral perfection in which he saw the sole meaning of life for himself as for others.

And what could be better, from the point of view of the Christian-Doukhobor, than communal, brotherly life where people, guided by love for one another, divide equally among themselves—where there are no hungry, poor people depressed by fate and by rich people? Potapoff dreamed of this ideal "real, just life" day and night. He lived and breathed it. It was his vision. And while he did not like to battle uselessly over this matter, everyone could see it in his bright thoughtful eyes, his open, inspired face and his gentle smile.

The first question in the notice—"How must we subsist?"—concerned the structure of external material life; that is, where to find earnings whether to seek loans for purchase of livestock, whether to buy it on credit, and so on. It was very important. It had to be considered—that was true. But important as it was, Potapoff's idea expressed in the second point—"And since we are brothers as one so we must eat as one"—was a thought that lived in the depth of the soul of every Doukhobor, yes, and probably in every person. Its importance overshadowed the first question. It had been sounded powerfully like a trumpet calling people to the fight. It had brought responses one way or another in all hearts and had compelled many to feel guilty before the brotherhood and before their conscience. And, of course, it was the reason why the elders so punctually in good time began to prepare for the appointed date in the South Settlement where the conference was to take place.

Canada
Assiniboia
South Settlement
July 6, 1899.

The elders who had something to say to the meeting sat at a long table which stood outside, by the wall of one of the buildings. There, also, sat C. St. John and V. Bonch-Bruevich. On the rows of benches opposite, about sixty respected elders were crowded. When he left for Europe, D. Hilcoff handed over matters to me, and so I used the meeting to talk to the Doukhobors about earnings, taking land, purchase and delivery of provisions, livestock, and other matters. It had been suggested also that I keep the minutes of the meetings.

On the front benches, motionless as statues of Mammon, sat the figures of the Elizabetpol and Kars elders. Dressed in new jackets, good Russian boots, red-faced, haughty, grand, an air of coarseness, stubbornness and spiritual cold wafts from them. Among them in their worn remnants, much knocked about by the world, sat the Cyprus and other Wet Mountain people, with pinched nervous faces and attentive, though calm, eyes. And the elders from Thunder Mountain (North Settlement) sat quietly behind the table on the ground, leaning their backs on the logs of the building.

"We can hear very well here," said H. Zeebarev quietly, sitting down beside Melesha and smiling at him broadly.

Melesha sat with weary face shrunken into a little lump, his feet, covered in torn moccasins, pulled under him. His worldly eyes laughed as he examined the Elizabetpol people sitting opposite him.

"What about Vasya Popoff? Did he not come to the meeting?" one of the Cyprus people asked.

"No, it seems he has done his part," answered Melesha quickly.

"Yes, he has become a very old man," explained Zeebarev. "It is uncomfortable for him to travel such a distance. After all it must be sixty versts here—is that an easy matter? Only such a lively creature as this can come to you here." Zeebarev said this, lovingly glancing at Melesha.

"Easy! What can one say!" Melesha reproachfully shook his head.

The conference at first began to discuss small matters. The holes dug for clay must be filled. Wells must be fenced, we must discuss certain household questions, and so on. Among other things the elders spoke of iron stoves which had been placed in the blockhouses for common use. What is to be done with them? After a little consultation, it was decided to divide them among villages since they were purchased with the bonus funds.

Discussing the question, "How shall we subsist?", the elders expressed the thought that it was essential for all to take work. Although it was not a fitting thing—these different kinds of hired work—nevertheless, until the loan comes we must feed ourselves somehow. One of the Cyprus people said "If our flour lasts a month, that will be good, or it may not last even that. And then where will we get flour?"

"All the same, I will tell you," disagreed a moody elder with a sad face, "we will never get on our feet from these right of way cuts and pegs.* Our work is land working. Plough and harrow—these are our tools. But as long as we have no livestock and equipment, there will be nothing."

"The elder is speaking the truth; that's right."

"That's it," voices are heard.

"And where will we get the livestock and equipment?" a short man asked, turning to the meeting, and at once answered himself. "I think the one hope is a loan; nothing else."

"In a word," said one man sitting at the table nodding his head affirmatively and positively after each word, "in a word, the whole community must take up the case, to hurry up a loan to speed up this matter as much as possible. Otherwise, we will all perish. Do I speak right or no?"

"It is absolutely necessary to hurry the matter. There is nothing more to be said about it."

"Everything rests on realizing a loan."

After a lively discussion of this theme, the Wet Mountain people resolved to ask McCreary, Archer and the Russian friends to hasten a loan for them as the state of affairs did not permit delay.**

---

*Surveyor's pegs for marking earth for moving.
**The discussion here is about a loan which the Doukhobors wanted to arrange with the Canadian government or some banks for all Doukhobors without exception. They had in mind acquiring livestock and land equipment with this money, to begin working the land without loss of time for earnings. Earnings, it seemed to the Doukhobors at that time, would not only fail to provide equipment but would not even be enough to feed them. The Doukhobors were not accustomed to work outside, other than land work, and came to it very reluctantly. This loan, which was to be made against the land taken up by the Doukhobors at 8% per annum (the normal Canadian interest), did not take place. The Doukhobors rejected it themselves as by winter their affairs were so improved that they no longer needed the loan.

"If we could only write to grandfather* or the Quakers," a timid voice murmured.

"To write what?" the elders turned to him.

Before them was a famished, worn figure, with grey emaciated face and with dark circles around his eyes. For some moments he did not answer, shifting from one foot to the other.

"About our extremity," his sad, monotonous voice was heard. "Perhaps somehow donations would come or something."

There was an awkward silence.

"Who knows what?" The elders glance at one another undecidedly.

Zeebarev, grimacing bitterly, turned his head.

"Good grief," he said, with pain in his voice. "That's enough about donations! This is only temptation, nothing more. He speaks of things that are embarrassing to hear. What kind of donations do you want? Have people not helped a great deal? Do you need livestock? Let all the village go out to the right of way cut or to the pegs (for earth work). You will have livestock and flour and everything. Oh, no! Everyone wants to go to some farmer to hire out in order to be farther away from the community so as to put money in his pocket where no one will know how much money he has. Each hiding from the other—what good comes of it? Nothing good—only bad! One might have lots of money, but no good will come of it. It will go for trifles. But let the whole village go and take firm hold of wage earnings. There's your start! Do not worry that there is no donation! You cannot have enough donations for our community. Is it possible to bring in enough to feed all our people? Think for yourself. From them there would only be quarrelling, anger; nothing else. Why should one sit and wait for donations? Come to us at Thunder Mountain—we now have work. As long as we have hands, we will live!"

"No use talking. If the whole village would take hold, there is nothing better."

"Yes, but can you get along with our people?"

"True," everyone looked around. "The people have weakened greatly, greatly weakened. All the trouble comes from that."

"There is no harmony of any kind," grumbled the elders.

For the hundred thousandth time the endless argument that livestock and wagons bought from the bonus had been divided unfairly among the villages began again.

"Now what have they given us? A pair of oxen and a horse for one hundred and seventy persons. And what will we do with the horse? Tell me, please? In Spasskaya village there are fewer souls and they have a

---

*L.N. Tolstoy

shorter distance to travel and they were given two pairs of horses and a wagon that is not like ours."

"Why say that?" the Spasskaya villagers defended themselves. You know yourself what kind of teams they are. Our foursome is not worth your oxen. One horse is entirely useless, a cripple. There is no harness for him. He pastures with the other only for appearances. I said we should not take it or it would be counted as if we have three horses and that's the way it has turned out. Can anything be hauled by it? Tell me, is it possible?"

"Why do you talk so foolishly? Look at the record. How much was paid for your horses and how much for our oxen and horse? How can one compare them? It's completely different!"

"Again, the record does not tell all. Agreed, that for ours more had been paid, but how much have they hauled for the whole society— baggage and provisions—how much have they moved? How much have they been harmed by changing drivers before they came to us? You know yourself. And yours had just been bought."

The argument was endless. Figures were mentioned to the last cent. The amount was divided by the number of persons in the village. Then all this was applied to animals, wagons and finally there was not a village satisfied with what had come to it by the division of the elders.

"The best thing would be if one were to cut with an axe, into equal parts, the horses, cows, harness and wagons. Then we would have a fair division," laughs Melesha good-naturedly.

To hear these endless quarrels from the outside was gloomy and depressing, and after hearing them for whole days, it was not difficult to accuse people of greed, quarrelsomeness and pettiness. But one needed only to imagine the conditions under which the Doukhobors were living at that time, all that they had lived through till this moment, and then instead of making accusations you would wonder how people quarrelled so little and why they had not fought and fallen out permanently among themselves.

Let us take for example the village of Laybomirovka (North Settlement), where for one hundred and fifteen persons there was not a single horse, and only one cow and a pair of oxen, of which one has fallen sick. And the people there must build, and skid logs from the woods, and plough, and more important, haul provisions for sixty or seventy versts or further. It went without saying that the Laybomirovka villagers did not go without bread. Other villages helped them load their bags, but how much could they help one another when for all thirteen villages, with 1403 inhabitants, there were in all eighteen teams of livestock, even less, because some of them were always sick. If one looked more thoroughly into their conditions, I repeat, one could only marvel how little these people complained and quarrelled.

The conference continued with people divided up into several groups. Then Vasili Potapoff began to talk on the point that "being brothers as one, we must all eat as one." He spoke briefly, simply, without pathos, without "pitiful words," with a calm, slightly vibrating voice, striving not to become agitated, as this is not allowed for a Doukhobor—it is considered bad form. Behind this calm and almost indifferent intonation was felt deep unshakable confidence in the rightness of his idea and a passionate desire to see it put into practice.

He showed that the differences between Doukhobors, first of all, interfere with their getting on their feet to acquire necessary equipment to become real masters.

"It is a difficult time now and all must gather strength and, gathered together in one whole, must struggle with need, hunger and cold."

He proposed to all Wet Mountain, Elizabetpol and Kars people, to all Doukhobors living in Canada, that they unite into one community, with one treasurer for all its members. Every earned cent would be brought to this official and an elected committee of elders would look after this money for the needs of the whole community. Provisions purchased from earned money, crops taken off their own fields—all this would be divided evenly among all.

"Who are the Kars Doukhobors, or Elizabetpol, or Wet Mountain? What are these divisions for?" he said. "Now they have divided into villages and each village seems to be another people or nation. Well, then, if a hungry brother is in Spassovka and you are from Michailovka, do you have no concern for him? Are you concerned only about the Michailovka people? Are the others foreign, or what? It is high time we forgot about these Michailovka, Effremovka, Kars, Wet Mountain people if we in our hearts wish to be genuine Christians! As we call ourselves the Christian Community of Universal Brotherhood, we must live up to this in detail. There is no place for further division— enough of jealousy, quarrelling, discord of all kinds. We have forgotten about our precepts, and now, like sheep we struggle vainly. We have become confused. Let us live in one Christian community so that one brother will have no jealousy of another. All should live together as befits genuine Christians."

Potapoff's eyes burned with a bright light. He had forgotten the "good tone." His swarthy cheeks turned red from excitement. The setting sun gently embraced his well-formed figure with its caressing golden rays and, penetrating among long, lilac, stretching shadows for the last time, cast over him its warm sinking light.

"Well then, elders, do you accept my word or not? What do you say?" he asked of the silently sitting elders.

The Elizabetpol and Kars elders could be seen to squirm uncomfortably in their tight jackets. During Potapoff's speech they exchanged significant glances many times. The silence became strained. Finally, "What could be better than one community?" said a sturdy Elizabetpol man, with coarse greying moustache and shining face. His grey eyes flitted from object to object, carefully avoiding the figure of Potapoff.

"For all to be together," grunted his neighbour.

"The most important thing, in truth, by Christian law," undecided comments were heard. These phrases, it was apparent, came with difficulty, being pulled out of the throat to hang in the air without purpose. The situation was not easy. Not to agree to live a community life, to disagree publicly, to speak against the community out loud before all brethren, would be entirely impossible. It would be unseemly in the peasant sense of the word; that is, it wouldn't belong.

Fortunately for the Elizabetpol and Kars people, H. Zeebarev began to speak.

"You are thinking very well, Vasya. There is no need to look for anything better," he said in a thoughtful voice, a tone of deep sympathy. "That is true, only I think to do this will be difficult."

"Difficult, yes," agreed Potapoff.

"My brother, there is a long distance between us. Just look at where you are and where we are. How is a common treasury to be kept? Or, let us say, some matter needs to be considered by the whole community—when can the elders gather to a meeting? Now we have come here by travelling fifty to sixty versts, and we must go the same to return. It is difficult and inconvenient. This must be considered as fully as possible."

"Must be considered, yes indeed," called the gladdened elders.

"It's not such a simple matter."

"Inconvenient—that is important!"

"Must be thoroughly considered!"

Some of the elders rose, some remained on the benches. All spoke at once, divided into several groups. Really only a few were deciding the question on its merits. With the majority, the matter had been decided long ago at the time of Potapoff's speech. They were occupied only with a search for a decent form of refusal.

It was late; soon it would be night; but the elders were still arguing, talking of the difficult matter and no one spoke directly.

"Well, then," began Melesha decisively and somewhat inquiringly, "have you thought of it, elders, or no? It is time to finish. It is already—"

"Yes it's time. It is night outside."

"According to us," continued Melesha, "there is no need to take much time. In a word, let every village say now: does it agree to a community, to community life as Vasya was inviting us all, to a single brotherhood, or no? Without evasion," he said with serious eyes. "After all, no one is pulling you unwillingly by the tongues, to prevent you from refusing."

"What about yourself? Can you give agreement to this for the whole village?" angrily asked an Elizabetpol elder with heavy eyebrows and covetous face. Standing near Melesha, he looked sideways at him scornfully over his shoulder from above, examining his thin figure in an old jacket worn through on one shoulder. He seemed to be greatly dissatisfied with Melesha for making such a decisive statement on the matter.

"Of course. Why did the people choose me? Why did I drag myself here? I vouch for my village."

"All the same, that will not do for us. We cannot give agreement without the village. We are not empowered to do this."

"And if we were now speaking of separate life? How would it be then? Then probably you would know what to say for your village," jokingly says Melesha, looking for approval from the elders of the North Settlement. "In a word," he almost shouted, jumping up from the ground with childlike simplicity, "Village of Troitskoye on Thunder Mountain; elder, Emelian Kanigan; agreed to community."

While his village was being signed up he stood alongside the table and followed the writing.

"Now let every village say how they wish to live."

All were uncomfortable. Separate voices were heard:

"We are not empowered for this!"

"There's no way to do this without consultation with the village."

"This would be alright for other matters but for this one must make proper enquiries so there will not be underhand behaviour afterwards."

After Melesha, several elders from the Northern Settlement came to the table and asked to sign up their villages for the community. Orlov and Tambov villages (Wet Mountain people from the South Settlement) also expressed their agreement though less decisively. The majority of elders said more and more loudly that they were not sufficiently empowered to give such decisions at this meeting. Finally the majority gained the upper hand. The Elizabetpol and Kars people insisted they had insufficient authority and some of the elders of the Northern Settlement did not agree to a single community because of the great distances separating their villages from the South Settlement.

For this reason the final decision on the question was postponed until July 25. Someone suggested that the decisions be given by a written statement rather than in person so as to allow greater freedom for expression of views. By July 25 each village was to deliver written lists in which each family would sign whether it was "agreed" or "not agreed." If the paper should not state, it would be taken to mean "not agreed." With this decision the meeting of July 6 concluded and the elders dispersed and went home.

Despite the fact that not a single voice spoke against Potapoff's idea of uniting all Canadian Doukhobors into a single community (except for several villages from Thunder Mountain, motivated in their disagreement by the great distances separating them) Vasili Potapoff, Melesha, and other confirmed community supporters completely lost confidence in the success of their enterprise after this decision of the elders.

"Well, now nothing will come of it," said Melesha, waving his arms hopelessly.

Vasili Potapoff remained sadly silent.

Canada
Assiniboia
North Settlement
Village of Michailovka,
July 10, 1899.

After returning home, the elders of the North Settlement gathered on July 9, in the village of Michailovka, for a final answer to the proposal of Vasili Potapoff.

Here are the minutes of this meeting, the consequences of which were so important to the Northern Settlement.

"Meeting of Elders of North Settlement, July 9, 1899."
To the proposal of the Cyprus people to live as one community with a single treasury for all, we reply:
1) All thirteen villages of Thunder Hill will live a communal life and will have one treasury common to all thirteen villages, but independent of South Settlement, principally because of the great distances from one another, which would make it difficult to gather meetings for decisions of communal questions.
On the other hand, the elders request that at the first need in the South Settlement they turn to them for help, and promise that it will always be given provided they have the means.
2) Flour (carload in Yorkton, 620 bags) will be used for all who need it in the South Settlement without return. Those who need it must apply to the council of elders that meets Mondays in the village of Michailovka.
3) Money from all subsequent earning will go to the hands of the treasurer selected by the society, and will be spent only by general agreement.

4) A letter of thanks is to be written to Dr. Mercer for his help to the sick.

North Settlement is provided with flour to about August 22. Besides, there are about 600 bags of flour in Cowan, but due to lack of roads it cannot be taken into account. This flour must be used mainly for the railroad workers belonging to the North Settlement or South Settlement without distinction.

From these minutes it was clear that all thirteen villages of North Settlement from July 9 decided to join into a single community as proposed by Potapoff. If they separated from the South Settlement, this resulted from external conditions unfavourable for unity.

Several Words About the South Settlement

Canada
Assiniboia
July 26, 1899

As was to be expected, a single community was not formed in the South Settlement. Very few listings were gathered by July 25. Notes on them were very unclear and careless; all were written on scraps of paper. In general, it was apparent that people were evading the community and doing everything possible to suppress this question and forget about it completely. These efforts were successful. No one mentioned "a single community." Among the inhabitants of the South

Doukhobors of the Thunder Hill Colony moving supplies from Yorkton in 1899.

Settlement several villages developed with unusually harmonious, strong community structures, and the remainder represented, in the main, unorganized groups, sometimes with impossible routines for inner life.

It will be enough to describe what went on in Yorkton when carloads of flour arrived, to understand how undisciplined people had become. In Yorkton a large number of Doukhobor teams always stood awaiting trains from Winnipeg. As soon as a carload of flour was put in place, people drove up and, taking it by storm, loaded up as much as they could take away. As to whose flour it was, or who sent it there, no one asked. There were instances of flour sent by me from Winnipeg on behalf of Doukhobors working on the railroad or other places (which these workers were sending to their co-villagers) being taken by people who had nothing to do with these workers and who often were better off.

People of the Northern Settlement had to struggle for several days to reach Yorkton on their famished livestock to get bread (flour). All the time they were away, the women ploughed the land and skidded logs from the forest themselves. Arriving in Yorkton, the men found instead of a carload of flour merely several bags. The rest had been taken by no-one-knows-whom. Once I had to spend four months getting information about people who had taken away a whole carload of flour (400 bags) which had been purchased on credit for the workers of the Northern Settlement.

With time this was all straightened out, but I am speaking now of the early times. Whenever I came to Yorkton I heard endless complaints.

"There is no flour!"

"The bread is all gone! We borrowed an ox from the neighbours— ours had fallen sick—but by the time we got here, there was no flour. We waited until the next train but again got nothing; when the crowd fell to, we didn't get a crumb."

"Our flour was taken by the Elizabetpol people. What are we to do, wait some more or what?"

Sometimes I had to buy several bags on credit at the local stores and send it home with them, because by the time another train came there would be hunger in the village.

It was almost impossible for a person from the outside to help. After sending flour from Winnipeg for the Northerners I asked C. St. John or A. Bodnianski to look after the receiving of it, but this did not help at all. The majority of the Doukhobors during this trying time took no account of where the flour came from, who sent it and why.

There was some misunderstanding about the "bonus," the loan, the idea that the government was concerned, that friends had sent gifts, and so on. Few knew about the real extent of the "bonus." To them it appeared endless. That the government itself disbursed the bonus and did not sufficiently inform the Doukhobors about how much of it was left was Canada's serious mistake. Had it turned this money over to the Doukhobors, I am convinced they would have become established twice as quickly and they would not have had that difficult period of which I am now speaking, when the people hungered, ate only bread and at the same time by-passed excellent earnings, confident that today, or tomorrow, a loan or donation would come, or that friends would not let them down; and so on.

Canada
Assiniboia
Yorkton
July 27, 1899.

The Doukhobors were living through a critical moment—a time of let-down and weakness, both physical and spiritual. At meetings it became necessary to use all means to convince them that there was nothing to depend on besides earnings, that bread was being bought from the last of the bonus and that there was no money for further purchases. Calculations were made; flour on hands was checked; but none of this helped.

"Yes," one heard, "it is very, very difficult. Who knows how it will be later on?"

But one felt that they had their reasons, that they were depending on something. Sometimes after a meeting someone would confidentially shake your shoulder and say something like:

"Don't fear, L.A., we will not perish. You will write, Vladimir* will write, Sister Vera** will write, and again you will see, we will not perish."

When you began to disagree, they did not believe you.

"You won't let the people perish."

Where exactly to write? Few Doukhobors knew and besides, this wasn't their concern.

"Somebody, somewhere, somehow, will help."

Sometimes this led to curious results. Today in Yorkton I saw on the square in front of the station a young boy of sixteen years of age with a pair of huge oxen which it appeared he had just brought from somewhere far away. The oxen were dusty—the boy was, too. Of what

---

*Vladimir—V.D. Bonch-Bruevich
**Sister Vera— V. Velichkina

surprising beauty was this young man—tall, well proportioned, tanned as if cast in bronze! His face was innocent. Manly eyes breathed freshness and health. In the real meaning of the word, this was a child of nature. Together with the huge oxen, calmly looking ahead with beautiful, moist eyes, he attracted the attention of everyone. And hardly anyone glancing at this vital group bursting with life did not admire it. Several older Doukhobors had gathered around the boy. With a calm, somewhat naive look, he was telling them something. The elders looking at him smiled.

"And here comes L.A.," one of them said. "This is he himself," the elders pointed out.

The young man, together with the oxen, moved towards me.

"Good-day, L.A.," he began.

I greeted him.

"Our elders sent me here to you. I am from N. (he named a village) from Good Spirit Lake.*"

Elizabetpol people whom I didn't know at all lived there. It was very far away. I asked him what he needed.

"In our village we have begun to run out of bread. So they sent me for flour, because our neighbours refused to haul for us. Earlier the neighbours hauled, but now they have discontinued—so they sent me. We have only oxen," he pointed with his whip in the direction of the oxen, "but we have no wagon. So they asked me to find you without fail so that you would get us a wagon," he ended, looking at me seriously with simple eyes. He was so firm in his confidence that I could, by some unknown means find a wagon, that, regardless of the lack of logic, I could not laugh. I imagined how back in the village the elders who had sent him sat waiting for bread which the young man would bring in a new shiny wagon with red wheels.

I tried to find out from him where this wagon could be obtained. Perhaps his co-villagers were working somewhere and I could get the wagon on credit for their labour. There were no workers of any kind. And my questions embarrassed the young man. He didn't expect them. Regrettable as it was, I could not find a wagon. On being refused, the young man became embittered, and with a hurt look brought the oxen to a stand. Apparently he could not understand why he was not given a wagon—after all, he had nothing on which to haul flour!

Fortunately, exactly at this time there was a Quaker in Yorkton who had come to see the Doukhobors. He had helped several families and in conversation with me said that he still had some money which he would like to use to help the Doukhobors, and asked what he could do. I told him the story and the Quaker, laughing at the simplicity of the

*Good Spirit Lake—more popularly known as Devil's Lake.

young man and his elders, bought them a wagon in the nearby warehouse.

If only you could have seen the face of the young man when he hitched his team to the newly-varnished green wagon! Loading it to the top with bags of flour, he solemnly sat on the high springed coach box and started on his long trip. His face beamed with excitement which infected all those gathered around him with joy. Even the wagon itself, it seemed, laughed with a happy laugh, its varnish flashing in the rays of the setting sun. With the good wishes of all, the oxen slowly started, the wagon rolled gently and, sparkling with its bright red spokes, solemnly drove out of the town, taking with it the happiest person that I have ever seen.

*   *   *

When you asked the elders where they would get flour when the last reserves were gone, they usually answered that the government would send it to them on credit.

I had to fabricate a story that if the Doukhobors were to take even one bag of flour on credit, then the whole bonus would be considered a debt. This story produced a certain pressure on the Doukhobors; but until they understood fully the state of their affairs, until they became convinced that their salvation lay in earnings, things went very badly.

Of course, I am speaking in this instance of the mass of Doukhobors, of the majority. A few people like Zeebarev, Potapoff, Popoff, Chernenkoff and many other more prominent Doukhobors saw very well that no donations and "gifts," as the Doukhobors called donations, would help and did everything possible to bring the crowd out of this apathetic condition. They were literally straining themselves, striving to tell people of the real state of affairs. But they, too, had little success at this time. The crowd at meetings made strong people such as Zeebarev weep in frustration and anger. All the leading elders unanimously confirmed that among Doukhobors there had never been such weakness and dissolution.

"The people have weakened, greatly weakened," they said sorrowfully to one another, shaking their heads.

Fortunately, such prostration, if one may call it that, continued for but a relatively short time. And to blame them for this temporary weakness is not warranted if we remember in what impossible material conditions they have had to live for the past several years. One must take into account all the losses, deaths, sicknesses, poverty, hunger and finally—most important—that great loss of nervous strength, that stress in which they have spent the last few years, which, of course, could not have left them untouched. They were tired out by great deeds, as one of the medical assistants expressed it very accurately. Added to this were the depressing conditions of life in which they found themselves at the time of their settlement on the land, conditions seeming sometimes hopeless. You will see that it was difficult for people not to stagger at the accumulation of such sad circumstances.

The conditions of life really were difficult. Here, for instance, is a letter from one of the nurses [E. Markova] describing them:

> I went around all the villages under my care and wept—anaemia, undernourishment, signs of scurvy, and so on.
>
> They eat bread, only bread, some kind of pickled grass and now the menu is varied by strawberries.
>
> Where there is a community they work surprisingly harmoniously. Young women bring bags of clay up the hill. Old women bring water and mix the clay with their feet; then make bricks. Girls bring sticks from the forest, boys cut them and out of all this men build places to live. But I do not know whether it will be possible for them to spend a cold winter in these temporary dwellings.
>
> For the whole village there is only one pair of horses by which large logs are carefully hauled.
>
> Is there hope of receiving medicines? I have almost none now.
>
> If I take them from one of Yorkton's drug stores will someone pay, and will they give them to me? Of course all economy measures will be taken.
>
> My present place of living is Vasilievka. Anna Rabetz is in Effremovka which is near Armashi.

Whether the village communes of the Cyprus and other Wet Mountain people, and of several of the Kars people, were organized well or badly, nevertheless it was possible to live there. It was felt that the people helped one another as well as they could. And certain of these communities, because of the touching love existing among their members, and of their readiness to respond to the sufferings of others, actually reminded one of the time of the ancient Christians.

But among the Elizabetpol village disgraceful things sometimes occurred. At each meeting one could hear of wrangling among the Elizabetpol people and complaints of the poor about the pressures of the rich. Here, for example, is one story which dragged on for a long time taking up not a little time at each meeting until, thanks to the generosity of the Quakers, the poor, dependent on the rich co-villagers, received the means of freeing themselves from this Babylonian imprisonment.

In the Elizabetpol village "Novotroitskoe" there are in all 180 persons, 90 of them rich, 90 poor. While living in Selkirk where they wintered, the poor became indebted to their fellow villagers by forty-eight dollars and forty cents. After settling in their district, they borrowed from the rich another ten dollars and fifty-three cents for the purchase of shovels and forks. The total debt became $58.93. After moving to the villages, the poor borrowed another $448.50 for the purchase of horses. All this money the poor undertook to pay out of the big loan about which I wrote earlier. But when the creditors saw that the loan was being delayed and might never take place, they took from the poor the three horses they had bought with the borrowed money. The remaining $58.93 was still to be paid out of the big loan they expected.

Soon after this an Englishman, probably A. Maude, wishing to help the Doukhobors, sent them a sum of money as a loan. The village of Novotroitskoe received $250 of this money, with which two wagons and a horse were bought. Immediately after the purchase, the rich announced that they were taking the wagons and the horse for themselves.

"But there is our half in these wagons," cried the poor. "$125 of Maude's money belongs to us. How can you take it all?"

To this the rich answered that they were taking their half in payment of the debt.

"But our debt is only $58.93 and you are taking $125! There should still remain $66.07. At least give this to us. This way we have nothing on which to bring provisions or to plough—nothing!"

But the rich answered that they were taking the $66 for temporary use of the three horses which had been bought in the spring by the rich and taken back by them. They were taking this because the poor had brought provisions on them. And while the poor had hauled provisions not only for themselves but also for the rich, the matter remained. At all the meetings the Novotroitsky people raised this ugly matter and always without results.

And who could have helped them in the matter? The meetings of the South Settlement consisted mostly of the Elizabetpol elders and while the Cold Mountain people spoke more than once on behalf of the poor, their words did not receive attention.

All these squabbles, quarrels, eternal divisions of countless numbers of cattle (instead of combining the livestock and ploughing together and later dividing the harvest) gave the meetings an unpleasant character. The Cyprus people did not always attend the meetings of the South Settlement, nor did the Cold Mountain people, and the North Settlement, as has been said, fell behind the Southern Settlement and their meetings took on a disruptive character. One could not feel any organic connection among its members. The life of the Cyprus and Cold Mountain people of the South Settlement, based on community beginnings, went on independently of the Elizabetpol and Kars people. Among the Cyprus people lived Capt. Arthur St. John, an Englishman who had become attached to them and had done much for them in Cyprus. He continued to work for them and therefore they did not need my services. To work among the undependable, unstructured crowd of Elizabetpol and Kars people was exceptionally difficult and unproductive. Besides, this took a lot of time and it was physically impossible for me to go to all the places I was needed, a distance of 230 versts between Cowan and Yorkton, which had to be ridden on horseback. Because of this, matters were delayed in the North Settlement.

I completely gave up participation in any business of the South Settlement. It was possible to do this with a clear conscience, because at this time a certain A. Bodiansky arrived in Yorkton and took on the job of helping the South Settlement.

Later, I proposed to the South Settlement that they send workers to the railway earth work in the North area, where they could work under the same conditions as the Northerners.

*　*　*

Once, while driving past blockhouses where several Kars families still lived, I noticed nearby a small pointed tent.

"Who can be living here?"

When I came nearer a stout, good-natured Doukhobor woman came out. Thrusting her stomach forward, she place upon it a hand holding a sock and knitting needles; with the other hand she shaded her eyes from the sun.

"How do you do, L.A.?" she greeted me, smiling her widest good-natured smile. I greeted her.

"What are you doing here?" I expressed surprise.

I am knitting a sock, dear man. Here it is," she answered, showing it to me.

"I am not asking about that. I am asking why you are sitting alone here in the field."

"Oh, dear one, that is exactly my trouble," she spoke in a tearful voice. "I was overjoyed to see you, thinking you would take me to Orlovka. Look and see—I have little baggage," she said, raising a fold of the tent. There stood two huge iron-bound chests and a basket.

"But could your people not move you?" I asked.

"Heaven only knows! Nobody wants to put me on their team because mostly they pass by loaded and if it's the Orlovskys they say, 'Your husband is an Effremov man. Let the Effremov people move you. We have lots of our own.' But my husband is in Yakutia (Siberia) and, of course, I want to go to my relatives in Orlovka but they are sending me to Effremovka." The woman wept but continued to smile good-naturedly as if she were telling about a most pleasant incident. "Well, I have sat here a long time. The Effremovskys came along and I thought, let me go to Effremovka. From there it will be nearer, and perhaps I'll find a way to get to Orlovka. But they looked at me and didn't take me. They said, 'You belong to Orlovka. Let the Orlovskys take you.' So I sit here, my dear one; neither the one nor the other will take me. A little while ago an empty team passed and did not take me.

They say I am an Effremovka woman. 'Is it too difficult for them to move their own women?' Thank goodness the Kars people are nearby. I eat with them and sleep here. Their girl comes to spend the night with me. It is fearful for one alone in the field. If only you, dear man, would take me! Otherwise, how long will I sit here? Do a good deed—move me!" She bowed a deep bow to me, and looked in my eyes inquiringly with a kind friendly smile. "I am very tired of being alone."

With all my wish to help her, I could not do so. My narrow light buggy, designed for fast travel, could not accommodate one of her large chests, even were I as good natured as she herself. So she remained in the tent to knit socks, sitting on her goods, to await the Orlovka and Effremovka teams.

Life in the North Settlement
Canada
Cowan Station
August 1, 1899.

More than two hundred people came to the railroad earth works, as I wrote above, for the June 5 contract. After the meeting of the elders on July 9, it was decided that all thirteen villages would unite into one community with a single treasurer, and the earnings of these people would go to meet the needs of the whole community and become its common capital. At the same meeting, it was decided to use this capital solely for the purchase of flour. It was decided not to give money to anybody. The flour was to be stored in a provisions warehouse in the village of Michailovka, from which it would be issued to the villages. Such a state of affairs should have produced excellent results. In fact, most of the elders who participated in the meeting of July 9 looked to the future with the most joyous hopes. And what moral satisfaction they experienced taking such a decision, agreeing to begin in the new land a new life with the most righteous Christian ideals of community life!

All the same, reality did not justify these hopes. What happened was this.

The people did not come to work at once. They set off from each village in separate parties whenever they were able to get ready. The first to come to work was N. Zeebarev with the workers of his village. Some of the workers who left later than the others, arriving at the "little town" (Land Office, Swan River), lying half way to the place of work, did not go further. According to them it was more profitable for them to stop there and seek work from local residents or nearby farmers— more profitable because the money earned would become their personal property and would not be spent for flour which would later be issued to the villages. It was more profitable, too, because any Doukhobor could board in the place, which issued goods on credit from the warehouses. In every store one could buy whatever one needed. The traders readily issued the goods. They knew that their accounts would come out of the wages earned on the railway line. Trading in this way on the account of the rail line workers, they purchased butter, sugar, boots and, without going to work, wandered home. Some of the workers, remaining two or three days at work, came to the conclusion that the work was somewhat heavy and it would be better to drop it and seek something else.

In this manner the number of workers on the line kept decreasing. The more determined of them continued by having members meet not by the day but by the hour. In a couple of weeks they too dropped the work, gathered their belongings and wandered home. Eventually, not a single Doukhobor remained on the line.

When I arrived at the North Settlement, I noticed several Doukhobors who had left the work party. In answer to the question as to why they had left for home so soon they answered that the work was altogether impossible, that from such work one could perish and the earnings were six kopeks per day.

"How did you find this out?" I asked.

"The elders have figured this out. It comes to six kopeks or even less."

"There are such swamps that you can't do anything."

"Impossible!" confirmed another.

I did not yet know what the trouble was but in conversation with the workers I felt something was wrong. There was a trace of embarrassment, an unwillingness to develop the theme. Identical word-for-word explanations aroused suspicion.

"Why do others find it possible to continue this work?" I asked.

"Wait, all will soon return. Who would work in such dire straits."

Aware that something was wrong I went to the place of work to investigate on the site. All that I had heard so far from the workers seemed extremely strange. English workers, I knew, considered this work very profitable. A good worker earned on such work one to three dollars per day, depending on the kind of place he struck. Frequently an Englishman came to work with a boy, when the daily earnings went to four dollars. How could it happen that the Doukhobors, such good workers, earned only six kopeks per day? Along the road to Cowan, time and again I met groups of Doukhobors returning home. They went hurriedly, stopping to drink tea somewhere under a bush. To all questions they reluctantly answered, as if with a learned phrase, "Six kopeks per day." "Impossible swamps." And so on.

186

In the "little town" I met the last group of workers. What a pitiful sight this crowd presented! Sunburned, thin, in torn jackets, they were spattered with thin mud above the knees. Few had boots on their feet. One had high rubber galoshes tied everywhere with string; another had old Indian moccasins. On their backs they carried their belongings; burkas, their reserves of bread, salt, tea. Over their knapsacks some had their jackets. Especially pitiful were boys of twelve and fourteen who stood by, looking with the large tired eyes of people pushed to the greatest degree of physical weariness, when everything seems to be happening in a dream, in some dull depressing fog.

And again I heard from all sides:

"Six kopeks per day."

"Better to die on dry land!"

"They give the English a selection, and to us the very worst." And so on.

Elders complained that the engineer did not let the Doukhobors select the better places along the line but showed them where they had to work, and selected all the poorer places.

"He drove the Troitsky people into such a flood that they couldn't do anything. You take a shovelful of this mud and before you can throw it on the wheelbarfow, half of it runs off on the ground."

"And the English stop to work wherever they wish," in a thin voice said one of the youngsters. "He lets them choose."

"On this work one can lose one's life."

"That's for six kopeks."

I hurried on to Cowan.

Turnbull met me with a troubled face.

"Oh, yes, your Doukhobors are strikers, yes, they are strikers. I swear by Ivan," he said with terror, stressing the word 'strikers!' "They have all gone away," he continued, "and I was unable to explain to them as there was no interpreter here. The weather is beautiful but the work is going so slowly. Why did they leave? What is the trouble?"

I liked the idea given by the engineer explaining the leaving of the Doukhobors as strikers, and I did not wish to disabuse him of the idea that they were strikers.

"They went away," I said, "because you gave them the worst places to work and did not let them choose. Besides, you let the English do so. They are altogether in the right! Either all must work where you say, or all may choose their place for work."

"But then no one will want to work in the bad places," he cried naively. "How shall I then build the line?"

I asked why the Doukhobors should work the poorer places for the same pay as those selecting their places.

"I didn't given them the poorest places at all. That's not true! Of course, there are some bad places, but I am not at all as dishonest as they tell you."

I proposed that we go together to the line to examine the work of the Doukhobors. Before going, we calculated how much the Doukhobors had earned during this time. It turned out that the Doukhobors had earned a clear income, after deductions for provisions, of fifty-six cents per day. While this was not the six kopeks per day they had insisted, it was all the same, too little. To question why the Doukhobors had earned so little, Turnbull answered:

"They worked very poorly, your Doukhobors. Yes, whenever you come, you see them conversing about something. Always. Sometimes all dropped work and gathered to talk. They must have lots to talk about." He laughed.

On the line I was convinced that half of the Doukhobor work places were bad, wet places. Here and there pools stood along the grade. I drew Turnbull's attention to this.

"Oh, they have only themselves to blame for this," he said. "Several times I took some of them and showed how this work could be done. It is essential to dig a canal at a certain distance from the grade through which all the water will flow and it will be dry. The earth from the canal can be used for the grade. But for some reason they did not want to do this. Yet these canals are as necessary as the grade! Now I will have to call day workers here. In future I shall deduct for this," he answered.

True. Walking past the English workers I saw that they first of all dug a canal. The English did not go after dry places. They preferred places covered with water. Letting the water out down a canal, they could work the moist land easily in large pieces and the work went well. All the same, the Doukhobors had bad places consisting, for example, of clay in which shovels stuck, where there were roots and stumps interfering with getting earth for the grade.

Returning to the office I said to Turnbull, "The Doukhobors will not work under the previous conditions. They ask that they be permitted, beginning at some point, to do all of the grade, the good and the bad places together." Turnbull did not agree to this. After a long argument about different conditions of new work we agreed on the following:

The Doukhobors would send enough men for finishing one difficult place along the way. This would require about one hundred men. Every worker in excess of this would be allowed to go along the line and select his place of work. All the poor places, including that for which the one hundred men were required, would be paid for at sixteen cents per cubic yard; others as formerly, would be paid for at fourteen cents per cubic yard.

Concluding this agreement, I proposed to the South Settlement that they send one hundred and fifty men. From the North Settlement two hundred could come. From these three hundred and fifty, one hundred would stay to complete the flooded place and two hundred and fifty would finish the bad places at sixteen cents per cubic yard. This would be a good earning. The South Settlement agreed to this proposal but in fact sent fewer than one hundred people. Some of these, meeting others returning from work along the way, and hearing of the six kopek earnings, returned home and only thirty arrived at the Northern Settlement.

When this party arrived at the Northern Settlement they sat there several days awaiting the local workers so as to go to the line all together. But the Northerners did not hurry. Twice a meeting was called to discuss this matter but each time so few came that the meeting did not take place. It seemed that the people were embarrassed to gather after what had taken place. At last the thirty people went home as the workers of the Northern District finally rejected this work.

No one wished to go out to work where the earnings would be in full view of the whole community and would be expended as community capital exclusively on flour at a time when there were other high priority needs which could not be provided from any other source. Up to this time, for example, the houses stood without windows. Soon, however, a third meeting was called for the final discussion of the question of earnings, to which elders from all the villages came in large numbers.

Canada
Assiniboia
North Settlement
Village of Michailovka
August 3, 1899.

It was a noisy meeting. For some time the confused elders looked at one another in bewilderment, as if unable to understand how it all could have happened. But soon, blaming others for the bad behaviour to the community, everyone began to feel that he was in the right and that others were to blame for the falling apart of the community.

"And see, the Stradaev villagers sent only boys, and the older men all remained at home."

"But someone had to build huts," answered the Stradaev people.

"All need to build huts, not only you," others retorted.

"And you did well that you came, threw a shovelful each, and then, 'good-day!' " the Stradaev people insisted. "As long as there is flour."

"All the same, people are working."

And so it went, on and on.

It was requested that the accounts for different goods that were bought for the work be read. In these accounts it was not shown who bought what; but all the goods were listed. The reading was interrupted by exclamations, questions of who could have bought one item or another.

"Four pairs of warm gloves! What is this? Somebody made a reserve for the whole family."

"Well done!"

"Butter, sugar, low boots, socks, sugar, butter—" A long list.

"Two pounds of tobacco!" I read on.

"What's that for?" elders asked one another with surprise, exchanging glances. Doukhobors do not smoke and such a purchase amazed them.

"Tell me, please—someone needed tobacco?"

"Who among us is smoking it?" Legebokoff asked in an inquisitive tone.

"Foo! Abomination!" the elders spat.

"This was taken for medicine when—" an indecisive guilty voice was heard from the back rows and broke off at once, remembering that only he who bought it could know about the tobacco. "And perhaps for smoking, who knows?"

"That's the way it looks," said a broad-shouldered Doukhobor with a husky voice, with a wide lower jaw and little dry eyes. "That's the way it goes. One who doesn't work parades about in new low boots, has tea with butter to his heart's content and will have flour. Others work for him. And those who work come home ragged and get by with bread alone. Go to work then and live for the community!"

"Best of all, let each village work for its own community and for none others. Then probably an unlimited number of people will come out to work."

"Then you may be sure each will strive to provide bread for his community for the winter."

After a long and heated argument among the elders of the community of thirteen villages, with the elders proposing that each village live as an independent community, the latter fairly easily gained majority. The remarkable thing was that until a meeting decided to divide by villages no one agreed to go back to work on the line.

"Better to die on dry land," called the elders, already bored by the stereotyped expression.

But as soon as the meeting decided to divide by villages, enquiries sprang up on all sides about the new conditions of work and when they could go out to work on the line, and so on. There was no doubt that everyone would come out to work. At once new rules were worked out for those going to this work. The meeting decided:

The Community of the Northern Settlement is put aside.

Each of the thirteen villages from today constitutes a separate community entirely independent of the remaining villages. The earnings of each village becomes its property which the community of each village deals with according to its discretion.

It was decided by all to send to the railway earth works altogether not fewer than 180 persons and if possible, more. On the job each village will take a separate section of the grade for which it receives its wages. None of the workers has the right to take goods from the railway warehouses or stores for the work. For necessary purchases all the workers of the Northern District will elect one elder, Vasilie Chernenkoff, who alone will buy all that is necessary for them. He will keep an account of how much each of the thirteen villages has taken during the time of work. No one else can do this.

It was decided to warn the merchants in the stores and warehouses so that they would not issue goods on credit to anyone other than Chernenkoff, as such purchases would not be paid for. This was necessary also to protect themselves from abuse by the merchants.

Any worker leaving work before the whole party will receive nothing except in cases where work is left due to illness.

Then arose the question of what to do with the future earnings—to give them to each village in cash or to buy flour for this money? At this time, it must be said, the reserves of flour were very small.

"Flour! Flour! L.A.!" cried the majority. "Just buy flour with all the earnings. We will then divide the flour among the villages."

All the same, voices could be heard for the issue of cash.

"Is there not much that people need now? Just see how ragged the people are. They need needle and thread and other things."

"Also a few livestock must be bought."

"Glass and putty must be bought sometime. We cannot stay on without windows."

A clamour arose. Heatedly arguing all along, Vasilie Chernenkoff suddenly jumped up as if pricked, and called out, overcoming everyone else:

"This is needed and that is needed and the other! You speak like children or fools. And what will you eat? Tell me! Eh? Enough!" cried Vasilie Chernenkoff in a frenzy. His nervous thin face turned pale, his eyes restlessly jumped from one face to another and with his hands he gestured so decisively and severely as if he were about to throw aside all the elders sitting in front of him somewhere far to one side. "The children will soon swell from hunger. We must have flour. That is the prime concern!"

"But we have become very impoverished, brothers," some protested indecisively. "What will you do then? There is nothing with which to sew on a button. That will not do either!"

"Without a button you can get by for the time being. All money should be used for flour. Nothing else!" continued Chernenkoff, flashing his eyes.

"With an empty stomach a button will not hold you," one of the elders supported Chernenkoff.

Talking some more, the elders agreed with Chernenkoff.

"Money will be spent on flour. Each of the thirteen villages will receive its earnings in flour. If you take the money in your hands, it will run right through your fingers. Then there will be no flour and no money," the elders said.

Canada
Cowan Station
August 8, 1899.

This time a large number of workers came. They came to the work briskly, energetically. There was no mention of it being better to die on dry land. Each village sent everybody it could; some even sent women. Nicolai Zeebarev took nearly all the men from his village and even his twelve-year-old son. This thin boy with an intelligent, pleasant face walked beside his father with a pack on his shoulders to earn money for flour, horses, wagons. The villages emptied at once. At home there remained only women, old men and the sick, unfit for work. But even those remaining in the villages worked energetically, digging the fields, gathering wood for the winter, dragging logs from the forest for barns, granaries and other buildings, digging wells, plastering the buildings with clay which they mixed in big holes with their own feet for lack of livestock.

On the line a 'competition-to-the-death' developed among the villages to see who would earn most. People strained themselves, running ahead of others, seeking better pieces of the right of way so as not to get behind. The Doukhobors worked the long Canadian day, rising before dawn and stopping work in the late twilight. No one wanted to leave work first. Difficult places were taken by storm on the run.

In these energetic people, greedily seizing work, robbing themselves of sleep and rest for the benefit of work, it was difficult to recognize those limp, lazily-scratching workers who so recently sought all kinds of reasons for dropping the shovel and harrow on the grade to gather in a group and talk away endlessly to pass the day more quickly. Life throbbed like a spring. At once the usual energy of the Doukhobors awakened their thirst for creative labour, that irresistible stubbornness which is the main distinguishing characteristic of the Doukhobors, and thanks to which they soon become the wealthiest group in whatever area fate drops them.

So as to fully and fairly comprehend the single-minded energy with which the Doukhobors came to the railroad work after the above-described meeting, one must know to what degree they dislike hired labour, especially non-agricultural.

Instinctively, in their hearts, Doukhobors like only agricultural labour—labour in nature. Only in work on the land, which they attack with all their strength, do they see the straight, natural and sinless source of life. Only here each Doukhobor feels himself master; he is in his own sphere. Here he is subject to no one. Here he feels that walking behind the plough is fulfilling the will of his God, and that together with surrounding nature he constitutes one harmonious, indivisible whole, subject only to one Master who created all.

On the railroad where working conditions were better and the work itself was lighter, it is hard to recognize in this bored, pining, even though assiduous, day worker, that Hercules, Mikula Selianinovich*, walking with a strong bright look to meet the wind of the field with a scythe in his hands or behind the clumsy, heavy plough. They prefer pulling the plough themselves, hitching into it twelve pairs together with their wives, to doing incomprehensible, to them unnecessary, uninspired, work, where, according to them, "reigns Satan rather than God." This explains, in part, the indifferent, reluctant attitude of the Doukhobors towards earnings.

Canada
Fort Pelly
August 13, 1899.

I came upon this picture, yesterday, while passing near the village of Osvobozhdenie (Liberation):

A no-longer-young, bowed woman, with wrinkles on her hands and with a brown, dried-up face, together with a brown old man on bent legs, and a youth as long as a pole, with rope harnesses over their shoulders were silently pulling a home-made wagon on which lay a large, fresh pine log. They were so absorbed in this work that they did not notice me. Barely moving one foot past the other, all ragged and dusty they slowly moved down the road. The ropes cut deeply into their thin shoulders but they did not change position and continued to walk

---

*Folklore hero, defender of the peasants.

without stopping, looking at the ground with pale tired faces, on which streamed shining stripes of abundantly flowing perspiration. And with each turn of the crooked wheels the home-made wagon squealed sadly, as if it too were in pain.

As the group drew near, the youth raised his head and without straightening up, stopped. His companions also stopped and raised their heads. I asked where they were dragging the log.

"We want to build a barn. The oxen went to Yorkton for flour; it's already the eighth day since they left," the youth said with a breaking voice, blinking with little expressionless eyes and then went silent. "Who knows whether they will bring it or not," he added with an uncertain voice. "Meanwhile, we are bringing logs, little by little."

The old man and woman remained silent, breathing heavily, glad of the unexpected rest.

After a close look, I realized that I had known the young man earlier. This was Elia Soprikin. He had lain in bed more than a year with legs swollen by rheumatism. Only recently, a couple of months ago, had he begun to walk.

"Well, now you are able to walk?" I asked him.

"No, I still can't walk properly. When I step hard, they begin to ache."

"And you have become still thinner than before!"

"Yes," he calmly answered. "If the food were good I would be heavier, but with bread only and not enough of that . . . "

After talking a little more we said goodbye.

"Goodbye," said all three and, seeing me off with tired eyes, slowly turned and fell into their agonizing harnesses. Squeaking loudly as if sighing, the heavy log moved and the wheel squealed again, leaving a wide, crooked track on the dusty road. They had a long way to drag it, more than a versta.

The sun threw its burning rays. The grasshoppers chirped merrily. The air was full of the sweet aroma of honey and the sleepy smell of stirring aromatic plants. In such weather one wanted to lie down somewhere on the thick grass and look into the deep blue sky, not thinking about anything. But the three bent, ragged, thin people did not notice their surroundings. To the squeaking of the wagon they looked only at the dusty road, breathing intense heat and felt nothing but the cutting pain on their shoulders. In this way those who remained in the villages, unfit for real earnings, spent their time. The rest all went to the line after being seen off by their weeping women.

On the Line
Canada
Town of Cowan
August 19, 1899.

Working together, the Doukhobors finished the marsh unusually quickly and were now working on better, selected places. Each village strove desperately not for the stomach but to work more than the others. They pulled with all their might and only the village of Troitskaye sometimes got behind. There they were unable to get together on whether to live as a community or each for himself. This was the only black spot. The Troitsky people were persuaded and convinced and pacified and ridiculed—nothing helped. And the Troitsky people continued to get behind.

In general it now appeared that each worker, depending on the village, was earning a net of a dollar or more per day. After working a couple of weeks the whole party decided to take two dollars per person of the earned money to buy leather soles, material for pants, and so on. This was necessary as the people at this time had become terribly ragged.

Upon receiving the money, Chernenkoff, another Doukhobor and I went to Winnipeg for purchases. There was at this time an unusual demand for workers for the harvest. A few people from the South Settlement were in Winnipeg. They were quickly taken at twenty, twenty-five and thirty dollars monthly wages at the employer's keep. I had to conclude many such agreements between farmers and Doukhobors. Seeing how quickly the Doukhobors were taken by farmers on excellent terms, it seemed to me it would be good to move all Doukhobors here from the railroad. With this in view I asked the manager of immigration, McCreary, to get free passage for the whole party from Cowan to Winnipeg. If this was not possible I asked him to try to get passage at one quarter fare.

Unable to wait for an answer, I went back to the line. There it appeared that the English again ran ahead of the Doukhobors and took up the best places along the line, and again the most difficult and least satisfactory places remained for the Doukhobors. This, it seemed, could not continue any longer. I went to the engineer and announced that if he would not conclude with us another contract more satisfactory to us which would protect our interests from all kinds of "occurrences," as the engineer called this seizure of the better work by the English, tomorrow there would not be a single Doukhobor on the line.

"Oh, I am not afraid of that," he answered. "There are more than eight thousand people coming from Ontario for the harvest. This is too many and all that remain who do not find work with the farmers will come to me."

But I already knew that there were not eight thousand coming from Ontario, but many less, and that even if some of them remained without work, none of them would come to work on the railroad but would return home as they always did. Meanwhile, the engineer was in a great hurry and every delay was very harmful to him.

At this time a telegram arrived from McCreary which said that the railroad would not agree to give free passage nor one at a reduced rate for the Doukhobors. The ticket to Winnipeg cost nine dollars and fifty cents, a large sum. They thought of going on foot but some of the Doukhobors opposed this. Actually, to drag such a party through nearly empty terrain would have been a difficult job. It was a fearful risk. Next the English working on the line began to leave the work one after another. They all headed to Winnipeg to hire out to farmers for the harvest.

New negotiations with the engineer began. This time, feeling our strength, we decided not to move from our indicated conditions under any circumstances. For two days the engineer yielded a little, sending telegrams from time to time to the management in Winnipeg. Finally, after long negotiations, wringing one half a cent from the price proposed by us, he agreed to our terms.

By the new contract, all the earth work on the whole line would belong to the Doukhobors without exception. The Company would pay fifteen and a half cents for each cubic foot worked, without distinction for good and bad places. All that had been worked by the Doukhobors on the line before the conclusion of this contract would be paid for at the same price, fifteen and a half cents for each cubic yard all around. For the very difficult places, the Company would hire day workers. The seventy-five cents which the Company had been deducting from each Doukhobor monthly for doctors' services would not be paid any more, since they had their own medical help. We would be obliged to keep on the line not fewer than one hundred and seventy workers. The company was to take as day workers twenty of this number at one dollar per day, with all keep by the Company. Every Doukhobor, above the number coming to work on the line, could be taken as a day worker. If we did not manage to work quickly enough, the Company would have the right to invite workers other than Doukhobors for the earth work.

Canada
Cowan Station
August 26, 1899.

After the conclusion of the last contract, the Doukhobors, whose spirits had fallen, took up the work with renewed energy. One Doukhobor was sent from the workers to the villages to call all the other able-bodied to work. The engineer tried to gain something on the Doukhobors for his own benefit but he could not, thanks to the stubborn united resistance which they showed. In my presence he tried to get the Doukhobors to work one swampy place along the way, but the Doukhobors refused and demanded that according to the agreed terms he hire day workers for this job. The engineer threatened that if they did not work this swamp, he would not pay them for all they had worked so far and would not let them continue further work, saying that he would not pay them if they by-passed the swamp. But the Doukhobors stood firmly on their rights and, dropping all work, sat quietly along the line, not sending anybody to the engineer for further negotiations.

"Anyway, the people need to rest a little. They are very strained."

The Doukhobors rested for nearly three days. Toward evening of the third day the engineer came and authorized work that by-passed the swamp, which was worked by day workers—Galicians.

PA-22229 | Public Archives Canada

Swan River (end of steel) 1899. Doukhobor men working as railway construction workers.

Canada
On the Railroad Line Being Built Near Swan River
August 29, 1899.

If one approaches the place where the Doukhobors are working from the direction of the finished road, one sees first a huge steam machine standing a little to one side from the grade, looking like some hideous iron animal with a long stretched-out neck ending in a dull square head which it beats against a rising gravel hill in front of it with much squealing and rattling and scraping.

Beside the machine stretches a long ballast train of open flatcars brought here for the gravel. The steam machine, beating its huge scoop against the gravel hill, fills it with gravel and then, turning its neck together with the scoop, pours out the gravel on one of the flatcars. Three turns and the flatcar is full. A whistle blows and the train moves ahead to present the next flatcar for filling with gravel.

The loading is carried out unusually quickly, and the train moves off to the place where the gravel is to be delivered. The gravel is unloaded on the grade also in a special manner. Under the wheels of the front flatcar a block is placed to keep the train in one place. The locomotive is unhooked, a thick steel cable is attached to it which stretches the whole length of the train to the last flatcar. On the last flatcar a large blade of steel looking like a clothes iron is placed. When the cable is attached to the ring on the point of iron the locomotive moves and pulls the iron over all the flatcars and pushes gravel from the flatcars to the grade.

Later you see how the workers of another train, loaded with ties and rails, lay the railway. By means of special rollers set in a sloping position the full length of the train, workers sitting on a flatcar quickly drop rails and ties from the front flatcar. Workers stationed in pairs quickly pick these up and set them on the grade. When enough ties are laid for one pair of rails, one hears the crash of rails rolling off the load, the pounding of hammers and the way is ready. A worker raises a red flag and the locomotive driver pushes the train on to the newly laid rails right to the end. Again the ties are heard, rails squeal. All this happens so easily, quickly and noiselessly, that it seems people are playing some amusing game.

Standing not far to one side are big, two-storey coaches. Here the workers live. Walking farther, you will see large tents of thick canvas set up in strict order on both sides of the grade. Between the tents are scattered wagons and horses; odd sorts of boxes lie underfoot with empty tins of conserves. In the tents are beds covered with thick woollen blankets; on poles around the stove, all kinds of clothing hangs to dry. This is where the day workers live. In one of the large tents there is a long white table. This is the dining room; the kitchen is also located here. Around the hot cookstove a cook bustles, dressed all in white with a cap on his head; his helper is washing pewter dishes in a large basin.

Farther beyond the tents on space cut out for the right of way stretches a long, uneven hump of fresh grade. We are walking on a narrow path beaten on to it. But suddenly the grade ends. We have to go down and wander in sticky, cold swampland. At first you try to step on protruding hummocks, to jump from stump to stump, picking firmer places but slipping several times and getting muddy to the knees; then you begin to walk without regard to where your foot falls. Fortunately, ahead are the dark figures of people digging on both sides of a just-started grade. Soon you get safely to the grade and, with a feeling of relief, walk on a level space to the place of work.

Among shining square pools, in places where turf has been taken for the grade, dark tattered people covered with mud work hurriedly, their sleeves worn to fringes. They cut large pieces of turf and load wheelbarrows. When a wheelbarrow is loaded to the top, another Doukhobor pulls it to the grade over boards laid down. The boards shake, and hauling is difficult. Besides, they are covered with soupy mud and feet slip on them.

"Where are you going?" laughingly calls one of the workers, seeing how his companion, with feet apart, is sliding back with the wheelbarrow.

"From the Wet Mountains to Batum," he croaks in answer. "It's a bad job."

"He has forgotten where it is to be hauled," others laugh.

"He must have eaten a lot of beans and now they pull him back!"

A muddy boy jumps up to join the worker and silently helps to pull the wheelbarrow.

"That's handy," approves the worker. "It seems, Nicky, that you are stronger than I am. I was unable to pull it up and see how you pulled it up in one pull."

The boy looks around, satisfied.

"You are just talk!" he says condescendingly.

The Doukhobors begin their work at sunrise and finish it at sunset. Morning and evening they drink tea; at noon they eat soup and kasha with cow butter. This is all prepared over camp fires by appointed cooks. Nearby they have constructed bake stoves in which bakers bake very tasty bread for the whole party. Since the party continually moved as the work was done, the bakery fell so far behind that they had to build another. They get water in the woods; they dig at a spring and construct a little well. Upon moving to a new place they look for a new spring.

The most difficult aspect of their life is the absence of living quarters. For the whole party, there are only two tents in which there is room for no more than twenty persons. The others get by in their own way. Mostly they build something like a cabin out of the piles of ties, cover it with forest-dry grass and so on. They put hay on the bottom, cover it with a burka (felt cloak), and find it an excellent home. When there are no ties, many pick a dry hill, get under a bush and make out of their ever-saving burka something like a tent. Despite these difficult conditions, the Doukhobors of the North Settlement did not leave this work till the late autumn. And only when severe frost had bound the earth and it was impossible to work any longer did the thin, tanned workers go home.

Canada
On the Railway Line Under Construction
September 2, 1899.

The Doukhobors go to day work gladly. They are paid less there but it is comparatively good and they are fed excellently. Regardless of the ten-hour work day, they find that day work is harder than in the party (piece work). For day work, especially at first, the Doukhobors picked stronger people from among themselves so as not to be embarrassed before the English.

Once the Doukhobors were sitting chattering in one of their tents as a fine rain was falling and, glancing through the tent opening at the rainy, misty picture of the right of way.

"It seems Konobolov is coming from day work," someone said, looking at a dark figure which appeared unexpectedly from out of the mist.

"Well, he has returned soon," a voice was heard.

"How could he do otherwise, a very weak old man. . . . "

The figure in the large, wide-brimmed straw hat, with a pack on his shoulders, stepped heavily, picking dryer places. When he came nearer I saw this was an old man with a small, recently-sprouted beard. His somewhat protruding dark eyes looked as if he had just done something very important and his face bore an expression as if he wanted to say:

"Well, did you get it? That's what we are like."

Knowing that this was Konobolov, the Doukhobors laughed and exchanged glances. They exchanged greetings. Konobolov sat heavily. Everyone examined him silently, smiling modestly.

"Well, how is it there?" somewhat jokingly someone of the Doukhobors asked. Others silently examined the tired figure of the old man.

Konobolov turned sharply in the direction of the questioner and angrily exclaimed, "How? No-how—that's how!"

Someone carelessly snickered.

"Why show your teeth!" snapped Konobolov. "Once it was said I am a horse tender—because I am by birth a horse man. So I don't have teeth. All this from horses," he pushed his finger into the black hole in place of his front teeth. "I went because of horses."

"And what did they do—give you a shovel instead of a horse?" someone asked.

"They will give one if there are no available places for looking after horses!"

"I told you," an old Doukhobor entered the conversation. "Do not go, Grisha. The work there is difficult, unsuitable for us old men."

Konobolov wrinkled his forehead and examined the ground.

"That's enough of anger, Grisha; it's sinful: better tell us how it was."

"How it was?" Konobolov said in a softer tone, examining all with his dark eyes. "It was very simple. Yes. The English work very intently—that's the point. So intently, so intently. It's a bad job. I wanted to be a driver but there was no place. They pushed a shovel in my hands and I scratched away. And I tell you they work so intently! It's a bad job! They don't let you straighten up. Even though they begin late, no argument—the sun is already this high, as soon as you eat and take your place, you don't straighten up till dinner. Does that make sense? And if you straighten up a bit, at once, 'Kadam,'* he calls. I took it for two days but don't wish any more. 'Are you a Turk?' I thought, 'The important thing is, I am a horse tender!' "

"Well, and how are our other people? Will they be running away too or not?"

"Others. Some are alright, but all complain. It is strict and the worst thing is the Kadam plagues."

"What kind of word is that? Tell me, please," asked one of the Doukhobors.

"When he gets very angry he at once calls 'Kadam!' This is their first word—nothing else—Kadam and that's it."

"You ought to know how I managed to get paid off," said a good-natured old man recently returned from Cowan. "We finished a little work there in Cowan, day work unloading rails. We wanted to get our money and go home. But he doesn't give it, do what you will. We waited a day, then another. So I said, 'Fellows, let's follow him and cry 'Kadam!' When he gets angry he cries 'Kadam' and so we are angry when he doesn't give us our money.' So we went. I say to him in our

---

*Goddamn—widespread English curse.

language, of course, 'So you will not give us our settlement today.' I showed with my hands the receiving of money. He took his pipe out of his mouth and said, 'The treasury is in Winnipeg,' and waved his hand in that direction.

" 'Well, then, if so, here is for you—Kadam!', I said. Here every-one cried out 'Kadam! Give us money! Kadam! Kadam! What are you going to do here?' He looked at me, at another, at a third and we are all calling, 'Kadam!' He opened his mouth, then raised his shoulders, threw out his hands, meaning 'I can do nothing.' 'Send a telegram,' I say, 'to Winnipeg. If you can't do it yourself, Kadam to you.' He went and we after him, calling 'Kadam!' Then he got into his cabin and sat there. But we are not to be put off. As soon as he appeared we at once called 'Kadam!' to him. We laughed among ourselves that we were calling we know not what. All the same, we saw him come out of his cabin and show with his hands that he would send a telegram! And, true, he went to the telegrapher and the next day the treasurer came and paid us. Without that, who knows when he would have settled with us?"

The English were very satisfied with Doukhobors as workers. They gladly took them to their farms and for day work, regardless of the fact that ignorance of the language sometimes produced money difficulties, especially on railroad work, and greatly diminished the productivity of their labour. They received the same wages as the English workers and if sometimes less, only a little less. On day work on the line they received the same wages as the rest.

There were some things the English did not like about the Douk-hobor day workers for example, their custom of greeting one another on meeting. They would be working somewhere on the grade. The Doukhobors work well, attentively. The supervisors of the day workers so trust the Doukhobors not to "lie down on the job" that they usually go to their tents, paying no attention to the Doukhobor workers. Everything goes beautifully. But then a party of workers comes wandering somewhere past the day workers. The workers stop, turn to face the day workers deliberately, take off their caps and bow, "How do you do?"

All the party stops work at once and equally deliberately bowing, answer:

"God be praised. How are you?"

The passers-by answer.

"Thank you. Your home folks send you greetings," and again a bow and so on. All this takes place unhurriedly, with dignity.

At first the English pay no attention to this. But someone else comes by and again, "How do you do?", again the work is stopped, again the inevitable answers and bows. Finally such proceedings begin to irritate them.

"Goddamn!" they cry. "Let thunder strike you. Are all these your relatives passing by?"

But the Doukhobors were unable to understand for some time what the English were angry about. Least of all could they imagine that the reason for the anger was their fulfilment of their "Christian ritual." When they were told what the trouble was, the Doukhobors very simply answered that it could not be otherwise and the English had to give in. But every time they were present at such meetings, they angrily growled through their teeth, "Oh, these elephants are at it again," as they shook their heads and thrust their hands in their pockets.

All the same, such details did not interfere with the English behaving to the Doukhobors with the greatest respect. As I have said, they were considered excellent workers and were much prized. Since Doukhobors did not eat meat, despite the inconvenience, they prepared separate food for them without meat, under their direction. For them the Company even bought new pewter dishes so as not to give them those where meat had been, although as far as I can remember the Doukhobors did not ask for new unused dishes.

The English respect the Doukhobors' sense of personal worth, their rare persistence, their ability not to complain under difficult conditions. All this fortitude, the absence of quarrelling, arguments or fights between them, their complete restraint from drinking spirits and from tobacco, together with their religiosity, are much liked by the English. They look with satisfacton at the Doukhobors when the latter in unison rise before dinner and repeat to themselves their pre-dinner grace. At this time the noisiest Englishmen respectfully go silent, awaiting the end of the grace. One must add to this that the Doukhobors, in relation to the property of others, are ideally honourable people. Unfortunately, many other immigrants living in Canada cannot boast of this.

This attitude of the English to the Doukhobors can be appreciated especially if one sees how they behave to the unfortunate Galicians and Bukovinians working here sometimes side by side with the Doukhobors. They treat them unusually rudely and even beat them.

I once saw an old man, a member of a group of Galician day workers, working with unusual strain. In his every move there was such fatigue that it seemed as if he would dig once more and then collapse. A tall Englishman with a pipe between his large yellowed horse teeth poked him in the side, grabbed the shovel out of his hands and sharply growled:

"Go away from here, old dog, you are unable to work."

The old man did not object. But his dark, famished face was so defeated; so much sorrow was written on it that it was impossible to convey it in words. He silently looked at the supervisor.

"Go on," the supervisor repeated impatiently, nodding his head to one side.

The old man knew it was useless to talk and wandered off looking ahead. On his face, furrowed with deep wrinkles, streamed small lines of tears, and his lips helplessly, soundlessly whispered something. He saw at this moment his wife and children in their hut in the wild, foreign prairies. What would happen to them?

The remaining workers here—Galicians—did not say a word. Someone just noted in a tired voice that Boitsech had been fired, and each of them began to work more vigorously, slouching his shoulders as if defending them from the blows of fate.

These people live here the first years in shocking need. They settle here in separate families on homesteads selected by them, lost in the endless prairies without neighbours, without any kind of social assistance, since there is nothing in their lives to arouse them to unite one with another. They live in some absurd little hut with one crooked window hardly letting any light. Often the husband goes away for whole months somewhere for earnings while the wife and children sit at home striving to dig up as much earth as possible so as to plant potatoes, which for a long time to come will be their sole nourishment.

When you pass by such a box-hut which appears suddenly like a rough mushroom from behind a bush in the midst of endless desert hills and see the poor blonde head of a boy looking out in fear and curiosity from behind a dark-sided window at your horse, it becomes inexpressibly painful to see these people. And nearby on a piece of black, dug-up earth you see a dry bent figure of a woman with a spade in her hand. All day she turns the heavy soul-less earth. And in the evening she sits with the children at the window and looks with faded sorrowing eyes at the distant prairie, more than once beginning to weep from the sorrow of loneliness. Supping on fat-less potatoes, beaten down by such labour, need and sorrow, she turns to sleep, awakened only by the wailing wind and the distant howling of coyotes. In fear, pressing the children to her dry breasts looking with wide-open eyes into the darkness, she will whisper prayer after prayer until daybreak.

These unfortunate, forgotten people suffer all this without complaint, and with desperate submission. Only in Chinese coolies have I seen such hopeless sad faces, such apathetic eyes, such downtrodden, depressed figures. If you give a Galician even some most insignificant help, he and his whole family rush to kiss your hand. Apparently such form of gratitude is generally accepted among the Galicians, apparently it is fed into them with their mothers' milk.

How much humiliation these people must have suffered—need, slavery, oppression of all kinds—to produce such downtrodden, submissive faces, such numbness of all that is human. And these people had not come from the wild desert of Asia nor Australia but from the very centre of "enlightened," "cultured" Europe. Who made them this way?

End of the First Year
Canada
North Settlement
Village of Michailovka
October 3, 1899.

The winter stole up unnoticed. The trees have dropped their golden dress and now stand bare like brooms. Through them whistles a penetrating cold wind. The earth has stiffened in the embrace of a fresh frost. In the mornings the high dry grass is grey with thick hoar frost. On the prairies, wolves (coyotes) appear. At night they come close to the village, flashing their burning eyes in the darkness to examine the dark, hitherto unseen, buildings from which come such appetizing aromas; they yelp from hunger.

The outer appearance of the Settlement of the North has also changed greatly with the approach of winter. The villagers have built clean new log huts; barns have been built for livestock. Among the buildings rise large cones of logs, wood reserves for the winter are in sheltered corners. Among the barns and huts, stacks of hay are hidden. No one lives in the blockhouses any more; the elders divided them among the villages, and a large number have been taken apart for new buildings.

One blockhouse has been brought into repair; the cracks have been freshly plastered, and some work has been done inside. This is the hospital of the North Settlement; here also are the clinic and pharmacy.

In another, lower blockhouse, lives the thin little woman doctor, V. Velichkina, thanks to whom this hospital has been set up. Together with A.A. Satz who helps in the capacity of assistant, they treat tirelessly, prepare medicines, and distribute fish oil which disappears unusually quickly. Sometimes people from other villages come for V. Velichkina and she travels there to the sick in a heavy fur coat sewn for her by the Doukhobors. Living in conditions differing little from those of the rest of the village of Michailovka, lying above her blockhouse, she is able to find the strength to give treatment and organize the work.

Because there was not, and would not be, any means for supporting the weak and sick, V. Velichkina began to write all over the world about the necessity of help for the Doukhobors. From income received in this manner, she organized medical help and provided improved nourishment for the weaker ones in this first difficult winter.

Sometimes in long winter evenings we non-Doukhobors gathered and, to the howling of the wind and the crackle of the overheated stove, we recalled our native land. Lively Russian arguments proceeded. V. Bonch-Bruevich read to us some of the more interesting things he had managed to record among the Doukhobors. For whole days he had recorded psalms, sayings, poems. Sometimes the good-natured Melesha comes from Thunder Mountain and, looking at the sisters with caressing eyes, entreats them to care more for themselves.

"Not everything for the divine; you must think of yourselves too, and of earthly things; not everything for salvation of the soul," he says endearingly with innocent guile in his face.

Sometimes when we gathered we sang, and Doukhobors, passing by the blockhouse and hearing songs, probably shook their heads reproachfully, mentally criticizing the guides, as they call us, for "devilish tricks."

A Doukhobor village, 1900. Houses and animal shelters were made of prairie sod.

Canada
North Settlement
Village of Michailovka
November 5, 1899.

A light snow has fallen. There have been no heavy frosts, as yet, below eight degrees Reamur (–ten degrees C). In the North Settlement, along the roads, landmarks were put up in the autumn so that riders and walkers would not get lost in the snowy fields. On the South Settlement this had not been done and there have been some incidents where wayfarers have lost their way and wandered over the prairie until they came upon their own tracks or on some farmer who, after warning them, showed them the road.

And once came the news that on the South Settlement a lost wayfarer had frozen. It happened like this. Two Doukhobors set off on foot from one village to another. They had to go through empty prairie and soon saw that they had lost the road. Twilight came and they were still walking over valleys and hills, past clumps of thin forest and could not find their road. Towards night a wet snow began to fall, which wet them through as they were lightly dressed. A dark moonless night came and a frost stiffened their clothes.

"Walking was difficult," said one of them afterwards. "Our clothing turned white and rustled at every touch."

Finally, tired out by continual walking—they were afraid of resting for fear of falling asleep and freezing—half frozen they came upon the home of a farmer. The wakened farmer came outside. The Doukhobors explained by signs that they were lost and asked for shelter till the morning, as they were completely worn out and could go no further. But the farmer cried something into their faces and, waving his hands, told them to leave the yard and went inside his home. The Doukhobors went after him pleading with him not to drive them away, but he was adamant. The unfortunate pair went on their knees before the farmer and, weeping loudly, begged him not to let them die. But the farmer ran into his home and locked himself in. The unfortunates got up from the ground and went into the field. Upon walking a little while and seeing that death was threatening them, they returned to the farm and tried to get into the stable to wait for morning. But the Englishman, hearing them come into the yard, aimed a gun at them and demanded that they leave his farm at once or he would shoot.

"What could we do?" related the one who had survived. "We saw before us unavoidable death. He would shoot us—his face showed it! And so we went further into the field. Thanks to him for showing us with the hand which way to go! We walked and our clothes crackled from the frost. Our feet would not lift. I cannot say how long we walked. It all seems to have happened in a dream. But the old man with me had lost all his strength. He kept saying, 'Let us sit down and rest a little.' I argued, 'No, then we will certainly fall asleep,' but he was so weakened he wept and begged. And he walked as if drunk, rocked as if about to fall. And then I saw a light far away, as on a hill. 'Well,' I thought, 'Thank God. It must be our village,' I said to the old man, 'Gather your strength. We do not have far to go.' But he, dear man, had already lain down and said, while falling asleep, 'Go, my dove, alone, and send for me from the village. For me it is so-o-o good here, so-o-o go-o-od. . .' and his eyes closed. I began to carry him as far as I could but I became very weak. I carried him three paces and stopped. 'Well,' I thought, 'this could be worse. I could freeze him.' And he had become very sleepy. I laid him down on the ground and said that I would come back at once from the village with more people, that he should try as hard as he could not to go to sleep, but he was already hardly speaking—only when I was about to go he took hold of me with his hands, opened his eyes very wide and looked right at the light.

"There, there," he said "our sun is rising, rising and so bright, it seems to run through the veins," and he laughed. I saw there was trouble; I must hurry. I kissed him and wept, grieving that I was leaving him, dear man, in the middle of the bare field and hurried as fast as I could to the village. I ran and ran, it seemed to be near but turned out to be far. I thought the light was in a window but it was not. The people in our village had learned that I had not arrived at the village where I was going and decided I must be lost and hung a lantern from a long pole on a hill. So the lantern was visible from far away.

"By the time I arrived, wakened the people and they went. . . I wanted to go myself but was unable, as soon as I went inside my legs gave up on me and soon I lost my memory. Just managed to tell where the old man was lying. Well, when they got there the poor man was dead and wolves or a fox had gnawed at his hands and nose. . . ."

Canada
North Settlement
Village of Michailovka
November 12, 1899.

With the first frosts the workers were compelled to return from the line. "The earth hardened" (as they said) "it could not be cut with an axe." Actually, it was impossible to work any more; the English had left work earlier, and the Doukhobors were the last to leave. The railway line now passed within fourteen miles of Thunder Mountain and the nearest village of Michailovka. A new little town had been built there consisting of the residents of the "Land Office," in place of which now remained only a few piles of garbage.

Land for the town had to be cleared of the trees growing there. This work was done by the Doukhobors at good wages. This was the last good earning of the Northern Settlement this winter. The new station and the town built around it was named after the river on which it stood "Swan River." Now for the Doukhobors of the Northern Settlement all communication with Winnipeg, delivery of flour and all other goods would come through this station and not through distant Yorkton as it had before. Because of this the Doukhobors of the North Settlement sent several workers from each village who set off, under the leadership of Zeebarev, to open a new road from Michailovka to Swan River.

In several days a road as straight as an arrow was cut through the forest. In Swan River itself the same workers under Zeebarev built large communal barns in which teams from all thirteen villages could be housed; here too they built a communal warehouse for flour and other goods and next to the warehouse they established a large room in which Doukhobors coming to the town could spend the night. All this was done harmoniously, quickly, happily.

The Cooperative store which could not come into existence for so long finally began operations. One of the Russian people living in Canada gave the Doukhobors 2000 roubles for the opening of this store and Zeebarev set off for Winnipeg and, with this money, bought a carload of flour and all kinds of other goods.

One should know that during the first year the railroad hauled flour for the Doukhobors at a preferred tariff, with a discount of 50%. From the new year they would have to pay the full freight rate. Ordering the flour as goods for the Cooperative store, the Doukhobors would have a discount of 35%, since the railroads give such a discount to all trading enterprises.

Thanks to the Cooperative store the Doukhobors were able to acquire necessary goods in general one and one-half times cheaper than before, and some goods such as kerosene, even cheaper. Even English farmers came several times to the Doukhobors with the request to purchase something out of their reserves but this was difficult to do since at first the reserves were small and could not satisfy all the Doukhobors. In a short time the store made two or three turnovers of stock and had a solid footing. The business apparently "took" and in time will develop to large proportions, it seems.

All the same, its development did not come easily. Besides a shortage of free cash, needed for start up, the main drawback was the unsympathetic attitude of the Doukhobors to the building of the store. According to their understanding, trading was improper for Doukhobors and degrading to them as Christians. When I had to speak in one of the villages about the building of this store, one of the Doukhobors asked scornfully:

"And who will do the trading in this store?"

Knowing the feeling of the Doukhobors about this matter, I said "Well one of you people, even you for example."

"No-o-o," he drawled, smiling ironically. "This will not do for us, this trade. Trading is not suited to us; according to Christian law this is not possible for us."

"Business is not suitable to us, no use talking" confirmed others.

"Now, if one of the Russians should undertake this work" he said. Slowly looking in my direction and seeing that I was silent, he added, "If you did it for example, you or Vladimir* let us say, we would thank you for your efforts."

For us non-Doukhobors, in their view, it would be alright to take on this unchristian business. Here that sense of their superiority over all other people, which is common to the majority of Doukhobors, was apparent. Thanks to the heroism, if one may say so, of Nicolai Zeebarev, the store came into being and at once stood on solid ground. He finally took on the running of the store himself, personally scorning the opinion of the community which for a long time looked sideways at him as he measured fine goods with a yardstick.

Zeebarev himself bought all the goods in Winnipeg beginning with instruments, iron goods and ending with thread, needles and other small stuff. Some of the goods he brought from the warehouse to his home in the village of Voznesenie where the crowd gathered (elders, women and girls) to make purchases in "our store" for unheard-of low prices.

N. Zeebarev traded at home in his cottage. His tall, able figure moved all day among the customers around him.

"How much red calico for you?" he asks some woman and getting the answer, swings his yardstick measuring the needed quantity, and tears the cloth with his strong fingers.

His wife Annie Zeebarev, being in love with him and proud of her husband looks at him from a distant corner of the room, her hand supporting one cheek, and weeping silent, bitter tears.

"What is it?" I asked her.

"Can it possibly be decent for him to be doing such work?" she says, weeping even more. "Has it ever been known for our people to take up trading! Do not tell me anything," she waves her arms at Zeebarev, who has begun to explain to her that there is nothing evil in this. "It is so shameful, so shameful, one cannot talk about it! What is it

*V. Bonch-Bruevich

for? If they want to start a store, let them operate it, but no one will do it. . . . They have all become accustomed to 'let Nicolai, let Nicolai do this.' To put it simply, this business is immoral for us," she ends and weeps again.

"There, and you say I have an intelligent wife!" says Zeebarev. "But I cannot explain it to her in any way. What is there about it that even our elders cannot get it into their heads? Very well; it will get milled over and will become flour!" he ends.

His tired face shows that this business is not easy for him.

Canada
Northern Settlement
Village of Michailovka
January 6, 1900.

Properly speaking, the period of moving and first construction on the new land could be considered completed by New Year 1900. We outside people, whom the Doukhobors needed till this time in the capacity of interpreters, intermediaries between them and the government, arrangers of earnings and commissioners for the purchase and delivery of flour, etc., could consider our work done.

People were living in their own houses, supplied for the winter with flour. Many spoke and wrote English though not very well, but well enough that they could always explain; they had learned about earnings, wages for labour were known to them; maps had been made up of the lands which they wished to take; there was a Cooperative store and warehouses; and so on. Our help was no longer needed by the Doukhobors. Perhaps we could have been useful to them for further serving as secretaries, interpreters, and so on, but this did not appear essential, and we considered we had the right to go home.

For the purpose of communicating with the government and for conducting business which concerns the whole of the North Settlement a special committee had been set up to whom we handed over all the business, accounts and documents concerning the North Settlement. From each village a trusted elder had been selected; together they would discuss the business of the North Settlement and three of them would constitute a committee to carry out the decisions of the larger group, conduct all business in practice, and assemble the larger group as needed.

Letterheads, printed in English, had been ordered for the Committee:

Christian Community of Universal Brotherhood (Doukhobors)

COMMITTEE: Nicolai Zeebarev
                      Ermolai Legebokoff
                      Grigori Kanigan
Secretary: Grigori Kanigan

Here the address was shown.

Letterheads had also been ordered for the store:

THE DOUKHOBOR'S COOPERATIVE STORE.

This Committee worked very effectively. Construction of the aforementioned community barns, warehouses and the store in Swan River, repair and construction of the new road from the Settlement to the town—all this had been done by the Committee, of which the most active person was N. Zeebarev.

In the early days of its existence the Committee did not get by without certain minor failures due to lack of experience. For instance it happened that the flour which the Doukhobors ordered independently for the first time came very late and certain villages went without bread for a couple of days. In this case they were helped by the flour which was in the Cooperative store. It was taken out at once in expectation of that which had been ordered for the villages.

At first, at the request of the Committee, we supervised its performance and helped it with necessary advice and assistance. All 13 villages of the North Settlement were very sympathetic to the setting up of the Committee. They readily and willingly selected their elders, and carried out the Committee's proposals most agreeably. It was apparent that they liked this organization and it fulfilled their desires.

In the South Settlement there was neither a Committee nor a Cooperative store. I remember clearly, at the meeting called to discuss the question of organizing a Committee, the gloomy, distrustful faces with which the elders were discussing this matter. The main reason against the organization of the Committee was that it might try to control the Doukhobor society.

"We are all equal, no one can be a master over others!"

"We do not need masters."

"As we have been without masters, so we will continue. It is all only temptation!"

As to the community barns and warehouses which had been built so harmoniously and energetically in the North Settlement, none were constructed in the Yorkton area, though the South Settlement needed them badly.

It was useless to argue that the Committee did not represent authority; more than anything in the world the Doukhobors fear the idea of commanders and masters replacing elected elders. They resisted the slightest suggestion of some kind of independent power of decision without consultation with the whole village.

Of all the villages of the South Settlement only the 13 "Cypriot" (Cold Mountain) Villages appreciated properly what a Committee was, and clearly understood that it need not represent some kind of power. The representatives of these villages tried to convince the remaining participants of the conference of this, but without success. So only these 13 villages elected from among themselves a Committee, which did not last very long.

When it was suggested that letterheads be printed for the Committee as was done in the North Settlement, many objected. One elder with a pale face and frightened eyes, as if he was confronting something terrible, implored the conference, with quivering lips, not to print letterheads.

"As you wish, brethren; but do not print, this would be such a sin, such a sin!"

How it was a sin was hard to understand, but that this person feared print more than anything in the world was obvious. So the "Cypriots" decided not to issue letterheads for their Committee.

Business went unusually badly. After two or three months of awkward existence, the Committee ended its activity completely without hope of renewal. The Cooperative store likewise did not succeed. The first purchases were carried out by ignorant people, little interested in the concept, and they were very unsuccessful. Leather, for instance, was sold in the Cooperative store several cents higher than in the local English stores. Very soon, the store closed down, even before the Committee, and the Doukhobors divided the community funds, its basic capital, on a per-person basis and taking the money settled down quietly.

Such was the state of affairs when I left Canada for Russia. Now it remains for me to say a few words about how the well-known "Anarchist" movement, which has drawn the attention of the whole world, appeared among the Doukhobors.

Just before my departure from Canada I had to prepare, together with the Englishman Archer, maps for the lands which the Doukhobors were taking up. During this work certain elders asked several times whether we could propose to the government that they should not register each quarter-section to an owner, but simply put aside for each village enough land for each person in the village who has a right to a homestead (farm as the Doukhobor said); so that each farm should not be indicated as the property of an individual Doukhobor.

"Why do you wish this?" I asked them.

"Because, as we understand it, the land is God's. It belongs to God and no person can buy it and become its master," answered the Doukhobors.

"The same as air, or say, water," others explained, "no one can sell them, God has released them for the use of all creatures equally. Not only for man but for all insects. So it is with land. Work as much as you can handle, feed yourself, and other good people—that is the law. But to have a piece of land as your own or my own—that would be sinful. That's where sin comes from. Some, you see, have no idea how to plough and have never done work; but they also cry out, this is my land, don't anybody come near. He got it from his parents but where did his parents get it?"

At the request of the Committee I asked the government whether they would permit not registering a farm to an owner but to marking out for each village as much land as it had a right to receive. The government answered quickly that it had no right to permit this, as such permission would conflict with the laws of Canada. At the same time the government announced that the land on which villages were built need not be registered as homesteads.

Receiving this answer, the Doukhobors were saddened and expressed regret but at that time, there was no talk of any kind of protest to the government or of pressing demands to give them land by villages. The Doukhobors agreed to take the land on the basis of Canadian laws.

All went well. Maps of the land were drawn up and they were only awaiting the government surveyor and officer to register in a special book the names of the people and the farms being registered to them. This is how the matter stood when I left Canada. But the surveyor and officer delayed their arrival and, by the time they came, the Doukhobors sharply changed their views on this matter, with the result that a long struggle developed between the Doukhobors and the government.

The Doukhobors refused to take the land by farms, and refused to register births, deaths and marriages as the government demanded in accordance with Canadian laws. They demanded full independence from the state structure of the land in which they settled, agreeing only to pay the taxes required of them. In other matters they wished to live as a completely independent community submitting only to the unwritten laws of their community and long established custom—to live by genuine Christian law, by God's truth.

How this movement arose, how it developed, and to what it led—I did not see. Those wishing to familiarize themselves with this interesting period in the life of the Doukhobors, I refer to the beautifully composed articles of V. Olchowsky (*Education*—"Doukhobors on the

Canadian Prairies," 1903 April—August). These articles are written with deep knowledge of the subject. There the reader will find broad statistical data showing the degree of well-being that the Doukhobors reached after a few years in North America.

About the inner structure of their lives after the arrival in Canada of their leader Peter Verigin, and of the latest occurrences the well-known writer Tan has written in a bold and lively fashion in *The Russian Record* 1904. Recently the outlines appeared in a separate edition under the heading "Russians in Canada."

PA-22231 / Public Archives Canada

The first harvest at Thunder Hill Colony. The scythes were brought from Caucasia.